DRY DECIDUOUS FORESTS OF KARNATAKA

Adding Years to their Life, And to Ours

DIPAK SARMAH, IFS (Retd.)

**Formerly PCCF (HoFF), PCCF, Wildlife,
Secretary (Forest), Government of Karnataka**

notionpress
.com

INDIA • SINGAPORE • MALAYSIA

Notion Press

No.8, 3rd Cross Street
CIT Colony, Mylapore
Chennai, Tamil Nadu – 600004

First Published by Notion Press 2021
Copyright © Dipak Sarmah, IFS (Retd.) 2021
All Rights Reserved.

ISBN 978-1-63781-644-8

BOOKS FROM THE AUTHOR

Status of Forests of Karnataka (2018)

Forestry in Karnataka – A Journey of 150 Years (2019)

Forests of Karnataka – A Panoramic View (2019)

Wildlife Management in Karnataka – A Forester's Perspective (2019)

Forestry in India during British Era – Karnataka Case-Study (2020)

Agroforestry in Karnataka – A Golden Opportunity for
Green Growth (2020)

Author's Contact Details:

Dipak Sarmah

245, NTI Layout, 8th Main

Vidyaranyapura, Bengaluru – 560 097

Mob: 9986232094

e-mail: sarmahdipak1@gmail.com

CONTENTS

Preface   7

Chapter 1   Introduction   13

Chapter 2   Classification of the Dry Deciduous and
Thorn Forests of Karnataka   17

Chapter 3   Dry Deciduous Forests of Karnataka –
A Historical Perspective   39

Chapter 4   Distribution of Tree Species Across the Dry
Deciduous Forests of Karnataka   121

Chapter 5   Present Status of the Dry Deciduous
Forests of Karnataka   141

Chapter 6   Restoration and Rejuvenation of the
Dry Deciduous Forests of Karnataka   161

Annexure-I   *Forest*   179

Annexure-II   *Health of a Forest*   191

Annexure-III   *Forest Encroachment*   199

Annexure-IV   *A Few Photographs of Dry Deciduous
and Thorn Forests of Karnataka*   213

References   217

Book Review   221

PREFACE

In the map of natural vegetation of India, the southern peninsular region appears more or less as an expansive, barren and dreary-looking patch dotted here and there with a few tiny green specks, and flanked on the west by a fairly broad, almost continuous and bold green strip, and on the east by a disjointed, somewhat patchy, light green strip. The green strips are the forested regions of the Western Ghats and the Eastern Ghats, respectively. However, the vast landscape lying in between the Ghats was not always bereft of tree growth as it is now. In the distant past, say about 500-600 years ago, this patch was almost entirely green, being covered with luxuriant forests with their types changing from place to place corresponding to the precipitation (rainfall) received and the underlying soil. In order to appreciate the various factors that contributed to the near decimation of these forests, a peek into how growth of human civilization has impacted the forests of India in general and those of the peninsular India in particular will be of some relevance.

In the history of human civilization, the earliest settlements came up along river-banks, and India was no exception. The banks of some of the major rivers in the Indian subcontinent such as the Sindhu, Ganga, Yamuna, Brahmaputra, Narmada, Tapti, Mahanadi, Godavari, Krishna, Cauvery, Tunga-Bhadra, Periyar, etc. now harbor many cities and towns which in the distant past had started as early human settlements or villages. Along the Indian coast-line, estuarine areas also grew as popular human settlements. With the increase in population, some of the inhabitants from these early settlements ventured out to other favorable localities with adequate supply of drinking water, and as a result, more and more villages came into being. By and large, the villages were situated near perennial rivers or large water-bodies such as lakes, tanks, etc. The villages were surrounded by agricultural and pastoral lands which the inhabitants had developed by clearing the nearby forests. As the villages grew in population, the extent of adjacent forest areas cleared for cultivation and pasture also grew. Throughout this period, many small groups of people continued to live deep inside the forests, some of these groups continuing with their primitive life-style of hunter-gatherer, some pursuing the practice of shifting cultivation, and some gradually switching over to a mixed form of settled agriculture in tiny pockets adjacent to perennial water sources within the forests. However, as these semi-nomadic groups comprised small and scattered populations in the midst of vast forest areas, their footprint on the forests by and large continued to be insignificant for a very long time.

During the medieval period, the Indian subcontinent was Balkanized into many small states, often hostile to one another resulting in perpetual wars amongst themselves. The vanquished rulers along with their followers would escape into some interior and undisturbed forest located far away, clear some portion of the forest, and start new abodes. In the process more and more forest areas were cleared. Virtually every war took a heavy toll on the forests. The severity of damage to forest due to local internal fights was further aggravated during the Muslim invasions, when large numbers of people had fled from their villages to avoid the wrath of the invaders and took refuge in the forests, never to come back. Significant movement of people from their settlements started during the period of Muslim conquests that mainly took place from the 12th to the 16th centuries. This was the beginning of a phase of human migration to the forest. The uprooted villagers cleared vast stretches of forest to make way for settlements and agricultural lands. This period of political instability caused immense human sufferings and large-scale forest destruction. The foreign invaders were also accompanied by herdsmen with large herds of cattle, and vast forest tracts had to be cleared to make pastures for the cattle to graze which further accelerated the destruction of forests. During this period substantial portions of forest of the peninsular India were lost.

The peninsular region, which during the 15th and 16th centuries was administered by a number of Sultanates and the Hindu Empire of Vijayanagara, was also witness to many wars among the kingdoms. These wars had resulted in heavy drain of the forest resources besides loss of forest areas. The decline of the Vijayanagara Empire after the Talikota war in 1565 had resulted in assertion of independence by a number of local rulers and chieftains in various parts of the present Karnataka. In order to consolidate their positions and to shore up revenues, these rulers had encouraged the villagers to expand their agricultural and pastoral lands by clearing more and more forest areas. This was also to the advantage of the people whose hunger for more land had already been triggered by rise in their numbers.

As regards the trend of increase of population in the Indian subcontinent, it was modest till the beginning of the nineteenth century, and was estimated to be about 200 million by the year 1880. A number of factors such as wars, epidemics, famines, political instability, etc. had kept checks on the rate of increase in population. However, due to various factors including relative political stability, there was phenomenal increase in the population of the country since the beginning of the twentieth century: 238 million in 1901, 390 million in 1947, 1,072 million in 2001, 1,247 million in 2011, and 1,380 million in 2020. This had triggered large-scale expansion of agricultural lands throughout the country and millions of hectares of forest areas were cleared for this purpose. According to a study by Hanqin Tian, Kamaljit Banger, Tao Bo, and Vinay K. Dadhwal in an article published in 'Global and Planetary Change' [121 (2014) 78-88], during the period between 1880 and 2010, when human population in India had increased from 200 million to 1,200 million, the area under cropland increased by 47.5 million hectares from 92.6 million hectares to 140.1 million hectares. The study has revealed that the rate of cropland expansion had been the highest during the period from 1950 to 1970 at the rate of about 8 million hectares per decade. The study has also indicated that during this period of 130 years, forest land had decreased by 26.3 million hectares from 89.7 million hectares to 63.4 million hectares; majority of the deforestation had occurred during the British administration as well as early years after the Independence corresponding to the period between 1880 and 1960. As regards grasslands/ shrub lands, these had decreased by 20 million hectares from 45 million hectares to 25 million hectares during the period 1880 and 2010. The study has also pointed out that cropland expansion in the Indo-Gangetic Plains was primarily from grasslands/shrub lands and fallow lands, while in the central, eastern and southern parts of the country, it was mainly from the forest clearing. In another study conducted by Mr. J. F. Richards and Ms. E. P. Flint (Historic land use and carbon estimates for South and South East Asia 1880-1980), it has been indicated that during the 100-year period of 1880-1980, India's net cultivated area rose from 100.81 million hectares to 142.44 million hectares, and during the same period the total forest cover shrunk from 102.68 million hectares to 64.59 million hectares.

The adverse impact of population growth on the adjoining forests in the Indian subcontinent as depicted above was also visible in the areas which now constitute the state of Karnataka. For obvious reasons, this impact was more severe in the regions where population density was high. The central and eastern regions of Karnataka which cover about 75% of the state's geographical area saw large-scale decimation of forested areas. The western region in the lap of the Western Ghats was thinly populated and remained relatively safe from large-scale decimation of forest.

The book '*Dry Deciduous Forests of Karnataka – Adding Years to Their Life, and to Ours*' attempts at highlighting various aspects of the dry deciduous forests which once covered large parts of the state of Karnataka, and which now occur only in a few, scattered pockets, having been almost entirely wiped out from two vast regions covering three fourths of the state, namely, interior Karnataka and the Eastern Plains. Although not as imposing as the moist deciduous, semi-evergreen and evergreen forests that are met with in the western part of the state, the dry deciduous forests have high ecological value in terms of biodiversity, soil and water conservation, climate moderation, medicinal properties, protection of agricultural land, etc. Although now restricted in patches dispersed over an almost limitless landscape, these forests have tremendous impact on the surrounding environment. More importantly these are the last vestiges of natural vegetation in an expansive, open and parched region where the ominous signs of desertification are already perceptible. Conservation and development of these forests, by any means and before it is too late, is of utmost importance for the overall protection and amelioration of the surrounding environment of the state of Karnataka. An attempt has been made in the book in analyzing the various factors that were responsible for pushing these forests to their present dismal state, and in offering a few suggestions regarding restoration and rejuvenation of these vanishing forests.

DIPAK SARMAH

Chapter 1

INTRODUCTION

Dry deciduous forests, in combination with Thorn forests in certain patches, constitute a primary forest ecosystem of the peninsular India. Starting eastwards from the eastern fringes of the Western Ghats, these forests are found to occur in widely dispersed patches in the entire peninsular region, eventually merging with the western fringes of the Eastern Ghats. Although nowhere comparable in terms of density and stocking with the evergreen, semi-evergreen and moist deciduous forests of the Western Ghats, the dry deciduous forests are visible over a much larger landscape of the peninsular India. In the distant past, these forests had formed a continuous swathe covering the entire peninsular region connecting the *Ghat* forests. Centuries of anthropogenic pressure, most notably due to expansion of agriculture and settlements, resulted in fragmentation and contraction of the vast forests which are now restricted in small, scattered patches distributed sporadically over the entire peninsular landscape. Being subjected to relentless biotic pressures, these forests are by and large in severely degraded condition, the portions situated farther from habitations being a shade better in terms of growth and diversity.

In Karnataka, the interior parts of the state and the Eastern Plains primarily harbor dry deciduous forests along with patches of thorn forests in the driest localities. These two regions together constitute about 75% of the geographical area of the state, the remaining 25% area being occupied by the Western Ghats region*, also known as the *malnad* region that harbors all the evergreen, semi-evergreen and moist deciduous forests of the state, besides a sizeable portion of dry deciduous forests. Twenty out of the thirty districts of the state harbor only dry deciduous forests with sprinkling of thorn forests scattered here and there. Among the remaining ten districts that come within the *malnad* region (fully or partly), three districts, namely, Dakshina Kannada, Udupi and Kodagu do not harbor dry deciduous forests, whereas the remaining seven districts, namely, Belagavi, Uttara Kannada, Shivamogga, Chikkamagaluru, Hassan, Mysuru and Chamarajanagar harbor dry deciduous forests in varying extents. Major portions of Belagavi, Hassan, Mysuru and Chamarajanagar districts harbor dry deciduous forests. In respect of Uttara Kannada, Shivamogga and Chikkamagaluru districts, about one-sixth to one-fifth of the geographical area of each district comprising two to three taluks harbors dry deciduous forests. Some of the most luxuriant dry deciduous forests of the state occur in the *malnad* region, especially in Uttara Kannada district. It must however be added that, although the dry deciduous and thorn forests of Karnataka are distributed over an expansive landscape covering more than 75% of the state's geographical area, their distribution in interior Karnataka and in the Eastern Plains is highly scattered and their total extent is very limited, being only about 10% of the geographical area of these two regions. This compares poorly with the *malnad* region where forests occupy about 45% of the geographical area of the region. Large-scale clearances of forests for extending agriculture and settlements have led to rapid shrinkage of the forests, which, due to years of use, over-use and abuse, have always been under perpetual stress, never being able to rejuvenate, and have suffered further degradation year after year.

Various types and sub-types of the dry deciduous and thorn forests that are met with in the state of Karnataka will be discussed in more detail in the following chapter (*Chapter-2*). Suffice it to say that these forests, though limited in extent, exhibit tremendous diversity in terms of forest classification and species composition. In addition to the climatic climax formations^ and a number of edaphic (soil-related) and secondary variants, numerous degraded formations collectively referred to as scrub forests are met with in the state. Broadly speaking, three types of dry deciduous forests occur in the state: (a) a strip of dry deciduous forest with *Tectona-Anogeissus-Terminalia* association occurs along the eastern fringes of the

Western Ghats. Teak trees of low to medium girth are fairly dominant in parts of this forest type; such areas with preponderance of teak are also known as teak pole forests; (b) another strip of dry deciduous forest with predominantly *Anogeissus-Chloroxylon-Albizia amara* association occurs in the *maidan* region or the Eastern Plains, away from the Western Ghats. Teak is occasionally present in this forest also, becoming conspicuous in some favorable patches; (c) in between the dry deciduous forests of the Western Ghats region (represented by the districts of Uttara Kannada, Dharwar, Shivamogga, Chikkamagaluru, Mysuru, Chamarajanagar, etc.) and the dry deciduous forests of the Eastern Plains (represented by the districts of Bidar, Kalaburagi, Ballari, Kolar, etc.), another type of dry deciduous forests is discernible in the south interior areas of Karnataka where rainfall and soil conditions are somewhat intermediate between those obtaining in the above two regions. The dry deciduous forests of the districts of Bengaluru, Ramanagara, Mandya, etc. belong to this type with floristic composition that is an admixture of the floristic compositions of the other two types. [^ **Note** – A general introduction to tropical forest and its various climatic climax formations is appended at **Annexure-I**; the characteristics of a healthy forest are highlighted in a write-up at **Annexure-II**.]

As regards the thorn forests, these are primarily dominated by thorny *Acacias*; these forests occur in the easternmost parts of the state where rainfall is scanty and erratic, and the soil is very poor. It may however be added that there is no clear line of demarcation between the climax dry deciduous forests and the climax thorn forests. The secondary and degraded formations of both these types of forest are fairly similar. As a matter of fact, when a dry deciduous forest is subjected to severe biotic pressure, it exhibits signs of degradation and its floristic composition undergoes a change with the proportion of thorny species increasing, thereby giving the appearance of a thorn forest.

> [***Note:** The type and quality of growth of a forest occurring in an area is primarily determined by the rainfall received in the terrain. For a comprehensive understanding of the forests of Karnataka, the state can be broadly divided into three regions based on the intensity of rainfall received. For this purpose, the districts of Belagavi, Uttara Kannada, Shivamogga, Chikkamagaluru, Udupi,

Hassan, Dakshina Kannada, Kodagu, Mysuru and Chamarajanagar have been grouped as districts receiving high rainfall (*Malnad*). The districts of Dharwar, Gadag, Haveri, Davanagere, Chitradurga, Tumkur, Bengaluru (Urban), Bengaluru (Rural), Ramanagara and Mandya have been grouped as districts receiving medium rainfall (Interior Karnataka or Semi-*malnad*). The districts of Bagalkote, Vijayapura, Bidar, Kalaburagi, Yadgiri, Raichur, Koppal, Ballari, Kolar and Chikkaballapur have been grouped as districts receiving low rainfall (*Bailuseeme* or *Maidan*). The geographical areas of the three regions are 70,723 km², 51,666 km² and 69,430 km², respectively, totaling 1,91,819 km² for the whole state. It may however be mentioned that, out of the ten districts included in the *malnad* region, only six, namely, Uttara Kannada, Dakshina Kannada, Udupi, Kodagu, Shivamogga and Chamarajanagar are located fully within the region. As regards the remaining four districts, only the portions that receive high rainfall can be said to truly fall within the *malnad* region. For example, in Belagavi and Hassan districts, only one taluk each, namely, Khanapur and Sakleshpur, respectively (along with small portions of a few adjoining taluks such as Belagavi, Alur, Belur and Arkalgud) falls within the *malnad* region. In respect of Chikkamagaluru district, the entire Kadur taluk and the eastern parts of Chikkamagaluru and Tarikere taluks fall outside the *malnad* region. In respect of Mysuru district, four taluks, namely, Hunsur, Periyapatna, HD Kote and Sargur are located within the *malnad* region, whereas the remaining taluks, namely, Mysuru, Nanjangud, KR Nagara and T Narsipur are located in the drier eastern parts, outside the *malnad* region. The combined area of the above taluks (some in full and some in part) that fall outside the *malnad* region is about 23,000 km². If this area is excluded, the actual area that falls in the *malnad* region comes to about 48,000 km² which constitutes roughly 25% of the geographical area of the state.]

Chapter 2

CLASSIFICATION OF THE DRY DECIDUOUS AND THORN FORESTS OF KARNATAKA

Dry Deciduous Forests of Karnataka

As per the "Revised Survey of the Forest Types of India" by Champion and Seth (1968), the dry deciduous forests of Karnataka come under the group 5 (Tropical Dry Deciduous Forests), sub-group 5A (Southern Tropical Dry Deciduous Forests). Champion and Seth have described this sub-group (5A) as follows:

"The upper canopy in the climax type is a closed though usually rather uneven and not very dense one. It is formed by a mixture of trees practically all of which are deciduous during the dry season, usually for several months, though some for a short period only. Most of the species also occur in the moist deciduous forest where they reach finer development, there, the height of the dry deciduous forest being typically 13-20 m. The number of species is much less than the foregoing types and although a few tend to predominate over any selected area, the majority are not particularly gregarious so that more or less pure associations can usually be traced to soil peculiarities or human interference. At the same time, the dry deciduous forests provide the clearest examples in tropical India outside the sal forest of natural single species crops. The lower canopy is likewise almost entirely deciduous as although evergreens or sub-evergreens are present they are inconspicuous and mainly confined to the moister and more sheltered spots. An undergrowth of shrubs is usually present but enough light gets in to permit of more or less grass growth, and with burning this tends to become more strongly developed resulting in savannah or park like forms. Bamboos are often present but are not luxuriant. Canes and palms are absent. Climbers are comparatively few but include large woody species which may be locally conspicuous. Epiphytes and ferns are quite inconspicuous."

The Southern Tropical Dry Deciduous Forests are found throughout the Indian Peninsula. These start from the leeward side of the Western Ghats where the rainfall is below 190 cm. As the rainfall decreases towards the east and drops below 75 cm, these forests merge into thorn forests. These forests cover parts of Gujarat, Madhya Pradesh, Chhattisgarh, Maharashtra, Tamil Nadu, Telangana, Andhra Pradesh and Karnataka. The annual mean temperature of the year varies from 29°C to 35°C and the annual mean minimum from 18°C to 23°C. The highest summer temperature may be as high as 48°C. The typical annual rainfall for this type of forest is from about 100 cm to about 130 cm occasionally down to 85 cm and frequently up to much higher figure, say 190 cm on dry soils or rapidly drained sites. The dry season is for about six months. These forests are found on virtually any variety of rock or soil. The soil remains dry most of the year. Sandy soils, lateritic soils and shallow clay soils are characteristic soils for this type of forest. These forests can come up in flat, undulating and hilly lands. However, most of these forests are now confined to undulating and hilly tracts as the forests on flat lands have mostly been cleared or destroyed for the purpose of agriculture.

The forests can be classified into two broad classes as teak-bearing and non-teak-bearing. The most characteristic species in the teak-bearing forests are *Tectona grandis* (saguwani/tega), *Anogeissus latifolia* (dindiga/dindal) and *Terminalias* [*Terminalia tomentosa* (matti), *Terminalia paniculata* (kindal/hunal), *Terminalia bellirica* (tare/ghoting) and *Terminalia chebula* (harda/alalekai)]. In the non-teak-bearing forests, the dominant genera are again *Anogeissus* and *Terminalias* accompanied by *Diospyros* (tupra/tendu), *Boswellia* (dhupa/chitta) and *Sterculia* (buthale/patala). Co-dominants are represented by many families having wider distribution and general adaptability. *Dipterocarpaceae* are virtually absent [except *Shorea talura* (jalari)]. *Dendrocalamus strictus* (medri bamboo) is the main bamboo. Grasses are of medium height such as *Heteropogon, Themeda, Saccharum spontanum*, etc.

In the revised classification of Champion and Seth (1968), following climax types are differentiated:

5A/C1 - Dry teak-bearing forest

5A/C2 - Dry red sanders-bearing forest

5A/C3 - Southern dry mixed deciduous forest

Among the above types, Dry teak-bearing forest (5A/C1) and Southern dry mixed deciduous forest (5A/C3) are met with in the forests of Karnataka. The third type, namely, Dry red sanders-bearing forest (5A/C2) occurs mainly in the state of Andhra Pradesh and, to a small extent, in Tamil Nadu.

Dry teak-bearing forest (5A/C1)

General description of this type of forest is as for the sub-group 5A given above but excluding the poorest parts of it. Unless considerably affected by human activities, the canopy is fairly complete and the trees are sufficiently large, tall and well grown to yield sawn timber. Teak of III and IV quality is included here, and the occurrence of teak in any quantity is indicative of this type. The majority of tree species occurring in this type coppice freely when felled. This type is met widely in South India. Rainfall is 100 cm to 125 cm but can be as high as 175 cm. The difference between this and the following type is usually due more to soil conditions than to rainfall and other climatic factors. This type of forest has been further sub-divided into two sub-types on the basis of floristic and environmental differences:

Very dry teak forest (5A/C1a): This sub-type occurs in areas with typical rainfall less than 90 cm. Soils are dry and infertile. It is an open forest of very poor quality on stony, detrital, truncated and shallow soils, usually derived from crystalline rocks or trap. Ground cover is scanty. Seedling regeneration is practically absent. Fires are very common. Grazing is heavy. Teak is present but not in high proportion. It is mixed with dry deciduous species. Characteristic species with *Tectona* (tega) are *Boswellia serrata* (dhupa), *Anogeissus latifolia* (dindiga), *Sterculia urens* (buthale/kempudale), *Cochlospermum religiosum* (Kadburuga/arasina buruga), *Acacia catechu* (kaggali/cutch), etc.

In Karnataka, Very dry teak forest (5A/C1a) is met with in some parts of **Bidar district**. Such forests occur in Changler, Karpakapalli and Karaknalli forests. In these forests, teak is found mixed with dry deciduous species such as *Chloroxylon swietenia* (mashwal) *Buchanania lanzan* (char/nurkal), *Terminalia tomentosa* (matti), *Anogeissus latifolia* (dindiga/dindal), *Albizia amara* (chujjulu/tugli), *Cassia fistula* (kakke), etc. In the past, this forest type appears to have been present in other dry districts also such as Ballari (Sandur), Kalaburagi (Chincholi), Yadgiri (Ashanal, Yeragera), Kolar (Royalpad forests), etc. However, biotic pressure and demand for teak for its prized wood resulted in its heavy exploitation; eventually the species has become occasional or sporadic in these forests.

Dry teak forest (5A/C1b): This sub-type occurs in areas with typical rainfall 90 cm to 130 cm. Soils are shallow or porous or clayey. Teak is present in high proportion, sometimes practically pure. Undergrowth is high and patchy. Seedlings are in groups and patches. Fires are frequent and grazing is heavy. It is a mixed dry deciduous forest with teak forming the major proportion of the crop on shallow porous or stiff clayey soils. Characteristic associate species are *Anogeissus latifolia* (dindiga), *Diospyros tomentosa* (tupra/tumri), *Hardwickia binata* (kamara/karachi/anjan) and other common dry deciduous trees. Champion and Seth have cited **a forest of Dharwar division** of Karnataka as an example of dry teak forest (5A/C1b) with the following floristic composition:

The tree species occupying the top canopy and second storey include *Tectona grandis* (tega) and *Anogeissus latifolia* (dindiga) as particularly characteristic species along with *Dillenia pentagyna* (kanagal), *Kydia calycina* (bhende), *Terminalia tomentosa* (matti), *Terminalia paniculata* (kindal), *Terminalia bellirica* (tare), *Terminalia chebula* (harda), *Lagerstroemia lanceolata* (nandi/nana), *Adina cordifolia* (heddi/yettiga), *Madhuca indica* (ippe/hippe), *Buchanania lanzan* (char/nurkal), *Salmalia malabarica* (buruga), *Grewia tiliaefolia* (tadasalu/dhaman), *Lannea coromandelica* (gojjal/godda) and *Pterocarpus marsupium* (honne). *Dendrocalamus strictus* (medri bamboo) is common, *Bambusa arundinacea* (dowga bamboo) is also found in moister localities. Shrubs include *Lantana* (chaduranga), *Santalum album* (srigandha), *Dodonaea viscosa* (bandarki) and *Carissa opaca* (kavali).

Dry teak forests (5A/C1b) are met with in a number of districts of Karnataka. These are: **Belagavi** (eastern part of Khanapur taluk), **Chikkamagaluru** (parts of Tarikere range and Lakkavalli WL range), **Davanagere** (parts of Channagiri and Shantisagar ranges), **Dharwar** (parts of Kalaghatgi range), **Haveri** (parts of Dhundsi and Hanagal ranges), **Shivamogga** (parts of Shikaripura and Soraba taluks, Bhadravathi, Sakrebyle, Shankar and Umblebyle ranges), **Uttara Kannada** (Haliyal range, parts of Sambrani, Bhagavathi, Kirwatti, Mundgod and Katur ranges). Due to heavy removal of teak in the past because of its prized timber, some of the forest areas which were earlier classified under 5A/C1b have lost the characteristics of a dry teak-bearing forest and are included in the following type (5A/C3).

Southern dry mixed deciduous forest (5A/C3)

This type (5A/C3) differs from the dry teak-bearing type (5A/C1) mainly floristically though some typical species (notably *Boswellia*) are more conspicuous. In this forest type, teak may be present but is not prominent. Thorny plants occur and tend to increase in proportion with heavy grazing, etc. to which most of the area is subjected. Bamboos are often absent and usually of poor quality when present. Grass is conspicuous till it is grazed down or burnt. Climbers are generally few, but may be heavy locally with species such as *Bauhinia vahlii, Acacia concinna*, etc. This forest type occurs throughout Peninsular India and is especially prevalent in the drier localities. Rainfall is 87.5 cm to 112.5 cm but can be as high as 150 cm on dry sites and soils. Well drained hill sides with shallow soils or undulating ground are typical. The most characteristic tree is *Anogeissus latifolia* (dindiga/dindal) with *Terminalia tomentosa* (matti) as a typical associate. *Diospyros tomentosa* (tupra/tumri) is also common. *Chloroxylon swietenia* (hurugalu/satinwood/mashawal), *Hardwickia binata* (kamara/karachi/ anjan), *Boswellia serrata* (dhupa/sambrani) and *Soymida febrifuga* (some/ swami mara) are very widespread and useful indicators as they are absent from the moist deciduous forests, but their occurrence is rather sporadic and often traceable to soil factors. *Acacia catechu* (kaggali/cutch/katha) is often present indicating the relation to thorn forests. The undergrowth is usually thin with a fairly dense growth of grass during monsoon. Champion and Seth have described a **forest of Dharwar forest division** and another **from Bhadravathi forest division,** both in Karnataka, as examples of Southern dry mixed deciduous forest (5A/C3) with the following floristic compositions:

Dharwar forest division, Karnataka

The characteristic tree species is *Anogeissus latifolia* (dindiga/dindal). Other species are *Acacia catechu* (kaggali/katha/cutch), *Terminalia tomentosa* (matti), *Soymida febrifuga* (swami), *Chloroxylon swietenia* (mashawal/hurugulu), *Albizia amara* (tugli/chujjulu), *Cassia fistula* (kakke), *Melia azedarach* (turukka bevu), *Hardwickia binata* (kamara/anjan/karachi), *Tectona grandis* (tyega/saguwani), *Santalum album* (shrigandha/gandhada gida). *Lantana* (chadurangi/lantana) is a common shrub. Growth of grass is fairly good.

Anthargange Sample Plot, Bhadravathi forest division, Karnataka

Top canopy trees: The characteristic tree species in the upper canopy are *Anogeissus latifolia* (dindiga), *Terminalia tomentosa* (matti), *Hymenodictyon* (doddathope/bogi) and *Sterculia urens* (buthale/kempu dale). Other species include *Terminalia chebula* (harda), *Lagerstroemia parviflora* (channangi), *Terminalia paniculata* (kindal/hunal), *Terminalia bellirica* (tare/ghoting/shanti), *Madhuca indica* (hippe/ippe), *Grewia tiliaefolia* (dhaman/tadasalu), *Tectona grandis* (saguwani/tyega), *Dalbergia latifolia* (beete/sissum), *Mitragyna parvifolia* (kalam/kadawal/kongu), *Stereospermum personatum* (padri/mukarti/malali), *Albizia odoratissima* (bilwara/goddahunase), *Albizia amara* (tugli/chujjulu), *Pterocarpus marsupium* (honne), *Schleichera trijuga* (chakota/kusum/sagade), *Strychnos potatorum* (cilla/chilla/chittadamara), *Lannea coromandelica* (godda/gojjal/moee/udimara), *Diospyros montana* (jagalaganti), *Schrebera swietenioides* (gante/kalgante), *Soymida febrifuga* (swami/some), *Dalbergia paniculata* (pachali/padre), *Adina cordifolia* (yethega) and *Gmelina arborea* (shivani/kumulu).

(**Note-** Champion and Seth have also indicated that in the above two examples, the patches in which teak is a prominent component of the crop could also be considered to belong to Dry Teak, 5A/C1.)

Second storey trees: *Zizyphus xylopyrus* (gotte/mullu kare/chotte), *Randia dumetorum* (kare), *Bauhinia racemosa* (basavanapada), *Ehretia laevis* (datrang/adak/bagari/tamboli), *Emblica officinalis* (nelli), *Gardenia latifolia* (kambi/kalkambi), *Flacourtia indica* (bilehuli/mulluthare), *Santalum album* (shrigandha), *Diospyros melanoxylon* (tumri/tupra), *Butea monosperma* (muthuga) and *Chloroxylon* (mashawal/hurugulu).

Bamboos: *Dendrocalamus strictus* (medri bamboo) is locally abundant.

Shrubs: *Holarrhena antidysenterica* (kuda/kudsalu/kadsoge), *Gardenia turgida* (bongeri), *Randia uliginosa* (kare/pandri/pindara), *Ixora arborea* (korgi/lokhandi/gorivi), *Gardenia gummifera* (dickemali/bikkegida).

Climbers: *Zizyphus oenoplia* (challa/sodli), *Acacia intsia* (kaad seege), *Celastrus paniculata* (bhavamga/jotishmati/kariganne/malkangoni).

Grass: There is complete cover of grass including *Aristida*.

(**Note -** On hill slopes, *Anogeissus latifolia* (dindiga) often strongly forms nearly pure associations.)

The general distribution of the forest type Southern dry mixed deciduous forest (5A/C3) in various districts of Karnataka is as follows: **Ballari** [parts of Sandur North, Sandur South, Hosapete and Kudligi ranges], **Belagavi** [part of Khanapur taluk, Kakti and Gujnal ranges], **Bengaluru Urban** (part of Bannerghatta national park), **Bidar** [parts of Bidar, Basavakalyan and Humnabad ranges], **Chamarajanagar** (most of the forests of the district other than the evergreen, semi-evergreen and moist deciduous forests that are met with at higher elevations, and excluding the eastern part of the district where the forests are relatively open and degraded; these forests cover about 2,00,000 hectares], **Chikkaballapur** [portions of the state forests such as Ittikaldurga (ID) Blocks, Narasimhadevarabetta (ND) Blocks, Vandamana, Vasanthapura, Haristala, KS Gida, Konaguntulu, Motamakalahalli, Gadare, Valasebetta, Adinarayanabetta, Talakai Kond, etc.], **Chikkamagaluru** [eastern parts of Chikkamagaluru and Tarikere taluks, eastern parts of Lakkavalli WL range], **Chitradurga** [Vedavathi valley in the western portions of Hosadurga and Holalkere taluks; some of the important forests are Marikanive, Kudurekanive, Lakkihalli, Devaragudda, Jankal, Nirthadi and Jogimatti], **Davanagere** [parts of Channagiri, Honnali, Davanagere, Jagalur and Harpanahalli taluks], **Dharwar** [parts of Kalaghatgi and Dharwar ranges], **Hassan** [parts of Alur, Arkalgud, Arsikere, Belur, Channarayapatna, Hassan and Holenarsipura ranges], **Haveri** [parts of Dhundsi, Hanagal and Hirekerur ranges], **Kalaburagi** [parts of the reserved forests of Chincholi range such as Chincholi B-I and B-II, Lachmasagar, Burugadoddi, Dharmasagar, Antawaram, Shadipur, Polkapalli, Bonaspur, etc.], **Kolar** [portions of the state forests such as Royalpad, Kamasandra, etc.], **Mandya** [parts of the state forests such as Basavanabetta, Dhanagur, Basavanakal, Konankal, Hasuvinakaval, Hulikere Lower and Upper Blocks, Narayanadurga, Mudibetta, etc.], **Mysuru** [eastern parts of Anechowkur and Doddaharave SFs, Muddanahally and Muthurayanahosalli SFs, western part of Veeranahosahalli SF, central part of Metikuppe SF, western parts of Sollepura, Siddapura and Chikkanahalli SFs, Somanathpura sandal reserve, eastern parts of Begur and Ainurmarigudi SFs, Alagachi and Katwal SFs and Naganapura I and II RFs], **Raichur** [parts of the reserved forests such as Bunkaldoddi, Galaga, Jalahalli, Kavital, Kumarkhed, Deodurga, etc.], **Ramanagara** [parts of the state forests such as Kombinakal, Narikal, Taylur, Chikkamannugudde, Kabbal, Makali, Tenginakal (in Channapatna range), Bettahalliwade (A,B&C), Gangadharanagudde, Muneshwarabetta, Banumanakal, Bananthamari, Siddarabetta (in Kanakapura range), Bantrakuppe (A&B), Chilur, Savanadurga, Siddadevarabetta, Chakrabhavi, Manchenabele (in Magadi range), Ramadevarabetta, Handigundi, Kumbalagod (in Ramanagara range), Chunchi West, Achal (RF), Arkavathi (PF) (in Sathanur range), Bilikal, Manjunatha, Ramadevarabetta (in Bannerghatta NP), Chowrakallu, Muggur, Chunchi East, Chilandavadi and Basavanabetta (part) (in Cauvery WLS)], **Shivamogga** [parts of Shivamogga, Bhadravathi, Shikaripura and Soraba taluks; some of the important state forests are: Anesara, Purdal, Devabal, Kunchenahalli, Muddinakoppa, parts of Shankar, Sakrebyle, Aldhara, Thammadihalli, Kukwada-Ubrani, Chandragutti, Chandrakala, Gangavanasara, etc.; a number of minor forests of the district also harbor this forest type], **Tumkur** [parts of Bukkapatna SF (in Bukkapatna range), Thirtharamapura and Extension SFs (in Chikkanayakanahalli range), Kolikal, Minchkal, Soolekal, Doddavadibetta and Kavaragal SFs (in Koratagere range), Ujjani, Huliyurdurga and Extension SFs (in Kunigal range), Madhugiri Extension, Byalya, Ramadevarabetta and Basmangi SFs (in Madhugiri range), Ranganathapura SF (in Sira range), Manchaldore and Extension SFs (in Gubbi range), Vadanakal SF (in Pavagada range), Devarayanadurga SF (in Tumkur range)], **Yadgiri** [parts of the reserved forests of Yadgiri range such as Minaspur B-I and B-II, Ashnal, Horancha, Yeragola, etc.]

It may however be mentioned that although widely distributed across the state as indicated above, the forests belonging to the climax type Southern dry mixed deciduous forest (5A/C3) are quite vulnerable to degradation especially in the Eastern Plains as well as in interior Karnataka, having been subjected to decades of overuse and maltreatment. As a matter of fact, the forests in some districts such as Chitradurga, Tumkur, Bidar, Hassan, Raichur, Kolar, Chikkaballapur, etc. have been so severely degraded that these now appear more like scrub forests. A number of districts such as Bagalkote, Vijayapura, Gadag, Bengaluru Rural, Koppal, Yadgiri, etc. have practically lost this forest type and various formations of deciduous scrub forest have taken over. Remnants of the original type (5A/C3) are occasionally met with in areas away from habitations, especially in valleys and depressions.

In addition to the climatic climax dry deciduous forest types mentioned above, the following degradation stages (DS) along with a number of edaphic (E) and secondary (S) types with characteristics of dry deciduous forests are found in Karnataka:

Dry deciduous scrub (5/DS1)

This type is characterized by shrubby growth on low broken soil cover. The shrubby growth, 3-6 m high, also includes some tree species, usually many-stemmed from the base due to heavy human and cattle interference. Many of the shrubs are unpalatable to cattle (*Holarrhena, Dodonaea*) or thorny (*Randia, Carissa*). Thin grass occurs throughout. The stunted growth of trees is attributed to maltreatment, felling, over-grazing, lopping and frequent fires. These forests are found throughout the dry deciduous zone.

Champion and Seth have described **three forest areas of Karnataka** as examples of Dry deciduous scrub (5/DS1) with the following floristic compositions:

Mysore plateau: Coppice shoots of dry deciduous forest species, i.e., *Tectona* (dry teak), *Pterocarpus, Albizia, Terminalia, Chloroxylon, Hardwickia,* etc. with thorny species *Atalantia monophylla* (kadunimbe/kadumbi), *Flacourtia* (bilehuli/mulluthare), *Dichrostachys* (wadu/waradu), *Randia* (kare), *Acacia chundra* (kempu jali). [*Atalantia monophylla, Dichrostachys, Randia* and *Acacia chundra* are characteristic species.]

Southern Mysore plateau: Main species are *Albizia lebbeck* (bage), *Albizia amara* (tugli/chujjulu), *Chloroxylon swietenia* (mashawal/hurugulu/satinwood), *Acacia chundra* (kempu jali), *Azadirachta indica* (bevu/neem), *Zizyphus mauritiana* (borehannu/bugari-mara/elachi), *Zizyphus oenoplia* (pargi/barige/karisurimullu/harasurali), *Dichrostachys cinerea* (wadu/waradu), *Euphorbia antiquorum* (mundukalli/chandara galli), *Pterolobium indicum* (travelers' terror/badabakke). Species occurring in stonier places include *Gyrocarpus jacquini* (kadu bende/thanaku), *Sterculia urens* (buthale/kempu dale), *Cochlospermum religiosum* (kaduburuga/arasina buruga), *Commiphora caudata* (konda mavu/assuaru) and *Givotia rottleriformis* (bilitale/butala/bettathaware/poliki). *Hardwickia, Feronia limonia* (bela/wood apple) and *Dendrocalamus strictus* are occasionally met with. [*Albizia amara, Dichrostachys cinerea, Euphorbia antiquorum, Gyrocarpus jacquini* and *Commiphora caudata* are characteristic species.]

Motebennur: *Butea* (muthuga), *Hardwickia* (kamara/anjan), *Cassia auriculata* (tangadi/tarwad) *Lantana, Dodonaea viscosa* (bandurki), *Cymbopogon* species. [*Cassia auriculata, Lantana and Dodonaea viscosa* are characteristic species.]

The dry deciduous scrub (5/DS1) now constitutes the major forest type in many districts of interior Karnataka and the Eastern Plains. While the forests of the districts of Bagalkote, Vijayapura, Gadag, Bengaluru Rural, Koppal and Yadgiri almost entirely belong to this type, substantial portions of the forests of the districts of Chitradurga, Tumkur, Bidar, Hassan, Raichur, Kolar, Chikkaballapur, Bengaluru Urban, Kalaburagi and Ballari also belong to this type. In these districts, there is no distinct line of demarcation between the climax formation (dry mixed deciduous forest 5A/C3) and the scrub forests (5/DS1), and these often overlap on each other. Shreds of the climax vegetation usually occur in areas with better soil, especially in valleys and depressions. Most of the forests are in various stages of degradation resulting from years of maltreatment of repeated hacking, over-grazing and recurrent fires. The districts of Belagavi and Hassan also harbor extensive scrub forests in all the taluks with the exception of Sakleshpur, Khanapur and Belagavi (part).

The scrub forests also occur in the remaining districts of the state such as Uttara Kannada, Shivamogga, Chikkamagaluru, Mysuru, Chamarajanagar, Dharwar, Haveri, Davanagere, Ramanagara and Mandya. Such forests are generally met with in areas adjacent to villages and other habitations where they are under constant pressure from both human and cattle populations.

Dry savannah forest (5/DS2)

This type of forest is represented by open grassland with fairly heavy grass interspersed with single or groups of fire hardy trees. The trees are short, usually crooked and unsound or hollow. Stem-less *Phoenix* is particularly characteristic. Thorny shrubs are common. The tree species include *Anogeissus latifolia* (dindiga), *Hardwickia binata* (kamara/anjan), *Butea monosperma* (muthuga), etc. Shrubs include *Cassia auriculata* (tangadi/tarwad), *Dodonaea viscosa* (bandurki), *Lantana camara* (chadurangi/lantana), etc. Among grasses, *Cymbopogon* species is very abundant. This type is found throughout the dry deciduous forests. Champion and Seth have described a **forest area of Motebennur**, Karnataka as an example of Dry savannah forest (5/DS2) with the following floristic composition:

Upper canopy: *Hardwickia binata* (kamara/anjan), *Butea monosperma* (muthuga/muttal).

Shrubs: *Cassia auriculata* (tangadi/tarwad), *Dodonaea viscosa* (bandurki), *Lantana camara.*

Grass: *Cymbopogon* species.

Euphorbia scrub (5/DS3)

This type of forest comes up on rocky areas or stony sites. Such forest owes its origin to intense biotic pressure such as excessive grazing, felling of tree growth, recurring fires, etc. Various species such as *Euphorbia antiquorum, Euphorbia neriifolia, Euphorbia nivulia, Euphorbia tirucalli, Calotropis gigantea, Opuntia dillenii,* etc. are commonly found in this type of forest.

Dry grassland (5/DS4)

This type of forest represents the most degraded stage of a dry deciduous forest. The dominant grass cover in the dry deciduous zone is *Sehima-Dicanthium* type, the characteristic perennial species being *Sehima nervosum, Chrysopogon fulvus, Themeda triandra, Erempogon foveolatus, Heteropogon contortus, Cymbopogon* species, etc. in hills and hill slopes and *Dichanthium annulatum, Bothriochloa pertusa, Erempogon foveolatus, Cyndon dactylon,* etc. on plateau, valleys and deep soils.

The above three forest types, namely, Dry savannah forest (5/DS2), Euphorbia scrub (5/DS3) and Dry grassland (5/DS4) are met with in patches within the scrub forests (5/DS1) described earlier. The prevalence of these forest types is more in the Eastern Plains as also in the eastern parts of some of the districts located in the northern and central parts of interior Karnataka such as Dharwar, Gadag, Haveri, Davanagere, Chitradurga and Tumkur.

Hardwickia forest (5/E4)

This is a distinct edaphic type of the dry deciduous forest characterized by the gregarious occurrence of *Hardwickia binata* (kamara/anjan/karachi). Kamara is an extremely resilient and hardy species having the unique ability to thrive on a dry climate and to establish and grow on dry shallow soil and rocky ground where most other species would struggle, wither or succumb. It is also a very fire-hardy species. In view of these unique abilities, in patches of shallow, gravelly soils in the dry deciduous zone, *Hardwickia binata* often adapts itself to the prevailing hostile environmental conditions forming pure groups. The growing stock is of relatively recent origin though aged and gnarled trees are found scattered. In such areas, usually kamara does not have many associates, and it occurs in complete occupation of the ground. Fire-hardiness coupled with heavy periodical seeding enables the species to grow gregariously. The factors that sustain such forests do not encourage the growth of other species. However, in areas run over by habitual ground fire, kamara is found to occur in association with other fire-hardy species such as *Chloroxylon swietenia* (mashawal/hurugulu) and *Anogeissus latifolia* (dindal).

Hardwickia binata as a tree species has a fairly widespread presence in the dry and semi-dry tracts of Karnataka. However, certain districts are particularly well known for natural and gregarious (edaphic) stands of *Hardwickia binata*; these are: **Chitradurga** (Marikanive, Swarnamukhi, Gowdanahalli, Bagganadu, Bhandravi and Kamarakaval RFs and Yelladakere MF), **Ballari** (Gollalingamanahalli, Koilarghatta, Bandri, Chikkantapura, Sunkadakallu and Tumbinakere RFs), **Haveri** (parts of Ranebennur range), **Gadag** (Kappat hills in Mundargi range and also in Shirhatti range), **Chamarajanagar** (Sathegal Jagir, Mambetta and Chikkailur RFs), **Davanagere** (Southern base of Sogi hills), **Ramanagara** (parts of Sathanur, Kanakapura and Ramanagara ranges, especially on hill tops of Basavanabetta and Chilandvadi RFs), **Tumkur** (northern portion of Bukkapatna RF and Kudrekanive RF), etc.

Boswellia forest (5/E2)

Another edaphic type, namely, Boswellia forest (5/E2) is encountered in patches of dry deciduous forests with shallow and gravelly soil, especially on upper slopes and hill tops. It is an open forest in which *Boswellia serrata* (dhupa) forms an overwood to stunted trees and shrubs of dry deciduous forests. The Boswellia crop is generally of uniform growth attaining appreciable height in favorable localities. The species is highly resistant to fire and regenerates well from seeds in difficult and hostile environments, resulting in its localized predominance. *Anogeissus latifolia* (dindal), generally stunted, is a common associate.

This edaphic forest type is encountered in sporadic patches in the dry deciduous forests of Ballari and Haveri districts: Ballari district (Kakubal, Deodhari, etc.), Haveri (Parts of Hirekerur range). Patches of *Boswellia serrata* in association with *Hardwickia* forests are met with in Ramanagara district also.

Laterite scrub (5/E7)

This type of forest is an open scrub of stunted trees of deciduous habit, sometimes with thorny species dominating, with thin undergrowth including xerophytic evergreens. It is distributed on the west coastal plains from Kanara downwards to Kerala. The climate is that of semi-evergreen or even evergreen forest, but the type is determined by the dry shallow soil which is usually hard laterite, probably exposed, denuded and hardened by human influences. Champion and Seth have described a **forest of North Kanara** and another from **South Kanara**, both from Karnataka, as examples of Laterite scrub (5/E7) with the following floristic compositions:

North Kanara, Karnataka

The tree species occupying the top canopy include *Terminalia chebula* (harda), *Careya arborea* (kavalu) and *Santalum album* (srigandha). The genera/species of trees and shrubs occupying the lower canopy and ground floor include *Gardenia* (dickemali), *Pavetta* (pavati/papat), *Ixora coccinea* (kepala/gudde dosal/kisukare/patkali/podkali), *Glochidion* (kaadu kaapi/bhoma/sulle mara), *Flacourtia indica* (bilehuli/mulluthotti/tambat), *Flacourtia montana* (attak/kakkade hannu mara/hennu sampige), *Osyris wightiana* (paral/chimat/popali/Nepalese sandalwood), *Randia dumetorum* (kare/mangarikai/gelphala), *Canthium dicoccum* (therane/kakkarole/pyre), etc. Climbers include *Dalbergia sympathetica* (maradeeballi/muldi), *Jasminum malabaricum* (kadu mallige), *Celastrus paniculatus* (bhavamga/jotishmati/kariganne), and *Zizyphus* species (bore/gotte).

South Kanara (N. Mangalore division), Karnataka

The tree species in the upper canopy include *Acacia chundra* (kempujali), *Litsea wightiana* (keyenjee/mashe/badaga), *Buchanania lanzan* (nurkal/char), *Lannea coromandelica* (godda/gojjal/udimara) and *Anacardium occidentale* (cashew/godambi - planted or natural). The lower storey comprises *Santalum album, Gardenia gummifera* (dickemali/bikke mara), etc.

The laterite scrub forests (5/E7) are encountered along the coastal areas in the districts of Uttara Kannada, Udupi and Dakshina Kannada. These areas were originally evergreen or semi-evergreen forests and were degraded over a number of centuries due to shifting cultivation followed by continuous withdrawals, over-grazing and recurring fires.

Dry bamboo brakes (5/E9)

Dry bamboo brakes are sometimes found in sporadic patches within the dry deciduous forests. This forest type is formed by the species *Dendrocalamus strictus* (medri bamboo/gala). Such brakes are of relatively low height, rarely over 7 meters, and are fairly dense. These brakes occur mainly on dry hillsides but also on alluvium with rainfall of 90 cm or rather more. The soil is often shallow and stony and remains dry most of the year. As already indicated, *Dendrocalamus strictus* is the characteristic species with a scattered distribution of trees and shrub species prevalent in the surrounding forest such as *Tectona grandis* (teak/saguwani), *Boswellia serrata* (dhupa), *Sterculia urens* (kempu dale/buthale) and *Cochlospermum religiosum* (kadu buruga/arisina buruga). Sometimes, the brakes are devoid of any other growth.

Dry tropical riverain forest (5/1S1)

This secondary forest type occurs as a narrow strip on both sides of the larger streams passing through a dry deciduous forest. The overwood on this strip of forest is of greater height than that of the climax dry deciduous forest and forms relatively moist and dense patches/strips with other smaller trees and shrubby undergrowth. The foliage is more or less evergreen in several of the chief dominants. The soil is often bare sand, which may have been first colonized by shrubs and grass. Common species found in the Dry riverain forest include *Terminalia arjuna* (holematti/torematti/bilimatti/neermatti), *Holoptelia integrifolia* (tapasi/aval), *Mitragyna parvifolia* (kalam/kongu), *Pongamia pinnata* (honge), *Tamarix ericoides* (jhao/serni), *Vitex negundo* (lakki/nikki), etc.

Secondary dry deciduous forest (5/2S1)

This forest type represents a secondary growth that has come up in a portion of a climax dry deciduous forest which had been subjected to more or less complete clearance at some time in the past for shifting or semi-permanent cultivation and has grown up again and is now subjected to heavy withdrawal for fuel, small timber and grazing. The forest is inferior to the climax type and comprises trees of poor shape and size. Sometimes old trees of inferior species are met with. Thorny species and species unpalatable to cattle are more common. Sandal is occasionally found. Champion and Seth have described **a forest of Dharwar taluk** from Karnataka as an example of Secondary dry deciduous forest (5/2S1) with the following floristic composition:

Dharwar taluk forests, Karnataka

The tree species occupying the top canopy include *Salmalia malabarica* (buruga/semal/savar), *Buchanania lanzan* (nurkal/char), *Grewia tiliaefolia* (tadasalu/dhaman), *Elaeodendron glaucum* (mukarki/kannur-mara), *Schleichera oleosa* (kusum/sagadi), *Lannea coromandelica* (godda/gojjal/udimara), *Semecarpus anacardium* (kadgeru/cheru/bibba), *Tectona grandis* (saguwani/thyaga). The lower storey comprises *Feronia limonia* (bela/wood apple), *Aegle marmelos* (bilva/patri), *Zizyphus xylopyrus* (gotte/mullu kare/kotte), *Careya arborea* (kavalu/kumbi), *Gardenia* species (dickemali/bikke mara), *Dolichandrone atrovirens* (oodimara/godmurki/mashwal), *Santalum album* (srigandha), etc. Shrubs include *Dodonaea viscosa* (bandurki/bandaru), *Carissa spinarum* (kavali/karvand), *Holarrhena antidysenterica* (kuda/kadsoge), *Lantana camara* (lantana/chadurangi), etc.

Shorea talura forest

Pure or nearly pure patches of *Shorea talura* (jalari) are occasionally found primarily in the dry deciduous forests of Karnataka. These gregarious forest patches are edaphic variants and are generally found on shallow, sandy or clayey, calcareous soil. Such forest patches are found in the districts of Mysuru, Chamarajanagar (Bandipur national park), Bengaluru Urban (Bannerghatta national park), Bengaluru Rural, Ramanagara, Chikkaballapur, Tumkur, etc. This forest type has not been mentioned by Champion and Seth in their book (1968). However, it is a forest type of significance and deserves to be recognized. Incidentally, *Shorea talura* is the lone representative of the *Dipterocarpaceae* family in the dry deciduous and scrub forests of Karnataka.

Thorn forests of Karnataka

As per the "Revised Survey of the Forest Types of India" by Champion and Seth (1968), the thorn forests of Karnataka come under the group 6 (Tropical Thorn Forests), sub-group 6A (Southern Tropical Thorn Forests). Champion and Seth have described this sub-group (6A) as follows:

"An open low forest in which thorny usually hardwood species predominate, *Acacia* species being particularly characteristic. The trees usually have short boles and low branching crowns which rarely meet. The usual height is 6 to 9 m. There is usually a mixture of species (though relatively few in number), consociations being the exception rather than the rule. There is ill-defined lower storey of smaller trees and large shrubs, mostly spiny and often with other xerophytic characters, extending down to low shrub growth of similar character. There is usually a thin grass growth which may appear fairly complete during the short moist season, but more or less the soil is bare. Climbers are few, also frequently showing xerophytic adaptations."

The Southern Tropical Thorn Forests are found throughout the dry peninsular tract to the lee of the Western Ghats from the extreme south up to Indore and Bhopal. These forests cover parts of Gujarat, Madhya Pradesh, Chhattisgarh, Maharashtra, Tamil Nadu, Telangana, Andhra Pradesh and Karnataka. The annual mean temperature of the year is about 25.5°C. A few places such as Ballari are hotter and Bengaluru with its extra 300 m of altitude a few degrees cooler. The hottest month is May when the monthly mean is usually 29.5°C to 32°C whilst the mean maximum is 41°C. The mean January temperature is a little over 21°C with mean minimum varying from 4.4°C to 13.3°C. The typical annual rainfall for this type of forest is from about 50 cm to about 85 cm. The dry season is for about six months or more. These forests are found on a wide range of geological formations and rocks. The soil is almost always shallow and dry, though it may be of fair depth if sandy. The type also comes up in black cotton soil. With higher rainfall, it comes up on hard laterite soil. In many localities the soil is quite alkaline. Most of the forest is on flat ground or low undulating hills and plateau.

The genus *Acacia* with a number of species is particularly characteristic of the Southern tropical thorn forests. Fleshy *Euphorbias* are generally present and may form a conspicuous constituent of the vegetation, and *Capparis* is also a typical genus. The genus *Zizyphus* is also fairly common in this forest type. *Opuntia*, though not indigenous, has naturalized over considerable extents of thorn forests.

In the revised classification of Champion and Seth, following four types are differentiated:

6A/C1   - Southern thorn forest

6A/C2   - Carnatic umbrella thorn forest

6A/DS1 - Southern thorn scrub

6A/DS2 - Southern *Euphorbia* scrub

Among the above types, Southern thorn forest (6A/C1), Southern thorn scrub (6A/DS1) and Southern *Euphorbia* scrub (6A/DS) are met with in the forests of Karnataka. Carnatic umbrella thorn forest (6A/C2) is restricted to southern part of Tamil Nadu.

Southern thorn forest (6A/C1)

This forest type is the most widely spread form of the Southern tropical thorn forest. *Acacia catechu* in one of its forms (*Acacia catechu* SS, *Acacia catechuoides, Acacia chundra*) is almost invariably present; quite often it is also the predominating species. It is associated with several other *Acacias* and allied thorny *Mimosae* and *Zizyphus*. Stunted specimens of a number of tree species of the dry deciduous forests such as *Anogeissus latifolia* (dindiga/ dindal), *Soymida febrifuga* (swami gida/some) and others are scattered in varying numbers throughout the forest. Patches of fleshy *Euphorbias* are met with in the shallow and rocky sites. The locality factors of the sub-group (6A) mentioned above are applicable to this type. Champion and Seth have cited **a forest of Dharwar-Bijapur area** from Karnataka as an example of Southern thorn forest (6A/C1) with the following floristic composition:

Characteristic species in the upper canopy are *Acacia catechu* (kaggali/ katha/cutch), *Acacia leucophloea* (bilijali) and *Acacia arabica* (karijali/ gobli). Other associates in the upper storey are *Aegle marmelos* (bilva/patri), *Chloroxylon swietenia* (mashawal/hurugalu), *Euphorbia nivulia* (dubbakalli/

dundukalli/elegalli/gutagalli), *Ficus asperrima* (garagatti/khargas), *Flacourtia indica* (bilehuli/mulluthotti/tambat), *Ixora arborea* (korgi/gorivi/lokhandi), *Strychnos potatorum* (chilla/chitta) and *Santalum album* (srigandha). The lower storey comprises *Carissa* species (kawli/karvand), *Cassia auriculata* (tangadi/tarwad), *Dodonaea viscosa* (bandara/bandarki), *Opuntia* (nagatali/dabbagalli/paapasu kalli - naturalized), etc. *Lantana* (naturalized) is a common shrub. Climber such as *Zizyphus oenoplia* (pargi/barige) is present.

Southern thorn scrub (6A/DS1)

This forest represents the degradation stage of the climax forest (6A/C1) mentioned above. Such degradation is the result of usual maltreatment meted out because of biotic interference such as heavy felling, recurrent fires, etc. This leads to formation of close almost impenetrable thorny thickets, about 4-6 m high. The number of stunted and scattered dry deciduous trees further comes down; very few surviving trees remain standing here and there. Spiny climbers are common. Further degradation of this type of forest may result in the formation of sparse thickets, about 2-4 m high in which grasses are more abundant. The floristic composition remains more or less unaltered.

Southern Euphorbia scrub (6A/DS2)

This forest type is a very open formation in which fleshy *Euphorbias* (kalli) are the most important constituents. The thorny *Acacias* and their associates also occur but are more than usually stunted, and form widely spaced rounded bushes. Much of the soil is bare but there is usually a thin cover of wiry grasses. This type of forest is found in the shallowest and poorest sites within the sub-group 6A. Soil is shallow and rocky, or alkaline. Important species are *Euphorbia tirucalli* (bontakalli/bontekalli), *E. antiquorum* (kontekalli/jadekalli/mundukalli), *E. trigona* (mandagalli/attimandu/kundigi), *E. nivulia* (dubbakalli/dundukalli/elegalli/gutagalli), *E. neriifolia* (malekalli), *Calotropis gigantea* (bili aekke/jilledi/arka), *Opuntia dillenii* (nagatali/dabbagalli/paapasukalli), *Dodonaea viscosa* (bandara/bandurki), *Cassia auriculata* (tangadi/tarwad), etc. Grasses such as *Aristida, Cymbopogon*, etc. are found.

In Karnataka, the Southern thorn forest (6A/C1) and its degraded formations (6A/DS1 and 6A/DS2) mostly occur in the Eastern Plains and in the eastern parts of some of the districts located in interior Karnataka such as Dharwar, Gadag, Haveri, Davanagere, Chitradurga and Tumkur. These areas receive scanty to very low rainfall. The Southern thorn forest is met with on the poorest soils in these areas. Its degraded formations occur in areas where soil is practically absent, or on sites that have been stripped of the soil mantle exposing the underlying rocks and boulders.

The line of distinction between the degraded formations (5/DS1, 5/DS2, 5/DS3 & 5/DS4) derived from climax dry deciduous forests (5A/C1 & 5A/C3) and the degraded formations (6/DS1 & 6/DS2) derived from climax thorn forests (6A/C1) is very thin. They exhibit near similar characteristics. At times, it becomes difficult to ascertain whether these formations originated from a dry deciduous forest or from a thorn forest.

Thorn Forest versus Dry Deciduous Scrub

Tropical thorn forest (6A/C1) is a climatic climax formation. This formation represents the highest/ultimate/final stage in the succession of a forest in areas with intrinsically poor soil and receiving very low rainfall (50 cm to 85 cm). Although the dominance of thorny species is an important indicator of a tropical thorn forest, it is not the sole criterion to determine the climax status. More specifically, a forest that has acquired the dominance of thorny species through a process of retrogression triggered by biotic disturbances does not qualify to be called a climax thorn forest.

In the Eastern Plains and interior Karnataka, due to intense biotic pressure resulting from centuries of use, overuse and abuse, many of the climax dry deciduous forests (5A/C1 or 5A/C3) have been severely degraded; so much so that the floristic compositions of these forests have undergone drastic change: most of the original species have disappeared, and hardier ones, primarily of the thorny types, have taken over. Presently, these forests actually belong to the type dry deciduous scrub (5/DS1). Quite often, such forests are assigned the status of climax thorn forest (6A/C1) merely because of the preponderance of thorny species. Such an assignment is not appropriate because these forests represent a degradation stage (DS) and not a climax state (C).

Before assigning the climax status to a forest as thorn forest (6A/C1), a review of its past history is essential. Sometimes, the residual/remnant vegetation in the forest gives sufficient clue regarding its past status. The ultimate clincher should of course be the average annual rainfall received in the area.

Chapter 3

DRY DECIDUOUS FORESTS OF KARNATAKA – A HISTORICAL PERSPECTIVE

In the introductory chapter we have indicated that although the dry deciduous and thorn forests of Karnataka have widespread presence over a vast landscape that covers more than 75% of the geographical area of the state, the forests together add up to only a small proportion of the geographical area. Here it may be mentioned that during 2006 the Karnataka State Remote Sensing Application Centre (KSRSAC), Bengaluru had provided detailed land use land cover statistics for each district of Karnataka state by interpreting satellite imageries pertaining to the period 1999-2000. This was one of the outputs of a project assigned to the KSRSAC by the Karnataka Forest Department (KFD) to develop and generate comprehensive database using Geographic Information Systems (GIS) and Remote Sensing (RS) to be used for planning and management by the KFD. The data regarding the land use land cover classification are enormous and provide a lot of information about our forests. The extent of each forest type in each density class has been indicated. As regards forest plantations, the extent in each category of plantation has been given. Similar information has been provided for croplands and other plantations like coffee, tea, areca nut, cashew, rubber, agricultural (mostly coconut) plantations, etc. District-wise details of scrub forests, forest blanks, grasslands, scrub lands, built up areas, rocky/stony areas, water bodies, waterlogged areas, mining/quarry areas, etc. have also been given. Based on the district-wise land use land cover statistics provided by the KSRSAC in their 2006 Report, the distribution of various types of forest in Karnataka is depicted in the following table (Table-3.1):

Table –3.1   District-wise distribution of various types of forest in Karnataka as per Land use Land cover classification by KSRSAC (2006)

(Area in km²)

Sl. No.	District	Geographical area (GA)	Recorded forest area (RFA)	Evergreen forest	Semi-evergreen forest	Moist deciduous forest	Dry deciduous forest	Scrub forest	Forest Plantations^
(1)	(2)	(3)	(4)	(5)	(6)	(7)	(8)	(9)	(10)
DISTRICTS WITH HIGH RAINFALL (*MALNAD*)									
1	Belagavi	13,415	2,063.20	285.42	82.67	434.74	119.56	902.56	75.13
2	Chamarajnagar	5,676	2,791.46	103.79	53.71	324.55	2,058.33	266.94	19.64
3	Chikkamagaluru	7,201	2,767.80	744.01	65.97	897.84	269.46	195.29	282.84
4	Dakshina Kannada	4,560	2,012.18	412.88	141.94	1,722.08	-	4.66	192.34
5	Hassan	6,814	880.60	231.12	41.47	30.16	4.66	154.85	129.30
6	Kodagu	4,102	2,870.99	949.90	44.67	274.99	183.82**	19.79	195.92
7	Mysuru	6,307	1,449.87	-	-	42.94	768.03	67.30	133.37
8	Shivamogga*	8,477	6,642.55	483.88	829.91	1,398.67	327.55	241.00	579.30
9	Udupi	3,880	1,720.57	386.00	260.45	342.59	-	14.53	93.22
10	Uttara Kannada	10,291	8,296.46	2,365.21	946.29	2,915.58	279.41	162.57	830.47
		70,723	31,495.68	5,962.21	2,467.08	8,384.14	4,010.00	2,029.49	2,531.53

	DISTRICTS WITH MEDIUM RAINFALL (INTERIOR KARNATAKA/SEMI-MALNAD)								
11	Dharwar	4,260	468.54	-	-	-	296.63	8.79	80.09
12	Gadag	4,656	333.37	-	-	-	0.77	290.00	31.70
13	Haveri	4,823	432.80	-	-	-	138.21	106.90	140.02
14	Davanagere*	5,924	544.34	-	-	-	173.64	412.02	105.59
15	Chitradurga	8,440	1,287.18	-	-	-	6.12	605.26	68.74
16	Tumkur	10,597	1,291.67	-	-	-	19.39	613.20	368.29
17	Bengaluru (Urban)	2,190	122.25	-	-	-	15.99	19.70	227.01
18	Bengaluru (Rural)	2,259	186.43	-	-	-	0.39	33.51	401.96
19	Ramanagara	3,556	978.42	-	-	-	432.52	159.28	145.40
20	Mandya	4,961	664.61	-	-	0.82	139.29	95.09	166.13
		51,666	6,310.25	-	-	0.82	1,222.95	2,343.75	1,734.93

Contd.

DISTRICTS WITH LOW RAINFALL (EASTERN PLAINS/MAIDAN)									
21	Bagalkote	6,575	838.93	-	-	-	0	687.36	31.67
22	Vijayapura	10,494	81.11	-	-	-	0	9.27	3.16
23	Bidar	5,448	456.16	-	-	-	10.34	62.79	33.83
24	Kalaburagi	10,954	480.93	-	-	-	94.03	92.73	32.56
25	Yadgiri	5,270	516.83	-	-	-	2.10	129.52	20.80
26	Raichur	8,386	327.47	-	-	-	18.16	256.77	20.70
27	Koppal	5,630	430.66	-	-	-	0	175.84	4.71
28	Ballari	8,450	1,378.52	-	-	-	305.60	1,138.59	72.00
29	Kolar	3,979	508.34	-	-	-	0	212.72	460.13
30	Chikkaballapur	4,244	557.88	-	-	-	9.92	516.90	307.99
		69,430	5,576.83	-	-	-	440.15	3,282.49	987.55
		1,91,819	43,382.76	5,962.21	2,467.08	8,384.96	5,673.10	7,655.73	5,254.01

[* The recorded forest areas of Shivamogga and Davanagere districts need reconciliation; forest areas of Channagiri taluk appear to have been included in Shivamogga district instead of Davanagere district. ** In the above table, Kodagu district has been shown to harbor dry deciduous forest; however, the district with an average annual rainfall of about 250 cm (210 cm to 330 cm) primarily harbors evergreen, semi-evergreen and moist deciduous forests; some of the relatively open moist deciduous forests of Somawarpet and Virajpet taluks appear to have been interpreted as dry deciduous forest. ^ Forest plantations include Eucalyptus plantations also with a total extent of about 2,120 sq km; about 50% of the Eucalyptus plantations are in private lands, mostly in the districts of Bengaluru Rural, Bengaluru Urban, Tumkur, Kolar and Chikkaballapur.]

Perusal of Table-3.1 indicates that the evergreen, semi-evergreen and moist deciduous forests of the state are restricted only in the *malnad* region, whereas the dry deciduous forests are distributed all over the state, although these are concentrated more in the eastern part of the *malnad* region (4,010.00 km²) compared with the interior Karnataka region (1,222.95 km²) and the Eastern Plains (440.15 km²). It may also be noted from the table [Column Nos. (4) & (8)] that the extent of dry deciduous forest (climax type) in the districts of interior Karnataka and the Eastern Plains is quite less compared with the recorded forest area (RFA) of the districts. Dharwar, Haveri, Davanagere, Ramanagara, Mandya, Kalaburagi and Ballari are the only districts that have some sizeable extents of dry deciduous forest. A few districts such as Gadag, Chitradurga, Tumkur, Bengaluru (Rural), Bengaluru (Urban), Bidar, Raichur, Yadgiri and Chikkaballapur have registered very insignificant extents under dry deciduous forest, and a few districts such as Bagalkote, Vijayapura, Koppal and Kolar have not registered any dry deciduous forest at all. It may also be seen that most of the districts of interior Karnataka and the Eastern Plains have large extents of scrub forests [Column No. (9)]. In these districts, it is the scrub forests and to some extent the plantations raised in forest areas, including eucapyptus plantations, that make up for the large gap that exists between the recorded forest area (RFA) and the area under dry deciduous forest. The extent of scrub forests is particularly high in the districts of Gadag, Davanagere, Chitradurga, Tumkur, Bagalkote, Raichur, Koppal, Ballari, Kolar and Chikkaballapur. Absence, or very limited presence, of dry deciduous forests coupled with overwhelming presence of scrub forests in most of the districts of interior Karnataka and the Eastern Plains is reflective of the severe maltreatment to which the forests in these regions were subjected to in the past. It will be of some interest to look into the various factors that led to transformation of vast extents of climax dry deciduous forests of the state into scrub forests. In this context, it may be mentioned that historical documents such as the Gazetteers written towards the end of the nineteenth century and during the beginning of the twentieth century give a fairly authentic account of the presence and status of forests in various parts of the state. An endeavor will be made in the following paragraphs to bring out the details regarding the dry deciduous and thorn forests that occurred in various parts of Karnataka including the Eastern Plains or the *maidan* region during that period.

Mysore State (princely state)

A fairly vivid and comprehensive description of the forests of the princely state of Mysore during the first quarter of the twentieth century has been provided in the Mysore Gazetteer (Volume I, Descriptive, 1927) compiled and edited by Mr. C. Hayavadana Rao. The description appears under the Chapter IV (Botany) which was prepared by Mr. G. H. Krumbiegel, Superintendent of Botanical Gardens and Economic Botanist to the Government of Mysore, Bangalore. The portion of the chapter pertaining to the dry deciduous forests (teak pole forests and fuel forests) of Mysore State is reproduced below:

> *"Deciduous teak pole belt.* – The strip of forest which extends from Anavatti in Sorab to Chamrajnagar is similar in composition to the above*, but the growth is very poor, the trees not attaining a girth of more than 4 feet anywhere. The average rainfall varies from 30 to 35 inches and the crop is open with undergrowth of grass. The forest yields small timber. The total area of this type of forest is about 262 square miles. The major portion of this belt has all conveniences in the matter of roads and labour. The principal forests that may be enumerated under this type are: - Kowdi, Chandrakal, Kunchenahalli, Kukwada-Ubrani, Antargange, Bhadrapur, Hadikere, Thyagadabagi, portions of Veeranahosahalli and Mettikuppe, Katwal, Naganapur, Bargi, and portions of Chamrajnagar. (* refers to the moist deciduous or high forest of Mysore State.)

> *"Dry deciduous fuel forest.* – This may also be divided into two definite strips of forests on account of certain characteristic differences.

> *"Superior type of fuel forest.* – This strip starting from about the south-western limits of Davanagere taluk extends to the north of Channapatna. Towards the east, it extends to the provincial boundary of the State in the Bangalore and Kolar Districts. The average rainfall over this tract varies from 25 to 30 inches. The principal species to be found are: - Kaggali/The Cutch tree (*Acacia*

catechu), Devadari (*Erythroxylon monogynum*), Chigare (*Albizia amara*), Channangi (*Lagerstroemia parviflora*), Dindiga (*Anogeissus latifolia*), Jalari (*Shorea talura*), Hunal (*Terminalia paniculata*), Some/The bastard Red Cedar (*Soymida febrifuga*), Banni (*Acacia ferruginea*), Karijali (*Acacia arabica*), Bilijali (*Acacia leucophloea*), Padarapachali (*Dalbergia paniculata*), Tupre (*Diospyros tupra*), Yeje (*Premna tomentosa*), Kodlimurka (*Acacia* Spp), Yelachi (*Zizyphus jujuba*).

"Inferior type. – This is confined chiefly to the northern portion of Chitaldrug and Tumkur Districts. It extends through Davanagere, Jagalur, Molkalmuru, Challakere, Hiriyur, Sira, Pavagada and Maddagiri Taluks. It is a dry arid forest tract, with very low rainfall, 15 to 20 inches. The growth is very poor. The characteristic tree growth is Kamara (*Hardwickia binata*) with a little Kaggali (the Cutch tree) and other inferior and scanty growth and Bode grass not yet identified for its under-growth. Among shrubs and useful bushes are: - Yekka/Giant swallow wort (*Calotropis gigantean*), Thangadi/ Tanner's bark (*Cassia auriculata*), Kakke/Indian Laburnum (*Cassia fistula*) and Maraharalu/Physic nut (*Jatropha curcas*)."

Among the erstwhile districts of the Mysore State, the districts of **Chitradurga, Kolar, Bangalore and Tumkur** appear to have lost substantial portions of the forests even before the advent of the British. The status of the forests of these districts as brought out in the Gazetteers and other documents during and after the British administration is briefly indicated below:

CHITRADURGA DISTRICT
(present Chitradurga and Davanagere districts)

In the Mysore Gazetteer (Volume II, Revised Edition, 1897) compiled and edited by Sir Benjamin Lewis Rice, the general topography of the Chitradurga district (then called Chitaldroog) has been described as follows:

"Physical features. – The whole of this comparatively arid District is included in the valley of the Vedavati or Haggari, with the Tungabhadra running for a few miles along the north-western boundary. The Vedavati enters the District in the south-west and flows in a north-east direction to a few miles beyond Hiriyur. From this point, where the stream begins to take the name of Haggari, it runs north, within a few miles of the main eastern boundary, and leaves the District near the eastern base of the Molakalmuru projection. During the hot months it is for the most part dry, but supplies a number of wells sunk in the sandy bed.

"The District is crossed from south-south-east to north-north-west by a belt, about 20 miles broad, of intermittent parallel chains of low hills, mostly bare and stony, through which are several *kanives*, or passes. The eastern line runs from the west of Hiriyur to Chitaldroog (3,229 feet), and thence, with a break for some distance, continues from Kankuppa hill (2,721 feet) to the frontier. The summit of Jogi Maradi to the south of Chitaldroog, one of the highest points in this range, is 3,803 feet above sea-level. The western parallel commences at Hosdurga (3,226 feet), and passes by Mayakonda to Anaji. Around Molakalmuru in the north are some detached clusters of rocky hills. Of these, Nunke Bhairava hill is 3,022 feet, Jatinga Ramesvara hill, 3,469, and Santigudda 2,595. This part of Mysore, says Mr. Bruce Foote, is 'occupied by a tract of country of singular beauty. The bold, rocky hills which rise out of it in every direction are divided from each other by equally picturesque valleys full of fine trees, amongst which tamarind trees, pre-eminent for their love of granitic soil, abound. The road from the travellers' bungalow at Hanagal (on the Bangalore-Bellary high road), which skirts the south side of the line of hills for the first five miles, and for the next four passes right through them, takes one through scenery not easily forgotten for its striking beauty in grand rocks and rich vegetation'.

"Except in the region of the hilly belt, the whole extent of the District north and east is open and level plain, entirely destitute of picturesque features, but presenting at certain seasons in favourable spots a vast expanse of verdant cultivation. Though there are no trees there is abundance of excellent pasture, while the black and dreary-looking soil seems only to require the contact of water to develop its productiveness. To the north and west of Chitaldroog the surface of the country is undulating and covered with thick and rich grass. Trees are few in number."

As regards the status of the vegetation including the forests of the district, the Mysore Gazetteer (Volume II, Revised Edition, 1897) provides the following information:

"**Vegetation.** – The District is almost throughout a 'dry and thirsty land'. It has no forest. Great undulating plains, covered frequently with nothing but stones and a dwarf species of mimosa (called locally *hote jali*, and armed with vicious looking and formidable spines from one to four inches in length), are dotted at wide intervals, with villages lying in the hollows, having sometimes a few trees round them. These are the characteristics of fully one-third of the District. The whole taluq of Challakere answers generally to this description, but where there is any water in the soil there are some fine cocoa-nut gardens. The pastures, too, during the cooler months of the year, are good, and the Amrit Mahal has extensive grazing grounds in Dodderi, Tallak, Hosdurga, and other parts of the District.

"Standing on the low range of hills near the Mari Kanave, the view which meets the eye is not, during the rainy months, altogether so desolate. Looking up the valley of the Vedavathi towards Hosdurga a few more trees are seen, and the country is not so very bare. To the south and south-east, along the Hiriyur hills, there are jungles of the karachi (*Hardwickia binata*). Again between Bommagondanakere and Hangal, in the taluq of Molkalmuru, is another tract of country covered with the karachi. In the same taluq, to the east of the kasba town and on the borders of the Bellary District, is a small fuel jungle among hills; and in the western corner of Jagalur taluq is another of tolerable dimensions. Not far from the town of Chitaldroog are a few small patches of acacias, and on the Jogi matti, a hill near Chitaldroog, are a few bamboos and some poor trees of second-class timber.

"Yet the soil would not be unproductive if it only had water. Near Jagalur and Bommagondanakere, and one or two other spots where irrigation is possible from either tanks or wells worked by *kapile*, heavy crops are taken. On the high lands where the soil is disintegrated rock, the dry crops, provided sufficient rain falls, are good.

"The quantity of timber for building purposes is, as may be supposed, very limited; and the large towns draw their supplies chiefly from more favoured districts. In the villages the huts are very poorly built. The stems of cocoa-nut trees and wood obtained from dead fruit-trees growing in gardens are very much used, and not unfrequently the scapes of the common aloe are used both as joists and uprights."

From the above descriptions provided in the Mysore Gazetteer (1897) it would appear that Chitradurga district did not harbor forest of much significance towards the end of the nineteenth century. The landscape primarily comprised rocky and barren hills interspersed with agricultural lands and pastures. Soil by and large was fertile and, when favored with irrigation or a good rainfall, produced luxuriant crop.

However, Chitradurga district in the distant past was reported to have harbored very good forests supporting fine timber trees. Most of these have since disappeared owing to the indiscriminate manner in which forests were cleared to make way for cultivation and human settlements. Massive clearance of forests in the region could be traced back to around the 16th century when the Vijayanagara kings had permitted the local chiefs, who reared numerous herds of cattle, to clear the forests to set up villages and bring the lands under cultivation and pasture. Continuous negligence towards preservation of forests coupled with the exploitative policies of the earlier rulers who had allowed very liberal diversion of forests in favor of agriculture, and the persistent efforts of the people to clear land for cultivation resulted in depletion of forest resources. Even today forests are considered dispensable in favor of agriculture and there is a tendency to encroach upon forest lands wherever some form of cultivation is possible.

That Chitradurga district had thick forest in the past is also corroborated by the following remarks of Mr. Bowring, the Commissioner of Mysore, quoted in the Mysore Gazetteer (1897) as reproduced below:

"It is not improbable that this portion of Mysore may have been less sterile formerly, as on many of the hills traces are to be seen of forests cut down long ago. In fact, old records mention the existence of fine timber where such has wholly disappeared, owing, no doubt, to the reckless way in which the cultivators have cut down whatever they required for agricultural implements, regardless of the destruction caused to young trees and saplings. No one ever thought of planting new trees to replace those that had been felled, and so, as population increased and agriculture spread, the few remaining forests rapidly disappeared. The denudation of trees under which the District suffers has probably had much to do with the prevailing drought, there being scarcely any vegetation to arrest the passage of the monsoon clouds, which float onwards without depositing their valuable contents."

The above remarks of Mr. Bowring are more or less in conformity with the observations of Dr. Francis Buchanan, the famous traveler who had passed through the Mysore State during 1800-1801. In his book titled 'A Journey from Madras through Mysore, Canara, and Malabar', Buchanan, while traveling from Hiriyur to Srirangapatna via Yelladakere, Banavara, Halebeedu, Hassan, etc. during the first week of May, 1801, describes the appearance of the region from Hiriyur towards *Ellady-caray* (Yelladakere) in the following words: 'The appearance of the country is desolate, and it is said never to have been much better, in the memory of man. The soil is entirely stony poor land; and the naked rocks, in a state of decay, come frequently to the surface. The grass in many places is long, but at this season it is quite withered; and the only things green, that are visible, are a few wild date palms (*Elate sylvestris*), most of which are young. In moist places they grow spontaneously, and produce juice, which is often boiled into *Jagory*. As Buchanan travels further and crosses hilly terrain, he comes across forests covered with trees: 'On the hills, there are a good many stunted trees.'

Buchanan in his book has mentioned in fairly great detail about the ongoing practice of mining and smelting of iron ore in various parts of Mysore State; furnaces for smelting iron were set up wherever iron ore was available. As regards mining in areas in the Chitradurga district, Buchanan mentioned about a number of places such as *Cudera Canavay, Buca Sagurada Canavay* and *Doda Rashy Guda*. He also referred to the place called *Ellady-caray* in *Heriuru* (Hiriyur) where smelting works had been discontinued long back owing to shortage of fuel (May 2, 1801):

> *"Iron was formerly smelted in Ellady-caray from black sand, which was brought from a hill about two miles to the westward. Much of the vitreous scoriae remain where the furnaces stood; but the work has been abandoned these sixty years; the want of fewel is indeed a sufficient reason."*

While referring to mining and smelting iron ore in the above-mentioned areas, Buchanan provided the following information (May 3, 1801) which throws some light on the forests of the region:

> *"At Chica-bayli-caray is a furnace for smelting iron ore, brought from a mine called Cudera Canavay, and which is supplied with charcoal from the hills to the westward. The ore is brought upon buffaloes and asses. It is in small slaty fragments that are broken to pieces with a stone, and thus separated from much sand and earth. These small pieces, when fit for the furnace, are about the size of a hazel-nut. The operation ought to be performed at the mine, to lessen the expense of carriage; but the danger from tigers prevents the people from staying there longer than absolutely necessary. The number of these ferocious animals having increased of late, has forced the people to relinquish a mine Buca Sagurada Canavay, which is distant from the other one coss toward the N.W. Even Cudera Canavay has now become very dangerous, and in the course of the last year three people have been destroyed."*

The presence of tiger in the forests of the erstwhile Chitradurga district in the beginning of the nineteenth century as mentioned above by Buchanan is a pointer to the fact that the district indeed had dense forests in the past. Smelting of iron ore in the forges required a lot of charcoal which was prepared by carbonizing firewood obtained from clearance of the nearby forests. Smelting of iron had reached its peak during the reign of Hyder Ali and Tipu Sultan, who had required a lot of iron for making military armaments. In addition, there was increasing demand for iron for making agricultural implements. Manufacture of iron, with some steel, was carried on in the district even during the British period 'in the Hiriyur, Hosdurga, and Chitaldroog talukqs, in the neighbourhood of the central hill ranges'. Such activity that continued for centuries could not have been possible in the absence of thick forest in the vicinity of the mines located in the district.

Regarding the condition to which the forests of Chitradurga district were affected due to smelting of iron has been described in the Mysore Gazetteer (1929) as follows:

> "Even greater ruin was caused in the Chitaldrug District from the same cause. Almost barren waste has taken the place of former wooded tracts, and that too in a district with but scanty rainfall. Luckily some forests were preserved by not being easy of access and they are now most carefully conserved."

During the first half of the nineteenth century the forests of the Mysore State including the forests of Chitradurga district had suffered a great deal in the absence of scientific management. Scientific conservancy came into being with the establishment of a separate Forest Department in 1864; the newly formed department during 1865 introduced preliminary forest rules for preservation of tree growth, prohibiting fires, removal of forest produce and grazing of cattle. These rules were further revised in 1869. The Forest Department assumed control of forest management and brought some order into the way the forests were exploited. Nevertheless, development of agriculture continued to receive higher priority over forest conservation. During that phase of forest conservancy, forests were primarily looked upon as a source of revenue. The revenue potential of the forests of Chitradurga district was much less when compared with that of the forests of the other districts of Mysore State, such as Asthagrama (Mysore) or Nagar (Shimoga and Kadur), or even Nandidoorg (Bangalore, Tumkur and Kolar). Indiscriminate extension of agriculture resulted in the destruction of forests by stripping the land of its natural defenses. Whatever forested areas were spared, being hilly or unsuitable for conversion to agriculture, were subjected to heavy biotic interferences including removal of forest produce, fire, grazing, etc. Mining of iron ore in various parts of the district also resulted in degradation of whatever forests were left, as vast quantities of firewood were converted to charcoal and used in the iron forges set up near the mines. In Buchanan's own words, 'The fuel used is charcoal prepared from any kind of tree that grows in the country, except the *Ficus Bengalensis*, and the *Chloroxylon Dupada* of my manuscripts'. Evidently, large-scale felling of trees for preparation of charcoal was inevitable, and it had resulted in the denudation of the forests in the district. Destruction of forest was so severe that sometimes smelting of iron ore itself was given up due to non availability of firewood in the vicinity and as the cost of procuring charcoal/firewood from faraway places became prohibitive and economically unviable.

Except for the reserved forests of Jogimatti (7½ square miles) and Nirtadi-gudda (5½ square miles) that were notified towards the end of the nineteenth century, most of the reserved forests of the district were constituted during the first quarter of the twentieth century. However, the forests of Chitradurga were not brought under regular working plan for a very long time, even after the Independence. Some of the reserved forests were worked under provisional schemes which had prescribed either 'simple coppice' or 'coppice with standards' system. The regeneration of the felled coupes was far from satisfactory because of inadequacy of after-care and heavy biotic interferences. The forests continued to suffer on account of heavy exploitation to meet the needs of firewood, charcoal, small timber, poles, tent pegs, grass, etc. The then prevailing 'pre-paid license' or permit system for removal of firewood had done a lot of damage to the forests. [The pre-paid permit was discontinued in 1974. The first regular working plan for the district was written by Mr. Mohammad Ataullah for the period 1980-89.]

JOGIMATTI WILDLIFE SANCTUARY – A CASE OF 'BETTER LATE THAN NEVER'

Amidst the generally scrub-like forests of Chitradurga district, the forests atop the Jogimatti hills near the town of Chitradurga provide a welcome relief. Reported to be a tiger habitat till the 1950s, these forests are perhaps the last remnants of the climax dry deciduous forests that in the distant past had occupied substantial areas of the district. Some of these forests were in existence, at least on hill tops, until about the beginning of the nineteenth century.

As early as 1955-56, a proposal to constitute an area of three miles around Jogimatti Forest Lodge as a game preserve was formulated and submitted to Government (Administration Report of the Mysore Forest Department for the year 1955-56). However, orders notifying the Preserve had not been issued. Again during 1977-78, another proposal was submitted to constitute Jogimatti Sanctuary under the provisions of the Wild Life (Protection) Act, 1972 (Annual Report of the Karnataka Forest Department, 1977-78). However, this time also, the proposal of the Forest Department did not find favor. Eventually, Jogimatti Wildlife Sanctuary covering an area of 100.48 sq km was notified on 23-12-2015.

During the last 15-20 years, the forests around Jogimatti have shown perceptible signs of recovery, thanks to intensive conservation efforts of the Forest department complemented by popular support and increased public awareness. It is hoped that the exalted status of a wildlife sanctuary that has been accorded to these forests will accelerate the process of their restoration and rejuvenation.

RANGAYYANADURGA FOUR-HORNED ANTELOPE SANCTUARY

The easternmost part of Davanagere district primarily harbors dry deciduous scrub forest along with patches of thorn forest in the driest localities. However, the Rangayyanadurga state forest in Jagalur taluk harbors dry mixed deciduous forest interspersed with patches of scrub and thorn forests. A very large number of tree species are found in this forest; these include *Hardwickia binata, Albizia amara, Anogeissus latifolia, Azadirachta indica, Cassia fistula, Chloroxylon swietenia, Soymida febrifuga, Emblica officinalis, Buchanania angustifolia, Ailanthus excelsa, Diospyros melanoxylon, Diospyros montana, Dalbergia paniculata, Tectona grandis, Pterocarpus marsupium, Santalum album, Terminalia tomentosa, Terminalia arjuna, Syzygium cumini, Pongamia pinnata, Mangifera indica, Vitex negundo, Lagerstroemia parviflora, Wrightia tinctoria, Grewia tiliifolia, Albizia lebbeck, Albizia odoratissima, Holoptelia integrifolia, Bridelia retusa, Givotia rottleriformis, Madhuca latifolia, Mitragyna parvifolia, Semecarpus anacardium, Butea monosperma, Acacia catechu, Acacia nilotica, Acacia sundra, Acacia latronum, Acacia leucophloea, Zizyphus jujuba, Carissa carandas, Cordia dichotoma, Dichrostachys cinerea, Prosopis juliflora, Gardenias, Randias, Euphorbias,* etc. and many more. The forest is also very rich in medicinal plants.

Rangayyanadurga state forest is one of the few wildlife habitats of Karnataka harboring the Four-Horned Antelope (*Tetracerus quadricornis*). This animal is facing extinction because of rapid fragmentation and loss of the dry deciduous forests which constitute the principal habitat of the animal. Rigid protection of the Rangayyanadurga forest from all forms of biotic interference is of utmost importance if the last few surviving four-horned antelopes present in the terrain are to be saved from extinction. Besides the four-horned antelope, other wild animals found in the forest include leopard, wolf, sloth bear, hyena, jackal, pangolin, wild cat, wild boar, porcupine, spotted deer, common langur, mongoose, hare, etc. and varieties of reptiles and birds. Situated in the arid region of Karnataka, Rangayyanadurga state forest is ecologically very significant as an important habitat of both flora and fauna. Considering its importance, the state forest was declared as a wildlife sanctuary in 2011 covering an area of 73.22 sq km.

KOLAR DISTRICT
(present Chikkaballapur and Kolar districts)

The erstwhile Kolar district of Mysore State (comprising present Kolar and Chikkaballapur districts) was one of the driest districts of the state with virtually no valuable forest. Although the temperature regime of Kolar district is more or less similar to that of the adjoining Bangalore district, there is perceptible difference in the rainfall between the two districts, doubtless due to the influence of the mountain range running between the two districts. Much of the rain brought by the south-west monsoon is intercepted by the mountain range resulting in drought-like condition in the Kolar district situated on the leeward side. The Kolar district is mainly dependent on the north-east monsoon, not adequate for the growth and sustenance of good forest.

In view of the absence of potential forest areas, the Kolar district was not considered important from the point of forest revenue. This district was a part of the then Nandidroog (Nandidurg) Division which also included the districts of Bangalore and Toomkur (Tumkur). It is interesting to note that in spite of the forests of these districts being very poor in character, the Government of India considered their protection as of utmost importance from the point of environmental conservation. In this context, the following comments of Mr. E. P. Stebbing taken from his book 'The Forests of India (1921)' are relevant:

> "As an outcome of the remarks made upon the formation of reserves in the Nandidroog Division already referred to, Van Someron, who had been confirmed as Conservator in 1868, wrote a special Report on the division in 1869, giving a clear account of the resources in respect of timber, bamboos and firewood of the three districts of the division, Kolar, Bangalore and Toomkur. This Report confirmed the expression of opinion of the Government of India on these forests that though poor in character they were of great value in this dry and comparatively barren part of the country, and therefore required to be carefully husbanded, the most promising forests being demarcated as State forests. The Government of India requested, therefore, that their previous suggestions with reference

to these forests should be carried out. Brandis had advised the formation of village forests. The Chief Commissioner of Mysore did not consider this practicable; he was therefore directed to include a larger area of jungle land within the limits of the State forests than would have otherwise been necessary."

The status of the vegetation (including forests) of Kolar district towards the end of the nineteenth century as brought out in the Mysore Gazetteer (Volume II, Revised Edition, 1897) compiled and edited by Sir Benjamin Lewis Rice is reproduced below:

"**Vegetation.**-The only forest containing trees of large growth is in the neighbourhood of Nandidroog. On several of the hills in the District the soil is a shallow blackish vegetable mould lying on rock, and though trees and bushes grow abundantly they never attain any size. In the northern taluqs near Gumnayakanapalya and Gudibanda the hills are very barren, and produce only stunted bushes of bandrike, tangadi, dodonaea, barleria, small devadari (*Sethia indica*), beppale (*Wrightia tinctoria*), and a few bushes of *Butea frondosa* and *Cassia fistula*. In portions of these taluqs wild tamarinds are abundant, and in the plains are topes of mango, mohwah or ippe, and tamarinds. The reserved forests of 142½ square miles in the Narasimhadeva hill consist principally of bamboos and stunted dindiga trees.

"The hills in the south-east corner of the Bowringpet taluq are covered with a profuse but small growth of various common fuel trees, among which tamarinds are not uncommon. In the Chik-Ballapur taluq the babul and topal (*Acacia leucophloea*) grow freely, and near Nandidroog there is much jalari (lac tree), chiefly in the west and south-west of the hill. The vegetation up to the fort walls is frequently dense, but of no size. Within the enclosure are several fine champakas, and the growth of all trees are better. Acacias are also common in groves in Kolar, Mulbagal, Sidlaghatta, and Srinivaspur. In this last-named sub-taluq is a jungle covering in all perhaps some 11 square miles, besides the Rayalpad forest of over 34 square miles. At the bases and on the lower slopes of the Rayalpad hills the scrub is of superior description, several bushes of *Cassia auriculata* running up to six and seven feet in height. The trees hereabouts average 20 feet; they consist chiefly of pachari, cheninge, navaladi, small devadari, huluve, yenne maddi, rale, wild tamarind, jalari, a few shisham, a few karachi, while high up on the Mudimadagu hill is some bad teak. Near the top of the hill, and all round and about the large Sunnakal hill, bamboos are abundant, also jalari or lac trees.

"In the Malur taluq there are fewer trees, and the uncultivated plains are covered with the ordinary scrub, mixed with euphorbias, which are also common in the Kolar taluq. Many villages in parts of this District are surrounded with stout and high hedges, in which banyans and bhair (*Zizyphus jujuba*) trees are common and well grown. Cocoa-nut trees are principally cultivated in the Mulbagal and Goribidnur taluqs, and areca in the latter. Near Mudavadi in Kolar taluq, there are good fuel tracts, which, as well as the Kolar hills, supply the town of Kolar with firewood. The sandal is scarce, but attempts have been made to propagate it in the Nandi forest.

"Besides the *State forests* reserved at Nandi, Narasimhadeva-betta, and Rayalpad, already mentioned, there are the Agara jungles of 15 square miles in Mulbagal taluq, the Kamasandra jungles of 26 square miles in Bowringpet* taluq, and the Valsebetta forest of 4½ square miles in Goribidnur taluq." [***Note:** Bowringpet was the earlier name of Bangarpet.]

In Kolar district, about thirty-five forest blocks were reserved during the late 1800s and early 1900s. These include Kamasandra state forest (1898), Karbele Plantation (1896), Kamasandra Block-V (1905), Byapanahalli Plantation (1896), Vokkaleri Plantation (1896), Yeshwanthpura state forest (1896), Plantations of Ramachandrapura, Mallapanahalli, Lakshmisagara, Dinneri, New Kurundahalli, Old Kurundahalli, Kadamuthasandra, Marasandra, Bellav and Kashipura (1896), Agara state forest (1900),

Srinivaspura state forest (1910), Addagal state forest (1910), Royalpad state forest (1896), Narasimha Devara Betta Blocks (1896-1908), Ittikaldurga SF Blocks (1911-1914), Konaguntulu (1915), Nandi SF (1911) and Kamashettihalli SF (1896). The remaining forest blocks of the district (about 100 in number) were reserved during the 1930s.

Detailed information about the management of most of the forests of Kolar district before their reservation is not available. The management of the forests was with the local Revenue officials. Sketchy information about only a few forests is available. As regards Srinivaspura state forest, it is reported that prior to 1887 it was treated as a common property of the surrounding villages and that reckless felling and grazing had reduced the forests into highly degraded areas. In 1887-88, it comprised the District Jungles of Kathaganahalli, Muruganahalli, Chepalli, Chintakunte, Avalakoppa and Srinivasapura villages under the management of the Amildar of Srinivasapura, with three watchers on monthly pay of Rupee 1/- per month to look after it. People were allowed to cut grass and to remove the same. Grazing was prohibited. Minor forest produce was auctioned village-wise. In 1895, the management of the forests was transferred from the Amildar to the Forest Department, and a Range Forest Officer was posted to look after the forests. As regards Royalpad state forest, prior to 1894-95 an Amildar was in charge. Licenses were issued for fuel at 0.36 paise per cartload and bamboos at Rs. 2/- per 100 numbers. With the appointment of a Range Forest Officer in 1894-95 to look after these forests, the Amildar's control ceased.

The forest areas of Kolar district, with the sole exception of Kamasandra state forest, were not brought under any regular working plan for a long time even after they were reserved. Details of the working plan of Kamasandra state forest* written sometime during 1900 by Mr. M. Ramaswamy Iyer are not available. However, a number of forests were brought under working schemes during the beginning of the twentieth century. These include the Ittikaldurga state forest blocks (IDB), Narasimha Devara Betta state forest blocks (NDB), Konaguntulu state forest, etc. The forests of Ittikaldurga state forest blocks were taken over by the Forest Department for management after they were constituted as state forests during 1911-14. The forests were divided into a number of coupes and the areas were leased out for fuel extraction and carbonization of charcoal. In 1919-20, a provisional working scheme was drawn for Konaguntulu state forest in which the forest was divided into two working circles, namely, Northern working circle and Southern working circle, with 20 and 15 felling coupes, respectively. The silvicultural system prescribed was 'coppice with standards' which, in the revised working scheme introduced in 1948, was changed to 'simple coppice' system. [* **Note**: Interestingly, the Working Plan for the Kamasandra state forest is one of the earliest working plans of the princely state of Mysore. Only three working plans, namely, those of Muthodi and Tegurgudda state forests of Kadur (Chikkamagaluru) district and Kukwada-Ubrani state forest of Shivamogga district (Benkipura/Bhadravathi forest division) had been written till then.]

The working scheme for the Narasimha Devara Betta state forest blocks (I to V) written in the Year 1902-1903 by Shri Y. Seetharamaiah, the then District Forest Officer, was fairly elaborate with different prescriptions for the five forest blocks. Blocks I and II had two working circles each, namely, Regeneration working circle and Protection working circle. Block III had only one working circle, namely, Protection working circle. Blocks IV and V had three working circles each, namely, Regeneration working circle, Firewood working circle and Protection working circle. The prescription under Regeneration working circle in respect of all the Blocks I, II, IV and V was artificial regeneration by 'Rab method'. Coupes were laid out and sold to lessees. Later as per the instructions of the then Chief Conservator of Forests, the prescription of clear-felling and natural regeneration was adopted, reserving only valuable trees of minor forest produce. The Firewood working circle for Block IV had two felling series and that for Block V had one felling series. Silvicultural system adopted was coppice with reserves. Rigid protection was prescribed for the areas included in the Protection working circle. While Block III was fully under Protection working circle, largest share of forest area in each of the remaining four Blocks was also kept under the Protection working circle. This is indicative of the fact that during that distant past, the forests of Kolar district were highly degraded. Heavy withdrawal for firewood and charcoal for many years in the past appears to have been the main reasons for such a degraded state of the forests of the district.

Large-scale plantations were raised in the forest areas of Kolar district since a very long time. It is also interesting to note that many of the state forests of the district were actually plantations, and their status was explicitly indicated in the state forest notification as 'Plantation state forests'. Due to poor soil and deficient rainfall, plantations of eucalyptus were raised quite extensively in the forest areas of Kolar district. This resulted in suppression of natural regeneration in extensive forest areas in the district. Some forests such as Kamasandra, Royalpad, Narasimha Devara Betta Blocks, and Ittikaldurga Blocks have retained patches of natural vegetation. [First comprehensive working plan for the forests of the erstwhile Kolar division (including the present Chikkaballapur division) was written for the period from 2002-03 to 2011-12)].

KAMASANDRA AND ROYALPAD STATE FORESTS

Forests of Kolar district by and large support stunted growth with poor stocking due to scanty rainfall and generally poor and shallow soil in the forest areas. In the past, most of the forests of the district were heavily exploited for firewood. Biotic interferences such as removal of biomass, grazing and fire have always been severe in these forests. As natural regeneration from seed and coppice was not encouraging, large scale planting, mainly with eucalyptus, was taken up to recoup the depleted stocking of the forests. This resulted in loss/suppression of natural vegetation in most of the forests of the district. Kamasandra state forest (19,774 acres) and Royalpad state forest (20,144 acres) are two large tracts with some original natural vegetation still intact. These forests were originally of tropical dry mixed deciduous type, but because of heavy anthropogenic pressure considerable portions have transformed into scrub type with preponderance of thorny species. The residual dry mixed deciduous vegetation is still visible in some undisturbed and favorable localities. The Royalpad forest had earlier supported some stunted teak and bamboo also. As per data furnished in the working plan of Kolar forest division for the period 2012-13 to 2021-22, 19 tree species have been identified in Kamasandra SF and 64 in Royalpad SF. The average basal area in Kamasandra SF is 2.11 sq m/ha and in Royalpad SF, it is 1.64 sq m/ha.

Both the forests are rich in wildlife and harbor sloth bear, leopard, spotted deer, black buck, slender loris, etc. Elephants also make occasional appearances. These forests, being contiguous with the forests of Andhra Pradesh and Tamil Nadu, serve as corridors for movement of wildlife across the states. Conservation of these areas as protected areas (PA) will not only help in safeguarding and propagating the existing plants and animals but will also mitigate the intensity of human-animal conflicts, especially with regard to human confrontation with elephants, leopards and sloth bears. Keeping this in mind, Kamasandra state forest has already been notified as a wildlife sanctuary in 2019. It is hoped that the Royalpad forests are also included in the protected area network of the state as early as possible.

BANGALORE DISTRICT
(present Bengaluru Rural, Bengaluru Urban and Ramanagara districts)

An account of the forests of the erstwhile Bangalore district in the by-gone days and their status towards the end of the nineteenth century have been provided in the Mysore Gazetteer (Volume II, Revised Edition, 1897) compiled and edited by Sir Benjamin Lewis Rice as follows:

"**Vegetation.**-*Forest*. - The earliest accounts describe the District as covered with forest, forming a part of the great Dandakaranya. The distinctive names have been preserved of some of the wooded tracts, such as the Chandanaranya (sandal forest) on the Arkavati near Nelamangala; the Ganjaranya (forest of the *Abrus precatorius*) around Sivaganga; the Kundaranya (jasmine forest) at Devanhalli, &c."

"As late as the sixteenth century, when Devanhalli, Dod-Ballapur, Hoskote and other chief places were founded, the original settlers are related to have commenced operations by clearing of surrounding forest.

"At the present day the hilly taluqs of Magadi and Kankanhalli contain the greatest proportion of jungle. Trees and bushes grow abundantly, especially in the ravines between the heights. In Kankanhalli there is much fuel jungle and good forest of karachi (*Hardwickia binata*). The best forests in the taluq lie to the east of the Arkavati. Besides acacias, the dindiga (*Conocarpus latifolia*) yielding a valuable gum, and the jalari or *lac* tree (*Vatica lacifera*) are abundant. The Channapatna taluq is also hilly, but the tree vegetation is smaller. The remaining taluqs north and east are fairly wooded with trees in the long and hollow valleys of the downs. The most common is the honge (*Pongamia glabra*), a valuable tree which fringes many tank bunds and often grows to a large size. Oil is extracted from the seeds, and the leaves are used as manure for sugar-cane. Acacias grow freely, and chennuge (*Lagerstroemia parviflora*) and huluve (*Terminalia paniculata*) are frequent. There is much scrub jungle around Ujani-betta and along the western border of the Dod-Ballapur and Nelamangala taluqs.

"The different kinds of ficus, the mango, tamarind, mohwah or ippe, jack, and jamun or nerle, all grow well, together with many varieties of acacia, the wood-apple, bael-tree and kusambe (*Carthamus tinctorius*); also the wild date (*Phoenix sylvestris*), which yields toddy.

"**Reserved Forests**. - The State forests cover an area of 312 square miles. The following are their names and areas:-

Bilikal (42), Savandurg (17), Handigundi (30), Chilandadi (37), Basavanbetta (37), Makali (39), Ragihalli (9), Dod Ballapur (13), Mugur (34), Kumbalgod (2), Kabbaldurg (12), Hultar (8), Tenginakal (16), Banantimari (6), and Mannugudda (10).

"**Arboriculture.** - *Plantations*. - The great demand for fuel created by the railway and the increasing consumption at Bangalore have led to the formation of fuel plantations both by Government and by private individuals. The common *Cassia florida* and the *Casuarina muricata* have been largely planted in the reserves. The former grows freely if treated as a pollard, otherwise it is apt to die out suddenly. The latter is the tree principally cultivated of late years. *Avenues* have been planted along all the public roads, 542 miles in length, the best growing indigenous trees being generally employed for the purpose. These consist of mango, figs, honge, and nerle, which are raised in nurseries and then transplanted.

"*Groves* of trees called topes are numerous. They are planted by natives near wells or tanks, as works of merit, for the shelter of travellers. The mango and the ippe appear to be preferred for the purpose in this District. The former is an umbrageous and handsome tree of symmetrical form, and grows well. *Village topes* have also been formed by order of Government, which should prove of great use as camping grounds, besides improving the appearance of the country. The number of topes in 1894 was 2,118, containing 106,103 trees."

FORESTS OF BANGALORE DISTRICT DURING THE BEGINNING OF THE NINETEENTH CENTURY

An idea about the diversity and richness of the forests of the erstwhile Bangalore district during the beginning of the 19th century can be made from Dr. Buchanan Hamilton's account of the tree specimens that were brought to him for examination while he was travelling through the forests of *Savana-durga* in Magadi (19th June, 1800) on his way to Bangalore from Seringapatam. In his book titled 'A Journey from Madras through the Countries of Mysore, Canara, and Malabar' which had been published in three volumes in 1807, he had mentioned about the presence of the following trees (the names indicated by Buchanan are in brackets): **Ixora arborea** [*Henna Gorivi, Ixora arborea*, Roxb. MSS.], an unidentified species [*Ghendu Gorivi*, or *Haydarany*], **Terminalia tomentosa** [*Cari Hulivay? Clutia forte stipularis?*], **Terminalia paniculata** [*Heb*, or *Bily Hulivay, Chuncoa Huliva*, Buch. MSS.], **Terminalia arjuna** [*Tor Mutti, Chuncoa Muttea*, Buch. MSS.], **Terminalia bellirica** [*Tari, Myrobalanus Taria*, Buch. MSS.], **Terminalia chebula** [*Arulay, Myrobalanus Arula*, Buch. MSS.], an unidentified species, perhaps **Lannea coromandelica** or **Garuga pinnata** or **Spondias mangifera** [*Amutty*, or *Gowda?*], **Diospyros Montana** [*Jugalagunti, Diospyros montana*, Roxb.], **Diospyros melanoxylon** [*Tupru, Diospyros Tupru*, Buch. MSS.], **Bauhinia** species [*Vana Raja*, or *Asha, Bauhinia*.], **Dalbergia lanceolaria** [*Hassur Gunny, Dalbergia?*], **Dalbergia paniculata** [*Pachery, Dalbergia paniculata*, Rox.], **Dalbergia latifolia** [*Biridy, Pterocarpus Sissoo*, Roxb. MSS.], **Pterocarpus marsupium** [*Whonay, Pterocarpus santalinus, L. F.*], **Pongamia pinnata** [*Hoingay, Robinia mitis* Lin.], **Chloroxylon swietenia** [*Hurugulu, Chloroxylon quod Swietenia chloroxylon*, Roxb.], **Boswellia serrata** [*Chandacalu, Chloroxylon Dupada*, Buch. MSS.], **Soymida febrifuga** [*Swamy, Swietenia febrifuga*, Roxb. MSS.], **Chukrasia tabularis** [*Gowda, Sweitenia trilocularis*, Roxb. MSS.], **Grewia orbiculata /rothii** [*Jani, Grewia*.], **Givotia rottleriformis** [*Bili Tali, Bilitalium farinosum*, Buch. MSS.], **Cochlospermum gossipium/religiosum** [*Betta Tali*, or *Betta Tovary, Bombax gossyppium*.], An unidentified species [*Nai*, or *Cag Neralu*.], **Syzygium cumini** [*Rudrashu Neralu, Calyptranthes Jambulana* Willd.], **Stereospermum chelonoides** [*Betta Padri, Bignonia chelonoides*.], **Dolichandrone falcata** [*Wullay Padri, Bignonia spathacea*.], **Vitex altissima** [*Navulady, Mail elou*, Hort. Mal. V. t. 1.], **Gmelina arborea** (perhaps) [*Shivuli*], **Acacia leucophloea** [*Topala, Mimosa leucophlea*, Roxb.], **Acacia catechu** [*Cagali, Mimosa catechu*, Roxb. Pl. Cor. N. 174.], **Acacia suma** [*Mugli, Mimosa Covalum*, Buch. MSS.], **Albizia amara** [*Wullay Sujalu, Mimosa Tuggula*, Buch. MSS.], **Albizia odoratissima** [*Betta Sujalu, Mimosa odoratissima*, L.], **Ficus** species, perhaps **Ficus benghalensis** [*Shalay, Ficus*.], **Ficus glomerata** [*Atty, Ficus glomerata*, Rox.], **Ficus carica** [*Cull Atty, Ficus rupestris*, Buch. MSS.], **Ficus infectoria** [*Birsi, Ficus*.], **Erythroxylon monogynum** [*Devadarum, Erythroxylon sideroxylloides*, E. M.], **Santalum album** [*Sri Gunda, Santalum album. Sandal-wood* of the English merchants.], **Shorea talura** [*Jala, Shorea Jala*, Buch. MSS.], **Anogeissus latifolia** [*Dinduga, Andersonia Panchamoum*, Roxb. MSS.], **Tectona grandis** [*Doda Tayca, Tectona robusta*.], **Adina cordifolia** [*Ursina Tayca, Nauclea cordifolia*, Roxb.], **Anthocephalus kadamba** [*Cadaga, Cadaba*, or *Cadava, Nauclea purpurea*, Roxb.], **Lagerstroemia parviflora** [*Chaningy, Lagerstroemia parviflora*, Roxb.], **Cordia macleodii** [*Hadaga*.], **Streblus asper** [*Mitly, Trophis aspera* Koenigi.], **Premna tomentosa** [*Easy, Premna tomentosa*.], **Azadirachta indica** [*Bewu, Melia azadirachta*.], **Wrightia tinctoria** [*Mara halay, Nerium tinctorium*, Roxb. MSS.], **Holoptelia integrifolia** [*Tapissa, Ulmus integrifolia*, Roxb.], **Zizyphus jujuba** [*Elichi, Rhamnus jujuba*, L.], **Saccopetalum tomentosum** [*Heb Hessary, Uvaria tomentosa*, Roxb.], **Polyalthia cerasoides** [*Chica Hessary, Uvaria cerasoides*, Roxb.], **Aegle marmelos** [*Timbu Bayala, Egle marmelos*, Roxb.], **Limonia crenulata** [*Nai bayla, Limonia crenulata*, Roxb.], **Dendrocalamus strictus** and **Bambusa bambos** [*Bideru, Bambusa*.], **Buchanania angustifolia** [*Muruculu, Chirongia glabra*, Buch. MSS.], **Antidesma zeylanicum** [*Hulu Muruculu, Antidesma alexiteria*.], **Atalantia monophylla** [*Cadu Nimbay*, or *Cadimbay*.], **Cordia monoica** [*Narwully, Cordia monoica*, Roxb.], **Gardenia latifolia** [*Hay Cambi, Gardenia latifolia*, Roxb.], **Jatropha curcas** [*Mara Haralu, Jatropa curcas*.], **Semecarpus anacardium** [*Gheru, Anacardium semecarpus*.], **Ochna obtusata** [*Mudali, Ochna squarrosa*.], **Emblica officinalis** [*Nelli, Phyllanthus emblica*.], **Cassia fistula** [*Cacay, Cassia fistula*.] and **Strychnos potatorum** [*Chillu, Strychnos potatorum* Koenigii.]

Buchanan also mentioned about the presence of fairly good forest with plenty of bamboos around Channapatna, although he later opined that the forests around Magadi (Savandurga) were better. While camping at Bidadi [Wiridy or Biridy], during the evening walk he came across a number of species such as **Wrightia tinctoria** [*Mara halaya, Nerium tinctorium*, Rox.], **Jatropha curcas** [*Mara haralu, Jatropha curcas*, Lin.], **Terminalia chebula** [*Alaygara, Terminalia myrobalana citrina* of *Koenig.*], **Erythroxylon monogynum** [*Devadarum, Erythroxylon sideroxyloides* of *Lamarck*], **Santalum album** [*Sri Gunda Chica, Santalum album*, Lin.], **Dendrophthoe falcata** [*Wotu, Loranthus falcatus, Lin.*], **Premna tomentosa** [*Easy, Premna tomentosa*, Willd.], **Acacia pennata** [*Ha-Shi-Cai, Mimosa pennata.*], and **Cassia fistula** [*Cacay, Cassia fistula, Lin.*].

During the reign of Hyder Ali and Tippu Sultan, mining and smelting of iron ore was prevalent in most of the districts of the kingdom wherever the ore was available, and areas around Magadi were no exception. Dr. Francis Buchanan provides the following information regarding the mining and smelting of iron in areas around Magadi that he had visited (June 13, 1800) in the following words:

> *"On my way, I examined some iron forges, of which there are many in the hilly tract of the country; and from a man, who employs twelve labourers, I procured the following account of the operations performed on the ore. The iron is made partly from the black sand which is found in the rainy season in the channels of all the torrents in the country; and partly from an ore which is found at Ghettipura, two coses from Magadi. During the four months of heavy rains, four men were able to collect as much sand as a furnace can smelt in the remainder of the year. In order to separate the earth and sand, which are always mixed with it in the channel of the torrent, it requires to be washed. These men get ten Fanams or 6 shillings 8½ d. a month, the nature of their service is similar to that of the farmer's servants, being bound by occasional advances of money to continue in the employment of the master. During the remaining eight months of the year, they work at the forge."*

Smelting of iron ore required enormous quantities of charcoal for which many trees had to be felled; this resulted in large-scale deforestation. Most of the dry districts of the kingdom had suffered heavily from the menace. However, the areas around Magadi, which during those days had harbored luxuriant forests, do not appear to have suffered as severely as districts like Chitradurga and, as we will see later, Tumkur.

The forests of Bangalore district were heavily extracted for supply of fuel, small timber, bamboo, etc. to meet the demands of Bangalore Civil and Military Station, the Railways and the growing population of Bangalore. Unregulated felling continued till 1902, when provisional schemes were drawn up for some of the forests in the early 1900s. This was followed by writing of regular working plans during the 1920s. The important forests covered under regular working plans were: (a) Basavanabetta, Chilandvadi and Muggur state forests - Mr. P. Krishnaswamy Rao (1922 to 1952), (b) Bilikal state forest – Mr. S. Venkatavaradiengar (1928-1948), (c) Bananthimari state forest – Mr. B. Narasimha Iyengar (1927-1943), (d) Makali state forest (1919-1949), (e) Chickmannugudda and Doddamannugudda state forests – Mr. B. Narasimhaiengar (1923-1932), (f) Ragihalli state forest - Mr. B. Narasimhaiengar (1923-1943), (g) Ujjani, Hulkadi, Maklidurga, Saslu and Melnayakanahalli state forests - Mr. B. Narasimhaiengar (1923-1943) and (h) Handigondi, Hulthar, Tenginakal and Savanadurga state forests – Mr. C. Abdul Jabbar (1918-1948). The provisional schemes had generally prescribed 'coppice with standards' system of extraction with a felling cycle of 30 years. The working plans were more elaborate. The silvicultural system continued to be the same i.e. 'coppice with standards' (except in case of Chickmannugudda and Doddamannugudda state forests for which 'improvement felling' was prescribed), but separate working circles were prescribed for fuel and small timber, sandalwood, bamboo and minor forest produce. Dibbling of seeds of various indigenous species such as bage (*Albizia lebbeck*), honge (*Pongamia pinnata*), bilwara (*Albizia odoratissima*), kaggali (*Acacia catechu*), banni (*Acacia ferruginea*), hunase (*Tamarindus indica*), chujjulu (*Albizia amara*), bevu (*Azadirachta indica*), sissoo (*Dalbergia sissoo*), kamara (*Hardwickia binata*), honne (*Pterocarpus marsupium*), neralu (*Syzygium cumini*), seegekai (*Acacia concinna*), bore (*Zizyphus jujuba*), alale (*Terminalia chebula*), karijali (*Acacia nilotica*), etc. was prescribed in the plans. Dibbling of sandal (*Santalum album*) was almost invariably prescribed in all the plans. However, only 18 forest blocks out of 146 blocks in the district were covered under working plans. After the expiry of these working plans in the 1940s, revision of the plans did not take place for a long time. The other forest blocks of the district numbering about 128 were not brought under any systematic working. As most of the forest blocks of the district were located nearer to habitations, these were subjected to uncontrolled felling, hacking, grazing, fires, encroachments, etc. Due to these biotic interferences, the unorganized forests, from the beginning, and the organized forests, since the expiry of the working plans in the 1940s, had started showing signs of deterioration. [All the forests of the district were eventually brought under Mr. N. V. Ramachandra Chetty's working plan (1976-1986).]

Dr. Krishnaswamy Kadambi in his 'Forest Types of Mysore' treats the forests of the then undivided Bangalore forest division under 'The Dry Deciduous type' and recognizes two sub-types:

a. Superior scrub type containing *Albizia amara* (tugli), *Acacia arabica* (karijali), *Anogeissus latifolia* (dindiga), *Albizia lebbeck* (bage), *Albizia odoratissima* (goddahunase), *Pterocarpus marsupium* (honne), *Terminalia chebula* (harda), *Zizyphus jujuba* (bore), *Feronia elephantum* (bela), etc.

b. Inferior scrub type containing mostly *Acacia* species, *Canthium* species, *Carissa* species, *Capparis* species, thorny succulent *Euphorbias* and species of *Cactus*. He also recognizes groves of *Phoenix sylvestris* (ichalu) as an edaphic variant of the scrub type.

From the above description of Dr. Krishnaswamy Kadambi, it is obvious that degradation of the forests of the erstwhile Bangalore district had set in quite earlier. The deterioration of the forests of the erstwhile district is more evident in the forests of present Bengaluru Rural and Bengaluru Urban districts, whereas these are in relatively better condition in the present Ramanagara district. The main reason for some of the forest blocks of Ramanagara district being in relatively better condition than the forests of Bengaluru Rural and Bengaluru Urban districts is perhaps the fact that Ramanagara district has a number of forests which are fairly large in extent. Most of the forest blocks of Bengaluru Rural and Bengaluru Urban districts, with the exception of a few, are very small, each block being less than 500 hectares in extent. The forest blocks of Bengaluru Urban district included in the Bannerghatta national park are larger. The effect of biotic interference tends to be severe on the peripheral area of a forest. As a result, the central or core areas of larger forest blocks are more secure from such interferences. This must have helped the forests of Ramanagara district to retain or restore fairly good vegetation in certain patches.

The extent of eucalyptus plantations raised in the forest blocks of Ramanagara district is also less compared with their extent in the forests of Bengaluru Rural and Bengaluru Urban districts. This has also helped in the retention of natural vegetation in the Ramanagara district. Biotic pressure on the forests of Bengaluru Rural and Bengaluru Urban districts has been so high that most of the forests in these two districts have turned into scrub forests. Bengaluru Urban district has been able to retain/rejuvenate some natural forest, thanks to the Bannerghatta national park which has been receiving strict protection since the 1970s. [Considerable extents of forest areas of Bengaluru Urban district are included in the Bannerghatta national park (BNP). These forests are Ragihalli SF, Ragihalli South Extension SF, Gullahatti Kaval SF, Mahadeswara SF, Bannerghatta SF, Karadikal SF, Bantanal SF, Bannerghatta and Suddehalla Lack Reserves. The total extent of these forests is about 10,274 hectares.]

One redeeming feature about the forests of Ramanagara district is that during the last decade or so, a number of state forests of the district have been included in the protected areas, namely, Bannerghatta national park and Cauvery wildlife sanctuary. The forests included in the Bannerghatta national park are Bilikal SF, Manjunatha SF and Ramadevarabetta SF. The forests included in the Cauvery wildlife sanctuary are Chowrakallu SF, Muggur SF, Chunchi East SF, Chilandwadi SF, Muneswarabetta SF and Basavanabetta SF (part). (The Basavanabetta forest block mentioned above is only a small part of the state forest, and the balance area of the state forest which is in the adjoining Mandya district is also included in the Cauvery wildlife sanctuary.) Another state forest of the Ramanagara district, namely, Ramadeverabetta SF (this SF is different from the SF bearing the same name that has been included in the Bannerghatta NP) has been notified in 2012 as a wildlife sanctuary for the conservation of vultures. This sanctuary, extending over an area of 346 hectares, is a part of the territorial division and is administered by the Deputy Conservator of Forests, Ramanagara forest division. Inclusion of substantial portions of the forests of the Ramanagara district in the protected area (PA) network augurs well for the future of these forests in view of the decidedly superior status of protection that is afforded to the protected areas (PA). There is a perceptible degree of reduction of biotic interferences in the protected areas as compared with the regular forest areas.

TUMKUR DISTRICT

Forests of Tumkur district had suffered a great deal of degradation and decimation before the advent of the British. The rulers of the past had encouraged setting up of villages/settlements and conversion of land for cultivation. By and large the people had maintained large herds of cattle. Extension of agriculture had resulted in shrinkage of forest, and biotic pressures including over-grazing had denuded whatever forest was spared of the plough. There were a number of iron ore mines in the district, and smelting of iron ore had been carried out around these mines. Such activities had reached their peak during the reign of Hyder Ali and Tipu Sultan due to huge demand of armaments. Iron smelting had consumed a lot of firewood (in the form of charcoal) which was procured from the nearby forests. With regard to mining activities in and around the present Tumkur district, Francis Buchanan writes (August 13, 1800) as follows:

"Iron is smelted in various places of the following Talucs, or districts; Madhu-giri, Chin-narayan-durga, Hagalawadi, and Devaraya-durga. In the first two districts the iron is chiefly made from the black-sand which the small torrents formed in the rainy season bring down from the rocks. In the two latter districts, it is made from an ore called here Cany Callu, which is found on the hill Kindalay Guda, near Muga-Nayakana-Cotay in the Hagalawadi district. A little of the same iron ore is also procured from a hill, called Kaymutty, near Muso-conda in the district Chica-nayakana-Hully.

"The manner of smelting the iron-ore, and rendering it fit for the use of blacksmith, is the same here as near Magadi. The people belonging to the smelting house are four bellows-men, three men who make charcoal, and three women and one man who collect and wash the sand. They work only during the four months in which the sand is to be found; and for the remainder of the year they cultivate the ground, or supply the inhabitants of towns with fire-wood. The four men relieve each other at the bellows; but the most skilful person takes out the iron and builds up the furnace; on which account his allowance is greater. In each furnace the workman puts first a basket (about half a bushel) of charcoal. He then takes up as much of the black sand as he can lift with both his hands joined, and puts

in double that quantity. He next puts in another basket of charcoal, and the fire is urged with the bellows. When the first charcoal that has been given burns down, he puts in the same quantity of sand, and one basket of charcoal; and does this again, so soon as the furnace will receive a farther supply. The whole quantity of sand put in at one smelting measures 617 cubical inches, and weighs, when dry, about 42½ lb. avoirdupois. This gives a mass of iron, which, when forged, makes 11 wedges, each intended to make a 'ploughshare', and weighing fully 1 82/100 lb. The workmen here, therefore, procure from the ore about 47 per cent. of malleable iron; but, as usual in India, their iron is impure."

Enormous quantities of charcoal were required for smelting of iron, and all the tree growth occurring in the forest lands around the iron smelting sites was cleared for the preparation of charcoal. The damages caused by the iron smelters to the tree growth of the forests of Tumkur district were described in 1854-55 by General Richard Stewart Dobbs, the then Superintendent of the district in the following words:

"The district generally is very bare of trees. The jungles were however extensive when I first assumed charge in 1835, but these are disappearing fast under the axe of the iron and steel manufacturers. When I first visited the beautiful range of hills running between Chikkanayakanahalli and Hagalwadi, they were clothed with trees from top to bottom; not a tree now remains except a few unfit for burning. In the immediate neighbourhood of Tumkur (Davaraidrug Hills) where three fourths of the wooding had disappeared, I stopped the progress of destruction by prohibiting iron forges altogether. The decrease of rain amongst the hills referred to has been very marked; no one who has not witnessed the process can conceive the destruction made by these iron forges."

Prior to the establishment of the Forest Department in Mysore State in 1864, the forests were under the control of the Revenue Department and people of the surrounding villages had free access to these forests and they could do anything they wanted. Even after the Forest Department took over the management of the forests, *ad hoc* arrangements continued for some time. Being entrusted with the responsibility of supplying firewood to the Railways and other local users including Tumkur town and the Civil and Military establishments at Bangalore, the Forest Department had to resort to large-scale extraction of the forests. Due to poor follow-up tending operations the forests were depleted. The forests around Devarayanadurga were brought under some sort of management during the 1870s under the supervision of a forester and six watchers. Subsequently in 1877, a head watcher was added. Firewood, bamboo and small timber were extracted from the forests. Sandalwood was also reportedly extracted on a large scale for 10 years from 1889. In 1882, the forest was roughly divided into compartments after a detailed inspection and improvement fellings were introduced. The converted wood was sent to Tumkur for sale. To set right the illegal grazing incidents the forest was thrown open for grazing except for the worked out coupes by levying fee for grazing. The sale of right to collect minor forest produce was stopped in 1886-87 and departmental collection was organized.

The status of the vegetation including the forests of Tumkur district towards the end of the nineteenth century as brought out in the Mysore Gazetteer (Volume II, Revised Edition, 1897) compiled and edited by Sir Benjamin Lewis Rice is reproduced below:

> "**Vegetation.**-The principal forest in the District is on the slopes of the Devarayadurga hills. Farther north the hills around Koratigere are clothed with good fuel jungle. Near Maddagiri the vegetation improves in appearance and variety. On the western range of hills running north from Kibbanhalli, there is a forest of karachi (*Hardwickia binata*), extending from Bukkapatna northwards to Gangarapente.

> "The following are the reserved or State forests in the District:-

	Sq. m.
Devarayadurga	30
Maddagiri	32
Bukkapatna	50
Huliyurdurga	30
Kudare-kanave	21
Kemplapura	1¼

"There are also nine Forest plantations, covering 963 acres, and three Revenue plantations. Of these, three are for sandal, and the others for casuarina and cassia.

"The best wooded taluqs are those which include the great eastern range of hills – namely, Tumkur, Koratigere, Maddagiri, and the old Huliyurdurga taluq. In these, too, sandal grows. The south-western taluqs are well occupied with trees in topes, and such as have planted themselves in the valleys and hedges. Cocoanut gardens are numerous, and in some parts the *Butea frondosa* grows abundantly in waste lands. The north and centre of the Sira taluq is badly supplied with wood, but the wild custard-apple grows in profusion in the plains.

"With the exceptions above noted the tree vegetation resembles that of the adjoining Districts on the east."

Reservation notifications of the forests of the district were issued during the last decade of the nineteenth century and the first quarter of the twentieth century. The first working plan for the Devarayanadurga group of forests was written by Mr. M. Venkataramanappa and it came into force in 1899-1900. [This working plan was one of the earliest working plans of the Mysore State along with those of Muthodi, Tegur Gudda, Kukwada-Ubrani and Kamasandra.] Mr. Venkataramanappa had prescribed 'improvement felling' with a felling cycle of 20 years. According to this plan the forest was divided into 20 compartments of varying areas. One compartment was taken up for improvement each year. A special arrangement for teak felling was made by clubbing the teak-bearing areas in different compartments into 5 groups and providing for very light and cautious improvement felling. The plan expired during 1919-20. The plan had mixed result. It was found that the fellings did not follow a regular sequence as the compartments were extensive in area and irregularly distributed on ground. By the end of the plan period certain areas were found to contain sound and somewhat vigorous re-growth whereas others were invaded by *Lantana* suppressing the regeneration. Improvement operations like climber cutting, thinning, clearing, etc. that were prescribed in the plan were not properly carried out.

Mr. M. Venkataramanappa's plan was revised in 1922 probably by the DFO, Tumkur who prescribed an 'improvement' working circle and a 'coppice with standards' working circle. He had introduced a method of temporary cultivation (*Hangami* or *Taungya*) to eradicate *Lantana*. However, as the *Lantana*-eradicated areas were not immediately afforested they were again invaded by *Lantana*. Eucalyptus planting was started in Tumkur division in the early 1930s, perhaps in an attempt to suppress the menace of *Lantana*. Dr. Krishnaswami Kadambi wrote the regular working plan for these forests in 1942 which was in operation up to 1951. He had prescribed Regeneration working circle, *Taungya* working circle, Firewood working circle and Bamboo (overlapping) working circle. By this plan the management of the forests was systematized to some extent and attempts of raising plantations on a large scale were made. The working plan was revised by Mr. M. W. Palekhanda (1952-62) who discontinued the *Taungya* method of regeneration as it was a failure. He prescribed a Regeneration working circle and a Protection working circle. Attempts for raising plantations on large scale were made during the implementation of this plan.

The Bukkapatna and Manchaladore group of forests of Tumkur district were worked under a working scheme written in 1907 which mainly dealt with cultural operations, grazing and minor forest produce, as there was no demand for firewood from these forests at that time. The first working plan for these forests was written by Mr. K. Revanna who had prescribed improvement felling system. Because of poor demand for fuel, the annual coupes could not be worked properly till 1945 and many coupes remained un-worked. However, from 1945 onwards there was sudden rise in demand for firewood and charcoal from Bangalore. There was also demand for large quantities of poles of kamara and other hardwood species by the Bellara Gold mine, which had just started functioning. To meet this sudden increase in demand, the forests were worked under 'coppice with standards' system. Revanna's working plan was revised by Mr. M. W. Palekhanda (1955-65) who had prescribed three working circles, namely, Regeneration working circle, Firewood working circle, and Protection working circle. Large-scale plantations were prescribed in the working plan.

The Devarayanadurga and Bukkapatna / Manchaladore groups of forests mentioned above comprised only eleven forest blocks of Tumkur district which had totally about 150 forest blocks. The remaining forest blocks of the district were not covered by any regular working plan. Even the approved working plans had expired by the 1960s. The forests of the district were not brought under working plan for a very long time until the working plan by Mr. Range Gowda (2001-02 - 2010-11) came into operation.

Being proximate to Bangalore, the forests of Tumkur district had suffered a lot, as Bangalore was a very promising consumption center of that time. These forests, along with those of Bangalore and Kolar districts, were worked heavily mainly for catering to the demand of fuel wood and small timber from Bangalore and other urban centers. As the demand grew with rising population, intensity of exploitation also increased resulting in degradation and depletion of the forests. Attempts at regenerating the forests were initially limited to sowing of seeds after felling under 'coppice with standards' system. As these regeneration efforts did not give encouraging results, planting of eucalyptus was started which yielded quicker results in terms of production of biomass. Planting of eucalyptus became quite common in these districts from the early 1930s. This practice was intensified after the Independence, reaching its peak during the period between 1960 and 1980. Although the eucalyptus plantations developed in the forest areas have by and large been successful and catered to the needs of the society for a considerable length of time, the biggest casualty has been the forests themselves. The presence of eucalyptus in most of these forest areas has become so dominating that the original species of the terrain were suppressed and gradually decimated. Eucalyptus has such an overpowering presence in these forests that most of the native species could not make a comeback even after the final harvest of eucalyptus (three rotations of 8/9 years each), the residual growth of the old eucalyptus trees still continuing to dominate the scene.

DEVARAYANADURGA AND SIDDARABETTA FORESTS

The Devarayanadurga state forest (DDSF) covering an area of about 4,160 hectares in Tumkur range was one of the earliest forests of Tumkur district brought under reservation. It was managed as a reserved forest since the 1860s and the final notification was issued in 1907. Due to very heavy working in the past and continued biotic interferences over the years, this forest, which originally harbored climax dry deciduous vegetation with teak and bamboo, has been reduced to dry deciduous scrub with preponderance of species such as *Dalbergia paniculata* (padarpachali), *Anogeissus latifolia* (dindiga), *Diospyros* (tupra), and eucalyptus (introduced). Shreds of the remnant vegetation are still met with in valleys and moister areas in the interiors of the state forest. Even in its degraded state, DDSF has fairly good stocking of trees with average basal area of about 2.95 sq m/ha, as against 1.86 sq m/ha for the district. The flora of Devarayanadurga SF was surveyed and documented in 1965 by Mr. RS Rao and Mr. AR Shastry who enumerated 209 species belonging to 59 families.

The Devarayanadurga state forest is rich not only from the point of tree diversity but also for harboring varieties of medicinal plants. The Forest department, with the help of the Foundation for Revitalization of Local Health Traditions (FRLHT), Bengaluru, has established one Medicinal Plant Conservation Area (MPCA) in the forest covering an area of 178 hectares. One hundred and fifty-seven (157) medicinal plant species have been identified in the MPCA.

Many eternal springs locally known as **"Theerthas"** originate in the hills around Devarayanadurga. The important ones are Ramatheertha, Dhanushtheertha, Parasharatheertha, etc. Medicinal plants are found in the wild around these springs and the mineral springs are believed to possess manifold healing properties.

The Devarayanadurga state forest is known to have been a tiger habitat till the 1950s. Stray sightings of the animal are reported in the forest now and then, although the present status of the forest as supportive of a resident animal is doubtful. Other animals found in the forest include leopard, wolf, sloth bear, wild boar, spotted deer, etc.

Siddarabetta is another hill range situated in Kolikal state forest in Koratagere range. This hill range is also famous for its floristic wealth including medicinal plant flora. People from various parts of South India used to visit the hill range because of their belief in the efficacy of the local herbs in curing various ailments. The hill range is known to have varied types of topographical features supporting different types of microclimatic zones from the foothill to the peak encompassing different floristic composition and genetic diversity. The hill range was reported to be unique for harboring some of the evergreen species like *Mangifera indica, Memecylon umbellatum, Vateria indica, Vitex altissima, Litsea deccanensis, Dipterocarpus indicus, Symplocos racemosa,* etc. It is feared that many of these species and other valuable medicinal flora have been lost or are on the verge of extinction due to over exploitation and gradual degradation of the forest over the years.

Conservation of both Devarayanadurga and Siddarabetta forests by bringing these into the fold of protected area network is of utmost importance.

BUKKAPATNA STATE FOREST

Bukkapatna state forest is another important forest of Tumkur district which has so far retained some fairly good patches of dry deciduous vegetation, although substantial portions of the SF have degraded into scrub types due to intense anthropogenic pressure. Notified in 1900, the Bukkapatna SF (13,154 ha) is known for harboring excellent trees of kamara (*Hardwickia binata*) including some gregarious patches of the species. Large stumps of kamara reminiscent of the bygone splendor of the forest are still visible here and there. Other important tree species found are dindal (*Anogeissus latifolia*), padarpachali (*Dalbergia paniculata*), padri (*Stereospermum personatum*), kaggali/kempujali (*Acacia chundra*), tupra (*Diospyros* spp), etc. Bukkapatna forests are also well-known for harboring the tree species maradi (*Buchanania angustifolia*). The kernels of the seeds of maradi are superior to those of nurkal/char (*Buchanania lanzan*) and are considered equivalent to almonds.

Large populations of the Chinkara (*Gazella bennettii*) inhabit the Bukkapatna forests, considered to be the southernmost limits of the antelope's habitat in the peninsular India. Other animals typical of the dry deciduous and scrub forests also occur in the confines of the Bukkapatna forests. Considering the ecological significance of these forests, and in order to protect the Chinkara from habitat loss, poaching and other threats, these forests have been notified as the Bukkapatna Chinkara Wildlife Sanctuary in 2019.

As regards the remaining districts of the erstwhile princely state of Mysore, i.e, **Mysore, Shimoga, Kadur (Chikkamagaluru) and Hassan,** these harbored substantial extents of evergreen, semi-evergreen and moist deciduous forests in addition to dry deciduous forests. As these districts had considerable extents of timber growing forests, the descriptions provided in the Gazetteer dwelt more on these forests that were considered more valuable at that time. References about the dry deciduous and the scrub forests were rather sketchy, as these were considered inferior from an economic point of view, being suitable for fuel wood or at the most some quantities of small timber. Besides, as the compositions of the moist deciduous forests and the dry deciduous forests in these districts are more or less similar, these have generally been described together.

MYSORE DISTRICT
(present Chamarajanagar, Mandya and Mysuru districts; also includes Kollegal taluk from erstwhile Madras Presidency)

A brief account of the vegetation along with the status of forests of the erstwhile Mysore district towards the end of the nineteenth century as given in the Mysore Gazetteer (Volume II, Revised Edition, 1897) compiled and edited by Sir Benjamin Lewis Rice is reproduced below:

"**Vegetation**. - In this District lies the great belt of forest which, commencing on the west at the Fraserpet* bridge, about 10 miles north-west of Periyapatna, extends continuously for 80 miles to a point a few miles south-east of Bandipura in the Gundulpet taluq. From the Fraserpet bridge to the Viranahosahalli jungle in Periyapatna, the Mysore portion of this belt varies from 1½ to 3 miles in breadth, and contains in abundance honne (*Pterocarpus marsupium*), matti (*Terminalia tomentosa*), arsentega (*Nauclea cordifolia*), dindiga (*Conocarpus latifolia*), navaladi (*Vitex alata*), udi (*Bignonia falcata*), huluve (*Terminalia paniculata*), banni (*Acacia ferruginea*), a few blackwood (*Dalbergia latifolia*) trees, and here and there patches of ill-grown stunted teak (*Tectona grandis*). Here the belt increases suddenly to 5 or 6 miles in breadth, and a portion of it is known as the Viranahosahalli jungles. The jungles of Metikuppa and Hunasekuppa adjoin the Viranahosahalli jungles, and between Bisalvadi on the west and Rampura on the banks of the Nugu in the east, is the portion of the Heggadadevankote taluq, which, measuring about 20 miles in length by 7 to 10 miles in breadth, contains the teak forests of Bisalvadi, Kakankote, Begur and Ainur Marigudi. Crossing the Nugu and passing through some thriving villages, a walk of about three miles brings one to the jungles of Berambadi and Bandipura in the Gundulpet taluk. From Bandipura to Yelandur the belt of forest again narrows. Much sandalwood is intermixed with it, very little teak is seen, open glades are common, and the country is very hilly. [*Note: Fraserpet is the old name of Kushalnagar.]

"The only other wooded portion of this District is the eastern taluq of Malavalli. There karachi (*Hardwickia binata*) is not uncommon round the Basavanabetta hill, and bamboos are abundant. Honne, matti, and ippe (*Bassia latifolia*) are abundant, but the vegetation generally is poor. The dindiga-tree, which yields a valuable gum, grows abundantly.

"The Hunsur taluq has a comparatively heavy rainfall in the west, where it borders Coorg, and several very fine specimens of mangoes, tamarinds and banyans grow round the villages. In this and the Heggadadevankote taluqs to the south, the fields are frequently divided by quick hedges or bamboo fences, among which bushes of various kinds have sprung up, and which much favour the growth of sandalwood. This marking off of fields by hedges is not common in Mysore. Parts of Periyapatna are covered with thousands of date-palm (*Phoenix sylvestris*), growing in the waste lands, and further south on the road to Heggadadevankote are two large fuel tracts known as Paduvakote and Janapanahalli jungles; much of the tree vegetation would, if enclosed, grow up into useful timber. The Heggadadevankote taluq has much forest in it, and the babul (*Acacia arabica*) is very common in fields.

"The taluq of Mysore has no forest, but babul-trees grow all over it in the fields. There are several planted topes of mangoes and banyans, and the jamun-tree grows well in many parts. Some thriving cocoa- and areca-nut gardens are scattered throughout it. The taluq of Seringapatam, is well irrigated by channels, and grows much rice and sugar-cane, as does the taluq of Tirumakudlu Narsipur in the east; but trees, except in planted groves, are scarce. Yedatore, another rice-growing taluq, is also bare of forest or large tracts of jungle; but the high waste-lands are covered with the *Cassia auriculata*, and frequently the *Cassia fistula*, both of which yield fuel for the use of the surrounding home population. The taluq of Mandya is very thinly wooded, and Maddur sub-taluq is not much better. Gundulpet and Chamarajnagar in the south are well off in this respect, the latter especially so, for in addition to the wood growing close by in the Ummattur hobli, and the jungles in the vicinity of Punjur, the Biligirirangan hills are near at hand. It is a well-watered land, full of paddy fields and rich gardens, strongly fenced in. The Nanjangud taluq has no lack of wood for home consumption."

"Attention has been directed to the great drain on the teak forests of Mysore District, which has been going on from the time of the taking of Seringapatam, or even before that, and which threatens to exhaust the supply. One cause has been that, while in many other parts of India the forests were comparatively untouched owing to want of roads, there were trunk lines of communication passing through several of the forests in the Mysore District, admitting of easy access and removal of teak and other timber. Teak seedlings are, no doubt, found more or less frequently in these forests, but the undergrowth and surroundings of an old forest seem not to be favourable to the raising of teak seedlings. The formation of regular teak plantations is therefore being carried out in places where the growth of this valuable timber, the demand of which is ever on the increase, may be free and unimpeded; the climate and soil of Mysore in certain parts being specially favourable for its propagation."

In the above description, while the forests of the present Mysuru district bordering on the then Coorg State (now Kodagu district) have been described in some detail, the remaining forests of the erstwhile Mysore district such as the forests of the present Mandya and Chamarajanagar districts have not been described in such detail, although these have been casually referred to as forests of mediocre or minor importance. This appears to be in view of the fact that most of the forests of the present Mandya and Chamarajanagar districts are either of the dry deciduous type yielding small timber or of the scrub type yielding mostly fuel wood. The forests of the present Mysuru district towards the west adjoining Kodagu district are high forests of moist deciduous type, gradually changing towards the east to dry deciduous forests of the teak pole type. Both these types of forest are mostly found in the Hunsur, HD Kote, Sargur and Periyapatna taluks.

Much of the forests referred to in the above description now fall in the protected area (PA) network comprising a number of national parks and sanctuaries such as Bandipur national park, Nagarahole national park (part), BRT wildlife sanctuary, MM Hills wildlife sanctuary and Cauvery wildlife sanctuary (part). It is interesting to note that all the reserved forests of Chamarajanagar district have been included in one or the other protected area. These are: Doddasampige RF, Biligiri Rangaswamy Temple RF, Chamarajanagara RF and Hardanahalli RF in **BRT wildlife**

sanctuary (tiger reserve); Kaniyanpura RF, Kaniyanpura Extension I and II RFs, Moyar RF, Bandipura RF, Beerambadi RF and Beerambadi north-east and south-east Extension RFs in **Bandipur national park (tiger reserve)**; Chikkaylur RF, Mambetta RF, Cowdalli RF, MM Hills RF (part) and Sathegal Jagir forest in **Cauvery wildlife division**: and MM Hills RF (part), Yediyarahalli RF and Hanur RF in **M.M. Hills wildlife division**. In respect of Mandya district, two important forest blocks of the district, namely, Basavanabetta SF and Dhanagur SF are included in the **Cauvery wildlife division**. In addition, Narayanadurga SF and Mudibetta SF of Mandya district are included in the **Melkote temple wildlife sanctuary**. With regard to the present Mysuru district also, a large number of forest blocks are included in one or the other protected area. These are: Begur SF, Ainurmarigudi SF, Alaganchi SF, Katwal SF, Naganapura I and II RFs in **Bandipur national park (tiger reserve)**; Kakankote SF, Kachuvanahalli SF, Veeranahosahalli SF and Metikuppe SF in **Nagarahole national park (tiger reserve)**; Lakshmanpura (Nugu) RF in **Nugu wildlife sanctuary**; and Arbithittu RF in **Arbithittu wildlife sanctuary**.

Inclusion of a very large number of reserved forests of the Mysuru, Chamarajanagar and Mandya districts in the protected area (PA) network as detailed above has been a blessing in disguise for the overall protection of the forests of the three districts. While protected areas constitute almost 100% of the recorded forest area of Chamarajanagar district, they constitute about 80% in respect of Mysuru district and about 25% in respect of Mandya district. [In Mandya district, the protected areas actually constitute about 75% of the reserved forests of the district; as the district has extensive area (443.33 km^2) under the category of 'Unclassified forest', the proportion of the protected areas as a percentage of the recorded forest area has come down.]

It is interesting to note from Table-3.1 that, while the districts of Mysuru, Chamarajanagar and Mandya together harbor about 3,000 km^2 of dry deciduous forests, they have only about 425 km^2 of scrub forests. This contrasts significantly with most of the districts in the interior Karnataka region and in the Eastern Plains where the extent of dry deciduous forests when compared with that of the scrub forests is generally much less. The presence of sizeable extents of dry deciduous forests as compared with scrub forests in the districts of Mysuru, Mandya and Chamarajanagar can be attributed to the fact that a large number of reserved forests in these three districts have been progressively brought under the protected area network comprising a number of national parks and wildlife sanctuaries where the status of protection is decidedly better than that in forest areas in the territorial divisions. In view of significantly reduced level of biotic interferences, the forests in the protected areas have shown signs of tremendous rejuvenation within a few decades.

SHIMOGA DISTRICT

As regards the Shimoga (now called Shivamogga) district, it harbors primarily evergreen, semi-evergreen and moist-deciduous forests. Dry deciduous forests are met with in the eastern part of the district in the taluks of Bhadravathi, Channagiri and Honnali, besides the eastern parts of Shimoga, Soraba and Shikaripur taluks. [Honnali and Channagiri taluks have since been transferred to Davanagere district.] A brief account of the vegetation along with the status of forests of Shimoga district towards the end of the nineteenth century as given in the Mysore Gazetteer (Volume II, Revised Edition, 1897) compiled and edited by Sir Benjamin Lewis Rice is reproduced below:

> "**Vegetation.** The Western Ghats and the country immediately below them are covered with magnificent evergreen forest. Many of the hills are heavily wooded up to their summits. In some parts the undergrowth is dense, elsewhere the forest is open, and on all sides trees with clear stems to the first branch of from 80 to 100 feet meet the eye. The great bulk of these trees can scarcely be realized except by actual measurement. The more valuable kinds are poon, wild jack, ebony, some heigni, erool, dupada mara, the large devadaram, gamboge and a species of cedar. The wealth of timber in these forests is almost entirely unproductive, owing to the inaccessible nature of the country.
>
> "More to the east, as far as a line from Anavatti to midway between Shikarpur and Honnali and thence to Sakrebail, is a rich and productive belt of vegetation, including the kans of Sorab, areca palm and cardamom gardens and the rich rice-flats of Sagar, Nagar

and Tirthahalli. Within this tract are the State and District forests. The more important trees are teak, black wood, honne, matti, sampaji, arsentega, alale, biridi, bilvara, bagi, sagade or chendala, jambe, dindiga, hulvati or namadari, hunal and mashi, jani, kadaga, kuli, kalteka, nelli, navaladi, nandi, pachari, shi-anvige, tapasi, and kendatsal.

"Teak, not the largest size, is found in Shikarpur, Kumsi and Sakrebail. Bamboo is abundant everywhere. Sandal is most plentiful in Sorab, Sagar and Nagar taluks. It also grows in parts of Shimoga and Shikarpur, and a little in Channagiri and Honnali.

"The taluq of Sorab abounds with kans, many of which are cultivated with pepper vines, and sometimes coffee. The sago palm (*Caryota urens*) is also much grown for the sake of its toddy. These kans are apparently the remains of the old forests, which appear once to have stretched as far east as Anavatti. At the present day at Anavatti itself there is no wood, and the surrounding country is clothed with either scrub jungle or small deciduous forest, generally pentapterous. Kans are found also in Sagar, Nagar, and other Malnad taluqs, but those in Sorab are, from their number, situation and accessibility, the most valuable.

"The Sagar taluq is not so thickly wooded as that of Sorab, except along the Ghats. The adjoining taluq of Nagar possesses heavy forests in the west (though several of the hills are cleared), but the wood grows generally in large kans, which are scattered unequally over the taluq. Going south to Tirthahalli much fine timber is found to the north of the Tunga, while to the south of the river the country is comparatively open. From Mandagadde in this taluq is a long stretch of wooded country, which runs north via Hannigeri through portions of the Shimoga taluq to the confines of Sorab and Sagar. In this strip there is good teak, much fine second-class timber, and a vast quantity of *Inga xylocarpa*, which is largely used for making charcoal for the iron mines that abound near Masrur, Shrigeri and other places in Anantapur and Shimoga.

"Between Shikarpur and Kumsi is a belt of jungle, parts of which have been placed on the State forest lists. In the eastern portions of Shikarpur and Honnali taluqs there is comparatively little wood. Between Shikarpur and Sorab is a quantity of small pentapterous jungle near Udagani and Siralkoppa, which only requires conservation to grow up into valuable second-class forest.

"The Honnali taluq is poorly wooded. Near Malebennur, in the low hills to the east of the Tungabhadra, are the remains of old jungles, which apparently yielded small timber and much fuel. In Channagiri there is very little wood; in the south west of the taluq is a small jungle.

The above description, which gives a fairly graphic narration of the luxuriant forests occurring in the western part of the Shimoga district, provides a very brief and average to poor account of the forests that are met with in the eastern part of the district. However, such a description should be viewed in the context of the presence of excellent and economically important forests in the western part of the district comprising Thirthahalli, Sagar and Hosanagara taluks, along with the western parts of Shivamogga, Shikaripura and Soraba taluks. As already mentioned, it has been generally observed that in respect of the districts that harbor both high forests and dry forests, some of the Gazetteers of the past have not provided as much details about the dry forests as they have provided about the rich, timber-bearing high forests. Perusal of Table-3.1 would indicate that the district has about 327 km² of dry deciduous forests and about 241 km² of scrub forests. These forests mostly occur in Bhadravathi, Channagiri and Honnali taluks and in the eastern parts of Shivamogga, Shikaripura and Soraba taluks. [As already mentioned, the forests of Channagiri and Honnali taluks now appear under the Davanagere district.]

The western part of Shivamogga district that harbors the best forests is relatively thinly populated. This region is fairly precipitous and the villages, located mostly in the valleys, are separated far and wide. On the other hand, the dry deciduous forests of the district are located in areas where the terrain is less undulating or almost flat. These areas are thickly populated with a large number of villages dotting the entire landscape.

Excessive biotic pressure has put very heavy toll on the forests of the region resulting in their severe degradation. Instances of forest encroachment are very high and have resulted in the fragmentation of many state forests. The minor forests of the district have suffered the most, many of them having been completely wiped out. The same has been the fate of many sandal reserves of the district.

KUKWADA UBRANI STATE FOREST

Kukwada Ubrani State Forest (KUSF) of Bhadravathi forest division was one among the largest dry deciduous forests of Mysore State. This state forest covering an area of 70 square miles (18,130.31 hectares) was notified in 1895 and is presently shared mainly between Channagiri taluk of Davanagere district and Bhadravathi taluk of Shivamogga district with a smaller portion in the Tarikere taluk of Chikkamagaluru district. This forest now defines the easternmost limits of climax dry deciduous forest in the Western Ghats region of central Karnataka. Although primarily a dry deciduous forest, patches of moist deciduous vegetation are also met with in the more favorable interiors of the forest. Surrounded almost all around by extensive arid tracts, the forest appears as an oasis, exhibiting rich floral diversity. In the past, the SF had good population of herbivores such as spotted deer and sambar, besides bisons in some moister pockets.

The flora of KUSF has been quite elaborately described in the book titled "Flora of Davanagere District, Karnataka, India" written by Mr. B. K. Manjunatha, Mr. V. Krishna and Mr. T. Pullaiah. In addition to most of the tree species that are generally associated with the moist deciduous forests of the Western Ghats, the book has mentioned about a number of species typical of evergreen and semi-evergreen forests of the Western Ghats that were reported from KUSF. These include *Dipterocarpus indicus, Vateria indica, Elaeocarpus serratus, Artocarpus hirtusus, Cedrela toona, Canarium strictum, Sapindus laurifolia, Hydnocarpus pentandra, Scolopia crenata, Hopea ponga, Sterculia guttata, Sterculia villosa, Euodia lunu-akenda, Euonymus indicus, Dimocarpus longan, Holigarna ferruginea, Spondias pinnata, Memecylon umbellatum,* etc. Although many of these species were occasional or rare in the state forest, and some of these may no longer be present there, the ecological significance of the KUSF as a heritage forest cannot be ignored or denied. KUSF may perhaps be considered as the easternmost limits to where the evergreen forests of the Western Ghats were extended in the distant past. In the above context, the need for taking up comprehensive ecological study of the KUSF may be very relevant. It may also be necessary, before it is too late, to protect the KUSF from contraction and fragmentation (signs are already visible, as old forest tracts or extraction paths have given way to asphalted roads), and to notify it as a sanctuary of ecological, floral and faunal significance in order to restore, protect, and develop its environment.

KADUR DISTRICT (now Chikkamagaluru district)

A brief description about the vegetation including the forests of the erstwhile Kadur district along with their status towards the end of the nineteenth century as brought out in the Mysore Gazetteer (Volume II, Revised Edition, 1897) compiled by Sir Benjamin Lewis Rice is reproduced below:

"**Vegetation**. - The west of the District is covered with some of the best forests of the country. This is especially the case with Lakvalli, which abounds in fine teak, and has for many years supplied the whole of western Mysore and the Bellary country with that timber, grown in the forests to the north of the Baba Budans. Throughout the Jagar valley and most of the Koppa and Mudgere taluqs is a continuous stretch of valuable forest, densely clothing the hill-sides and giving shelter to much coffee cultivation. Sholas and hanging woods occupy almost every ravine and hollow of the Baba Budans. The loftier heights are nearly always bare of trees, but clothed with much coarse grass and dwarf date. The tree vegetation east and south of Santaveri is as a rule poor, and, even when the soil is better and the growth is fair, there is but little good and useful timber. The eastern taluqs are generally devoid of trees. The date palm (*Phoenix sylvestris*) grows profusely in parts, especially in Kadur, and the grazing is good. In the north of Tarikere are the jungles round Ubrani, which, though not yielding large timber, are valuable as affording a supply of fuel in so poorly wooded a neighbourhood. The sandal grows on the slopes of the hills leading up to the Baba Budans from the south and east.

The above description reveals that the best forests of the district are met with in the western part. The forests on the eastern taluks were generally poor, at the most yielding fuel wood. The western part of the district comprising Koppa, Sringeri, Mudigere and NR Pura taluks, along with the western portions of Chikkamagaluru and Tarikere taluks harbors some of the best forests of Karnataka. These are primarily of evergreen, semi-evergreen and moist deciduous types, gradually turning to dry deciduous towards the east. The forests met with in Kadur taluk and in the eastern parts of Chikkamagaluru and Tarikere taluks are of dry deciduous type, turning to thorn forests at the westernmost limits of Kadur taluk. The dry deciduous forests occurring at the transition zone from moist deciduous forest are of a fairly high quality and are met with in the central part of Tarikere taluk.

YEMMEDODDI TIGER PRESERVE IN KADUR TALUK

Kadur taluk in Chikkamagaluru district now primarily harbors scrub forest. However, in not too distant past, this taluk had harbored dry deciduous forest that was also an ideal tiger habitat. As early as 1942, a tiger preserve was notified at Yemme Doddi in Kadur taluk covering about 140 sq km of forest area. In the tussle between the man and the beast, it is usually the man who comes out winner; and the Yemmedoddi Tiger Preserve was no exception, its fate as an abode of tiger having been sealed and pushed into the oblivion. The following is an extract from the working plan of Chikkamagaluru forest division for the period 2013-2023 written by Shri Mallik Fiaz Uddin:

"Yemmedoddi Tiger Preserve

An extent of 21,394 acres and 16 guntas was declared as a Tiger Preserve under Section 4 (b) of Game and Fish Preservation Regulation (Regulation No. II of 1901) vide No. AF3892-Forest 137-41-2 dated 4th February 1942. An area of 13,000 acres was again notified under Section-4 of Mysore Forest Regulation vide No. AF. 2365FT-71-42-2 dated 20/2/1942. This area is being shown till date as Yemmedoddi Reserved Forest. Forest was released twice to cultivation by Government vide G.O. 295/301 AH.7/56-3 dated 24/10/1956 - 2070.00 acres and vide G.O. 8295/301 AH.7/56-3 dated 24/10/1956- 7053.00 acres."

As in the case of Shivamogga district, the population density of Chikkamagaluru district is low in the western taluks where the terrain is mostly hilly, and increases considerably towards the eastern region that has extensive plain areas. Perusal of Table-3.1 indicates that the district has about 270 km² of dry deciduous forests and about 195 km² of scrub forests; these two forest types are mostly located in the eastern parts of the district. The presence of substantial extents of scrub forests is indicative of the severe biotic pressures that the dry deciduous forests of the district have been subjected to.

HASSAN DISTRICT

A brief description about the vegetation including the forests of the Hassan district along with their status towards the end of the nineteenth century as brought out in the Mysore Gazetteer (Volume II, Revised Edition, 1897) edited and compiled by Sir Benjamin Lewis Rice is reproduced below:

> **"Vegetation.** The upper slopes of the Ghats which form the western boundary of the District are clothed with magnificent virgin forests containing, among other trees, the poon (*Calophyllum angustfolium*), the some (*Soymida febrifuge*), and blackwood (*Dalbergia latifolia*). Some of these forests have been taken up for coffee and cardamom cultivation, but certain of them are

reserved by Government as State forests – namely, the Kempuhole Ghat, Kaganeri Ghat, Kabbinale Ghat, and Bisale Ghat, all in the Manjarabad taluq. Owing, however, to their inaccessible position, these forests have as yet been worked only on a limited scale. The timber found in the coffee jungles bordering on the Ghats is of little value, with the exception of the hone (*Pterocarpus marsupium*), the nandi (*Lagerstroemia microcarpa*), matti (*Terminalia tomentosa*), heswa (*Artocarpus hirsuta*), ebony (*Diospyros ebenum*), and wild champaka (*Michelia champaca*).

"Lying more inland, in that tract of country in which the pure Malnad (hill country) merges into Maidan (plain country), are the Gopigudda, Doddabetta, Hulkunda and Nagavara jungles. They contain chiefly inferior kinds of woods, with a quantity of nandi, matti and hone, much injured by indiscriminate felling. In the Arkalgud taluq, the only jungle worthy of mention is a strip of land lying on the borders of Coorg known as Menasabetta, the value of which is at present very small for its having been overworked. In the Belur taluq is the Arehalli jungle, containing wood of the above description, but of little value from want of a road. There are also low matti jungles of some size near the Maharajandurga fort, and scrub jungle near the Sige-gudda in the Hassan and Hirikalgudda in the Arsikere taluqs. The babul (*Acacia arabica*) is to be found growing in fields in parts of the Channarayapatna and Hole Narsipur taluqs.

The above description of the vegetation of Hassan district pertaining to the late 1800s is quite brief; the evergreen and semi-evergreen forests situated in the Ghat areas have not been described in detail as most of these forests were yet to be explored and exploited due to their inaccessibility. The description is more or less silent about the occurrence of moist deciduous or high forest in the district. Apparently, most of the areas which originally harbored moist deciduous vegetation had already been converted into coffee plantations; as a result, the extent of moist deciduous forests in the district was very limited. The forests occurring in the vast plain areas of the district have not been described fully as they were not very productive from the point of timber yield; these forests have been generally referred to as scrub jungle.

Although the forests occurring in the vast plains of Hassan district have not been fully described in the Gazetteer and detailed information about their working during that period is not readily available, whatever sketchy information about their management is available indicates that some of these forests were in fairly good condition and were therefore considered fit for exploitation of fuel wood and small timber. A working scheme for the Hirekalgudda state forest was prepared in 1902 dividing the forest into five blocks, each block having been further sub-divided into thirty annual coupes to be worked under 'coppice with standards' system. However, this scheme was reported to have not been followed systematically. A regular working plan was drawn in 1920 for Ramenahalli, Chakanakatte and Hirekalgudda group of state forests for a period of twenty years (1921-1940). Another working plan was drawn up in 1924 for a group of 26 forests of Hassan district. The forests were divided into annual coupes based on area. The number of coupes for each forest varied from 5 to 30 depending upon the extent of the forest. The silvicultural system envisaged was 'coppice with standards' prescribing retention of 20-30 standards per acre. Sandal and minor forest produce (MFP) yielding trees were prescribed to be retained and the blanks were to be afforested with indigenous species.

Regular working plan for all the eastern dry forests of Hassan forest division was written by Mr. K. Belliappa in 1964-65, which was approved during 1974-75 for the period 1975-1986. The plan covering an area of 30,138 hectares had prescribed a number of working circles such as coppice with reserves, protection-cum-improvement, teak conversion, soft wood conversion, afforestation and sandal extraction working circles. Going by the working circles prescribed in the plan, the forests appear to have been in fairly good condition about fifty years ago. Besides, Hassan district in the past was reported to have harbored natural teak in a number of forests such as Baktharahalli reserved forest, Doddabetta reserved forest, Kantenahalli reserved forest, Malasavara protected forest and Karjuvalli village forest; this is indicative of fairly high status of the forests as belonging to the climax dry deciduous type.

Going by the above account, it appears that until about fifty years ago, the district had extensive dry deciduous forests including patches of teak forest. These forests were distributed all over the eastern portion covering all taluks of the district with the sole exception of Sakleshpur taluk, which primarily harbors evergreen and semi-evergreen forests. However, most of these dry forests are now in various stages of degradation resulting from years of maltreatment of repeated hacking, over-grazing and recurrent fires. The proportion of thorny species tends to increase with further degradation of the forests. As a result, substantial portions of the dry deciduous forests of the district have transformed into scrub forests. Perusal of Table-3.1 indicates that the extent of dry deciduous forests in the district is less than 5 km^2 and that of scrub forests is about 155 km^2. Evidently, the dry deciduous forests of Hassan district have suffered a serious setback. A large extent (about 80 km^2) of the district's natural dry deciduous forests had been converted to eucalyptus plantations which have more or less suppressed the indigenous species.

HIREKALGUDDA STATE FOREST

Among the eastern dry forests of Hassan district, the Hirekalgudda state forest is the most prominent. A tiger habitat in the bygone days, this forest overlooking the town of Arsikere covers an area of 6,210.00 hectares. It was notified as a state forest in 1895 with an area of 92 square miles. Eventually, the area of the forest was corrected after resurvey. In the past, this forest was the best climax dry deciduous forest of Hassan district. Since 1902, it was worked for fuel wood and small timber under the silvicultural system of 'coppice with reserves'. The working plan for the Eastern Dry Forests of Hassan forest division (1975-1986) by Mr. K. Belliappa had included the Hirekalgudda forest in the 'Coppice with Reserves' working circle, prescribing retention of honne (*Pterocarpus marsupium*) and teak (*Tectona grandis*) as standards.

Although the present condition of the Hirekalgudda forest is quite degraded due to heavy working in the past and continuous biotic interference spanning many decades, and the forest has now been reduced to dry deciduous scrub in most parts, the remnants of the earlier vegetation are still visible in some pockets. Mr. Range Gowda's working plan for Hassan forest division (2001-02 to 2010-11) has mentioned the presence of 69 tree species in the forest; these include *Tectona grandis, Santalum album, Terminalia tomentosa, Pterocarpus marsupium, Terminalia chebula, Terminalia bellirica, Hardwickia binata, Shorea talura, Gmelina arborea, Chloroxylon swietenia, Lagerstroemia parviflora, Ailanthus excelsa, Givotia rottleriformis), Oxytenanthera monostigma*, etc. A study of flora and fauna conducted in selected areas of Hirekalgudda forest by Dr. T. V. Naik and others (2012) has revealed the presence of 201 plant species belonging to 71 families comprising a fairly wide diversity of species: trees (76), shrubs (70), herbs (45), twinners (5) and climbers (5).

As regards wildlife, the Hirekalgudda forest harbors leopards, wolves, jackals, black bucks, sloth bears, etc. There is a proposal to declare the forest as a sloth bear sanctuary. According the status of protected area (PA) to the forest will help in overall restoration and rejuvenation of this once-vibrant forest to retrieve some of its lost glory.

KODAGU DISTRICT (erstwhile Coorg State)

The deciduous forests of Kodagu district are located on the eastern portion of the district. These are located in Madikeri forest division, Virajpet forest division and Nagarahole national park. The forests of Madikeri division are Dubare, Anekadu, Attur, Malambi, Alur, Kattepura, Gangavara, Yedavanad, Janukallbetta and Nidthi reserved forests. The forests of Nagarahole national park are Nalkeri, Hatgat and Arikeri reserved forests. The forests of Virajpet division are Devamachi and Mavukal reserved forests.

The deciduous forests of Kodagu district are primarily of moist deciduous type. However, Mr. A. Akbar Sha in his working plan for Madikeri forest division (1986-1995) has kept only three forests of the division, namely, Anekadu, Malambi and Yedavanad RFs in the category of moist deciduous forests. The remaining reserved forests of the division, i.e. Dubare, Attur, Alur, Kattepura, Gangavara, Janukallbetta and Nidthi reserved forests have been kept in the dry deciduous category. Similarly, the relatively degraded and drier parts of Devamachi and Mavukal reserved forests of Virajpet forest division have been kept in the category of dry deciduous forest by Mr. Ajai Misra in the working plan (2001-2011) of the division. [In the KSRSAC report of 2006 also, Kodagu district has been shown as harboring some dry deciduous forests. Perusal of Table-3.1 would indicate the presence of about 184 km² of dry deciduous forests.] However, considering the rainfall and crop composition, the deciduous forests of Kodagu district need to be classified as moist deciduous forests. As large portions of these forests have been degraded due to biotic factors such as repeated fire, over-grazing and infestation by invasive weeds, they often give an impression of being of the dry deciduous type. These degraded patches of moist deciduous forests cannot be assigned the status of climax formation of Dry deciduous forest.

In the Western Ghats region, there is a distinct pattern in which transformation from one forest type to the next takes place. Starting eastward from the crest of the Western Ghats, we come across climatic climax formations of evergreen, semi-evergreen, moist deciduous and dry deciduous forests, in that sequential order. Among these forest formations, the distinction between the moist deciduous type and the dry deciduous type is very thin, as the species compositions of both these types are more or less similar. The main difference between these two types lies in the size of the trees: the trees of the moist deciduous forests are much larger whereas those of the dry deciduous forests are comparatively smaller, usually referred to as pole-sized trees. In a dry deciduous forest, some of the common hardwood tree species such as teak, matti, kindal, beete, etc. attain maximum average girth of about 1.20 m whereas the same species grow up to 4-5 m or even more in a moist deciduous forest. The difference in size of the trees in these two types of forest is brought about mainly by the difference in the average rainfall, which is about 150-200 cm in respect of the moist deciduous forests and about 100-130 cm in respect of the dry deciduous forests. The soil profile of the areas supporting moist deciduous forests is somewhat better than that in areas supporting dry deciduous forests. The average number of rainy days is also generally more in case of the moist deciduous forests.

Kodagu district has an average rainfall of about 250 cm. The average rainfall of the wettest taluk Madikeri is about 330 cm and that of the driest taluk Somawarpet is about 210 cm. From the point of rainfall distribution, the forest of Kodagu district is by and large evergreen. Moist deciduous forests occur in the eastern portions of Somawarpet and Virajpet taluks with preponderance of evergreen and semi-evergreen patches in the moister localities. These forests continue to be moist deciduous beyond the eastern boundary of the district and spill over to the Mysuru district (Hunsur, Periyapatna, and HD Kote taluks) for some distance before turning to dry deciduous forests.

At the field level, the surest way of finding the difference between a climax moist deciduous forest and a climax dry deciduous forest in the Western Ghats region is to look for the presence of *Bambusa bambos* (dowga bamboo). This species is ubiquitous and abundant in a moist deciduous forest, being present almost throughout the forest. In a moist deciduous forest, *Dendrocalamus strictus* (medri bamboo) is less frequent and starts appearing in the drier end of the forest; in the moister end, it appears only at higher altitudes. On the other hand, the occurrence of *Bambusa bambos* is restricted in the dry deciduous forest, being present only along depressions or stream banks. In such forest *Dendrocalamus strictus* (medri bamboo) is more common and sometimes abundant.

From a practical point of view also, it will not be proper to assign the status of dry deciduous forest to the forests of Kodagu district, because, in that eventuality, all the forests of Hunsur, HD Kote and Periyapatna taluks which are located further east of the Kodagu forests will have to be assigned the status of dry deciduous forest. As we have seen earlier, the above-mentioned taluks of Mysore district harbor some very fine moist deciduous forests along the border of Kodagu district and subsequently turn dry deciduous further east.

BELGAUM DISTRICT

As already mentioned, only one taluk of Belgaum (present name Belagavi) district, namely, Khanapur taluk, along with the western part of the adjoining Belgaum taluk, is thickly forested with various types of forest such as evergreen, semi-evergreen, moist deciduous and dry deciduous. The remaining taluks of the district harbor some dry deciduous but largely scrub forests. As per the Gazetteer of Bombay Presidency (Volume XXI) compiled and edited by Mr. James M. Campbell (printed in 1884), "Teak and blackwood forest began about six miles east of the Sahyadris and stretched through Ghotgali and Kakkeri. The teak had formerly stretched to Dharwar. Deep woody valleys under the hill of Sidh on the North Kanara border, about five miles south of Ghotgali, had suffered much from the spread of tillage. Of young growing teak there is still a respectable quantity in the west of the forest abutting on Sidh hill. Further east the trees though numerous, were stunted and would probably never yield more than rafters and small posts.---".

The Gazetteer further adds that the forests of the district can be broadly distributed in two categories as moist forests and dry forests. The dry forests lie on the east side of the Poona-Dharwar Road and include the forests of Chikodi, Sampgaon and Gokak sub-divisions. The moist forests lie on the west side of the Poona-Dharwar Road and include the forests of Belgaum and Khanapur sub-divisions. The forests are very unevenly distributed, the large sub-divisions like Athni and Parasgad having till lately little or no forest, while Khanapur sub-division has twice as much area as cultivated land. A brief synopsis of the forests of the district as given in the Gazetteer is furnished below:

In the moist forest the rainfall is heavy, from 50 inches to probably not less than 200 inches. About one-half of the moist area belongs to the Sahyadris (Western Ghats), 'a mass of laterite covered mountains, cut by deep densely wooded ravines and open to the full force of the south-west monsoon. Except an occasional patch of rice or *ragi* the forest is unbroken. Here the population is scanty and the area fit for plough cultivation is small.' In those villages which lie actually along the crest of the Sahyadris these conditions are most marked. The area culturable with the plough is insufficient even for the small population, and from time immemorial they have chiefly lived on the proceeds of what is known as *kumri* or wood-ash tillage. In view of the damage caused to the forest by the *kumri* cultivation, it has been abolished in the Presidency. However, considering the distress and hardship faced by the hill-tribes because of its abolition, *kumri* has been permitted in these areas under strict supervision of the government officials and on condition of mandatory planting of trees in the *kumri*-affected area. The commonest trees are the *jambul* (*Eugenia jambolana*), *kumba* (*Careya arborea*), *mati* (*Terminalia tomentosa*), *harda* (*T. chebula*), *hela* (*T. bellerica*), *pairi* (*Ficus cordifolia*), *kel* (*Ficus infectoria*), *umar* (*Ficus glomerata*), *kindali* (*Terminalia paniculata*), *bava* (*Cassia fistula*), *karanj* (*Pongamia glabra*), *anjan* (*Memecylon edule*), *nana* (*Lagerstroemia lanceolata*), *avla* (*Phyllanthus emblica*), and small bamboo. Common shrub is *karvi* (*Strobilanthus grahamianus*). There is sprinkling of *jamba* (*Xylia dolabriformis*), *sisva* (*Dalbergia latifolia*), *shemba* (*Acacia concinna*), and other *acacias, hasan* (*Pterocarpus marsupium*), *apta* (*Bauhinia racemosa*), *palas* (*Butea frondosa*), and *pangera* (*Erythrina indica*), but no teak. *Anjan*, a useful wood, is confined to very moist places on the crest-line of the Sahyadris where it forms unmixed wood of considerable extent. [Here, *Anjan* refers to *Memecylon edule*.] Here and there, dense *rais* or groves of huge evergreen tree, sometimes covering more than a hundred acres, stand out like dark islands in the grey sea of withered grass and leafless coppice. The commonest trees in these evergreen hill groves are soft woods, *nanas*, jacks, and mangoes with a sprinkling of *mari* palms (*Phoenix sylvestris*), whose sap is drawn for liquor, and of cinnamon trees whose bark is used as a spice. Along the Sahyadris there is comparatively little large timber, though large *matis*, *nanas*, and other valuable trees are by no means uncommon in ravines and remote places.

The eastern part of the moist forest is less hilly than the western part and is also partially sheltered from the fury of the south-west monsoon by the crests of the main range of the Sahyadris. Here the rainfall is relatively less, being roughly forty-five to sixty inches. In addition to the trees found in the purely Sahyadri forest mentioned above, the timber trees occurring in this part of forest include *dhamin* (*Grewia asiatica*), *honangi* (*Adina cordifolia*), *kalam* (*Stephegyne parvifolia*), *siris* (*Albizia* spp.), teak, and large bamboos. The commonest trees are *kumba*, *jamba*, *harda*, the dwarf-date palm (*Phoenix farinifera*), *palas*, *avla*, *jambul*, bamboo, *kindali*, *mati*, *nana*, and in the south a good sprinkling of teak and blackwood (rosewood). The produce is chiefly superior firewood poles from fifteen to thirty feet long, with here and there large standards of *savari* (*Bombax malabaricum*), *hela*, *pangera*, *karambal* (*Dillenia pentagyna*), and other softwoods, and less often of *mati*, *kindali*, *jambul*, and other hard woods. The forest increases in heaviness towards the south where are some fifty square miles of good timber, including much clean straight-stemmed teak, *mati*, and blackwood. These tracts are much better wooded than the main range. Probably one-fourth of the forest area is stocked. Teak occurs only in the south and is commonest on the granite hills south of Nandgad. It is generally mixed with *jamba* and bamboo. But between Tavarkatti and Bidi there is much pure teak of vigorous growth.

The dry forests on the east of Poona-Dharwar road are on the trap and sandstone hills of Chikodi, Gokak, and Sampgaon. These dry forests are located at an altitude of about 2,000 feet, similar to the moist forests. However, here the rainfall is much less, probably on an average not more than thirty inches. Cultivation is confined to the valleys and some of the flat-topped trap-hills. The forestland, about one-eighth of which is stocked with useful wood, is very poor and stony, yielding only firewood scrub with a sprinkling of small poles, fit for hut-building, and of an average height of about ten feet. The produce is chiefly cactus, four or five kinds of fig, *dindal* (*Anogeissus latifolia*), *mashval* (*Chloroxylon swietenia*), *bandurgi* (*Dodonaea viscosa*), *avla* (*Phyllanthus emblica*), *gorvi* (*Ixora parviflora*), *tarvar* (*Cassia auriculata*), *mati* (*Terminalia tomentosa*), *kindali* (*Terminalia paniculata*), *as* (*Hardwickia binata*), sandal, bamboo, and numberless thorns.

From the above description provided in the Gazetteer of Bombay Presidency it is apparent that the condition of the dry forests of the district was quite poor even at the time when the British had taken over the administration. Most of the thickly wooded forests of the district were confined to the Khanapur and Belgaum sub-divisions. While the western parts of these sub-divisions harbored evergreen, semi-evergreen and moist deciduous forests, the forests on the eastern part were dry deciduous of high quality. Good quality teak-bearing dry deciduous forests are now met with in the eastern part of Nagargali range of Belagavi forest division. These forests are also known as Teak pole forests. Some extent of dry deciduous forest without teak is also met with in the Kakti and Gujnal ranges of Belagavi forest division. Except for the above-mentioned patches of dry deciduous forest, the remaining dry forests of the district spread over the eastern and northern taluks such as Hukkeri, Bailhongal, Gokak, Chikkodi, Athani, Raibag, Ramdurg and Saundatti were poorly stocked capable of yielding fuel wood and some quantities of small timber. These forests have been under severe biotic pressure due to high population density and as a result got further degraded into dry scrub forests with preponderance of thorny species in the driest localities. Perusal of Table-3.1 indicates that the district has about 902.56 km^2 of scrub forests. Most of these scrub forests are met with in the above taluks of the district.

In addition to the expansion of agriculture and continuous withdrawal of biomass spanning centuries which obviously were the main reasons for the decimation, depletion and loss of forest in the eastern taluks of the Belgaum district, iron ore mining also had adversely affected the forests in the region. Smelting of iron was carried out in areas close to where these mines were located and large quantities of charcoal required in the iron forges were prepared from the fuel wood obtained by clearing the adjacent jungles. As the availability of fuel wood in the nearby forests came down due to over exploitation, it had to be obtained and carted from distant jungles incurring higher cost. As a matter of fact, increasing cost of fuel wood made iron smelting economically unviable, and ultimately iron ore mining was given up. As per information furnished in the Gazetteer of the Bombay Presidency (Volume XXI), 1884, iron ore mining was formerly taking place in a number of places in the district such as Kanur, Punare, and Patne in Belgaum, at Kaitnal and Tavaz in Gokak, at Kitur in Sampagaon, and at Ram pass (at Nersa, about six miles west of Khanapur). The ore was generally peroxide of iron with a mixture of clay, quartz, and lime. Iron ore was also smelted in Tegihal village from brown haematite found in the limits of Basargi village, both the villages lying on the left bank of Malaprabha, between Manoli and Torgal. The manufacture of iron had by then (1883) ceased, partly on account of the increased price of the fuel and partly because of the fall in the price of iron, as cheaper iron imported from Britain started becoming available.

BIJAPUR DISTRICT
(present Bagalkote and Vijayapura districts)

Among the four districts of Karnataka which formed part of Bombay Presidency, Bijapur district was situated wholly in the *maidan* region. Most of the plain areas of the district were under cultivation since a long time. As a result, the forests were distributed in widely scattered patches mostly restricted in the hill tops and steep slopes of the tract. A few forest patches in the plains were confined to the river banks and mid-stream islands. In the Gazetteer of the Bombay Presidency (Volume XXIII) compiled and edited by Mr. James M. Campbell (printed in 1884), the description of the forests of the Bijapur district as obtaining in 1883 has been given as follows:

> "Of 5757 square miles, the whole area of the district, 245 or 4.2 per cent have been set apart as forest land. On the 31st of March 1883 of the total forest area 155 square miles were reserved and ninety square miles were protected forests. Except small areas of grassland bearing *babhul* and *jambhul* in the bed of or near the bank of the Krishna, the Ghataprabha, and the Malaprabha, the

forest lands of the Bijapur district are on the hills to the south of the Krishna and between the Krishna and Dharwar. They stretch east to the Nizam's territories and west to the petty states of Mudhol, Ramdurg, and Torgal. That till recent times these hill-sides had an abundance of moderately sized trees and firewood is shown by coppice stools and decayed roots. The present barrenness is due to the recklessness of the people in dealing with forests, and to the drain which the old iron-smelting industry must have caused. The hills about Kaladgi and Bagalkote are bare. North towards Bilgi, south-east about Badami and Gudur, and north west towards Ramdurg and Torgal, there is a large stretch of rough country more or less covered with scrub and such small trees as *dhavda* (M.) *dindal* (K.) (*Anogeissus latifolia*), *bahava* (M.) *kakkai* (K.) (*Cassia fistula*), *nim* (M.) *bevina* or *bevu* (K.) (*Melia azadirachta*), *timburni* (M.) *balai* (K.) (*Diospyros melanoxylon*), *khair* (M.) *khairada* (K.) (*Acacia catechu*), *halda* (M.) *mashvala* (K.) (*Chloroxylon swietenia*), some armed and unarmed *acacias*, and numerous varieties of thorn bushes. The hills best clothed with wood and scrub are those of Badami and Hungund. Here many parts have much improved since 1874, when conservancy was enforced, and the bamboo, which in 1870 was all but extinct, makes a fair show on some of the hill-sides. The Bijapur forest may be divided into two sections, scrub forests and babhul or babli *Acacia arabica* reserves. The scrub forests, scattered over 238 square miles are composed chiefly of stunted *mashvala* (*Chloroxylon swietenia*), *kakkai* (*Cassia fistula*), *nim* (*Melia azadirachta*), *aval* (*Cassia auriculata*), *hulgal* (*Dalbergia arborea*), *khair* (*Acacia catechu*), *ippi* (*Bassia latifolia*) and *jaune* (*Grewia rothii*). These forests at present are valuable only as firewood reserves; wood required for minor building purposes and for field tools can also be obtained from the forests of Badami and from part of Hungund. The *babhul* reserves include the lands which yield *babhul*, *nim*, bamboo, *jambhul*, and *bor*. These lie in isolated patches and together do not spread over more than six square miles. Almost all are covered with both old and young trees grown artificially. Among the woods in the district the *nim* and *babhul*, which do not suffer from the attacks of white ants, are considered very strong and used by all classes as house beams, posts, ploughs, plough-staves, cart-wheels and cart-staves, and other field purposes. The wood of the *mashvala, kakkai, hulgal,* and *khair* is used for poles. Large beams, logs, scantlings, and planks of teak and blackwood, for good buildings, are yearly brought from the Kanara forests. ------"

The forests of Bijapur district were brought under working plan from 1920 onwards. Earlier, they were worked by carrying out fellings of irregular nature by laying out 'coupes' either departmentally or through the contractors. With the introduction of regular working plans, felling became systematic. The forests were worked under the silvicultural system of 'clear felling' mainly for extraction of fuel wood and some quantities of small timber, followed by natural regeneration from seed and coppice. Initially a rotation of 20 years was adopted which was changed to 40 years since 1936-37 in order to reduce the intensity of felling. Sound neem (*Azadirachta indica*) and a few young and sound mashwal (*Chloroxylon swietenia*) trees were to be retained as seed bearers, in addition to karanj (*Pongamia pinnata*), sandal (*Santalum album*) and medri bamboo (*Dendrocalamus strictus*). In addition, promising advance growth of and below six inches girth of all the important species such as mashwal (*Chloroxylon swietenia*), tugli (*Albizia amara*), dindal (*Anogeissus latifolia*), khair (*Acacia catechu*), chil (*Strychnos potatorum*), neem (*Azadirachta indica*), etc. was to be retained at the time of principal felling of the coupe. Artificial regeneration of mashwal, tugli, dindal, khair and neem was also prescribed. However, the results of both natural and artificial regeneration were by and large not successful due to a number of factors such as hard crust in the top soil, heavy grazing, and lack of sub-soil moisture due to inconsistent rainfall. Thus, as the existing natural forests kept on getting denuded as a result of continuous exploitation for supply of fuel wood to the people, commensurate recoupment of the forests did not materialize. Consequently, the forests got more and more degraded, and what once were dry mixed deciduous forests got transformed into dry deciduous scrub with increasing presence of thorny elements.

From the above description it is apparent that the forest area of the district was quite insignificant even during the beginning of the British administration. By the time reservation of forest was started under the provisions of the Indian Forest Act, 1878, expansion of agriculture had taken place in most of the areas of the district that were considered fit for cultivation. The extent of forest in the district was too less to be able to cater to the biomass needs of the people and their cattle; and due to intense biotic pressure, it became difficult to protect whatever little forest the district was left with. As a matter of fact, land hunger in the district continued to be so acute that some portions of the reserved forests had also been released for agriculture, both before and after the Independence. The extent of agricultural land in the present Bagalkote and Vijayapura districts is very high, being 77.97% and 87.72% respectively of the geographical areas of the districts. The extent of recorded forest area is low, being 12.76% and 0.77% of the geographical areas of the districts. When the erstwhile Bijapur district was bifurcated in 1997, lion's share of the forests went to the newly formed Bagalkote district, with practically no forest having been apportioned to the residual Bijapur (now Vijayapura) district. Perusal of Table-3.1 would reveal that both the districts now do not harbor any dry deciduous forest (climax type). All the forests of Bagalkote district have degenerated into scrub forests (687.36 km^2). Vijayapura district, which anyway did not have much forest, now harbors about 9.27 km^2 of scrub forests.

Smelting of iron also had affected whatever forests were available around the iron ore mines scattered in the district. As per the information provided in the Gazetteer of the Bombay Presidency (Volume XXIII) printed in 1884, iron ore was found in various parts of the Bijapur district south of the Krishna. During the 1820s, iron was manufactured at the village of Adgal, about four miles north of Badami. In 1873 iron ore was, and to a limited extent was still (1883) smelted at a number of places such as Siddapur, Jainmatti, Sidanhal, Haligeri, Raghavpur, Benkanvadi, etc. Since the famine of 1877, there was fall in the production of iron. The main reason was high cost of fuel resulting in higher production cost. The local iron was dearer than the foreign (imported) iron. Evidently, with the decimation of the nearby forests, fuel wood had to be cut and transported from distant jungles incurring higher expenditure, which in turn raised the cost of production of local iron.

YADAHALLI CHINKARA WILDLIFE SANCTUARY

The first wildlife sanctuary for the conservation of Chinkara (*Gazella bennettii*) in the state of Karnataka was notified in 2016 at the Yadahalli reserved forest in Bagalkote district. Covering an area of 96.36 sq km, the sanctuary falls partly in Bilagi taluk and partly in Mudhol taluk. The vegetation of the sanctuary is primarily dry deciduous scrub interspersed with thorny and rocky patches. Prominent tree species occurring in the forest include *Chloroxylon swietenia*, *Albizia amara*, *Wrightia tinctoria*, *Anogeissus latifolia*, *Azadirachta indica*, *Madhuca latifolia*, etc. besides thorny *Acacias* and *Euphorbias*, and a host of shrub species. As regards wildlife, besides Chinkara, the sanctuary harbors wolves, jackals, wildcats, stripped hyenas, and a variety of other mammals, reptiles and birds.

Considering that most of the forests in the Eastern Plains are generally of smaller extents, notifying a fairly large-sized forest as a protected area is a very welcome move. The Yadahalli sanctuary, the first in Bagalkote district, augurs well not only for the resident wildlife population in the reserved forest, but will also prove to be very beneficial to the once-ravaged forest. Because of increased protection and more conservative management in a protected area (PA), the highly degraded forest will be able to bounce back and retrieve some of the original vegetation of the tract. The overall quality of the forest will improve. [**Note:** Credit for the formation of the Yadahalli Chinkara Wildlife Sanctuary mainly goes to Mr. M. R. Desai, formerly Honorary Wildlife Warden, who has, for more than 30 years, relentlessly campaigned for the protection and conservation of the antelope, once thought to be extinct in Karnataka, and its habitat.]

DHARWAR DISTRICT
(present Dharwar, Gadag and Haveri districts)

During the earlier part of British administration, Dharwar district was thickly forested. Up to the middle of the nineteenth century, dense forests had extended to as far as the towns of Dharwar and Kod (near Hirekerur) from the border of its western neighbor, the North Kanara district. It is reported that 'in 1857, within three miles of Dharwar many parts of the country were covered with dense forests, the haunts of tiger, bison, and other wild animals'. However, the forests came under heavy exploitation because of proximity to habitations and a number of consumption centers, and degraded rapidly, the remnant forest cover being 'hardly enough for jackals, and some parts are under tillage.' As early as 1848, Lieutenant W.C. Anderson of the Revenue Survey Department had complained of forest destruction near Kod (near Hirekerur) due to timber extraction. 'Not a tree of more than a few inches in diameter was to be found within miles of the edge of the forest.' During those days, only teak and blackwood (*Dalbergia latifolia*) were safe, being protected by the Government. Other hardwood tree species such as matti (*Terminalia tomentosa*) and honne (*Pterocarpus marsupium*) were fast disappearing. The first plantation activity in the district had been taken up during the 1870s in Kalaghatgi area adjoining North Kanara district, where teak had been planted.

A brief account of the status of the forests of the Dharwar district as provided in the Gazetteer of the Bombay Presidency (Volume XXII) compiled and edited by Mr. James M. Campbell (printed in 1884) is given below:

> The forest area of the district as on 31-03-1883 was 426 square miles comprising 155½ of reserved forests and 270½ of protected forests. The western part of the district comprising Dharwar, Kalaghatgi, Bankapur and Hangal sub-divisions harbor moist forests covering 200 square miles of which 108 are reserved and 92 are protected forests. The eastern and southern parts of the district comprising Gadag, Karajgi, Ranebennur, and Kod sub-divisions harbor dry forests covering 224 square miles of which 47 are reserved and 177 are protected forests. Hubli and Navalgund sub-divisions have practically no forest, having only two square miles of forest between them. The process of forest reservation is in progress in the district.

As regards the moist forests, the forest lands in Dharwar, Kalaghatgi and Bankapur are hilly and undulating, and the Hangal reserves are mostly flat. The finest trees are generally found in valleys, which in some parts are thickly wooded, while the hill tops are generally thinly covered with trees. Teak prevails in the forests of Dharwar, Kalaghatgi and Bankapur; towards Hangal it almost disappears. Where teak prevails, the soil is light, loose, and is veined with quartz. Growth of teak is the best in the Kalaghatgi forests where it grows to considerable size in suitable localities. The reserved forests are by and large covered with fairly good growth of trees capable of giving building materials and firewood. However, these forests as a rule do not harbor very big trees but comprise pole crop. The forests of Dharwar sub-division which cover 29 square miles of reserved forests and 21 square miles of protected forests are of great value as the main source of timber and firewood to Dharwar town and the tree-less eastern part of the district.

The dry forests of the district occurring in Gadag, Karajgi, Ranebennur, and Kod sub-divisions are mostly dry stony hills. In this part of the district the existing forest or wood-bearing area is extremely small. Most of the reserves are in very poor condition, bare or at best with a covering of scrub and thorn. The tops of the hills are bare rocks. The most important species found among the scrub is *bandurbi* (*Dodonaea viscosa*), followed by the Acacias and Cassias: *khair* (*Acacia catechu*), *phulate babhul* (*Acacia latronum*), *babhul* (*Acacia arabica*), *tarvad* (*Cassia auriculata*), and *baya* (*Cassia fistula*). *Cassia fistula* is not plentiful, it is found chiefly along the banks of a few rivulets. Vigorous coppice shoots of teak are seen in some places, an indication that teak was formerly common. There is a natural forest of anjan (*Hardwickia binata*) covering about one square mile in Eklashpur village.

The erstwhile Dharwar district now comprises three districts, namely, Dharwar, Haveri, and Gadag. Among these districts, Dharwar and Haveri share their western boundaries with the district of Uttara Kannada (earlier North Kanara). The forests of Dharwar and Haveri districts adjacent to the Uttara Kannada district are of dry deciduous type of fairly good quality. These are also known as Teak pole forests. With the exception of these two patches of forest, the remaining forests of both these districts are now scrub forests. As regards Gadag district, most of the forests which originally were of dry mixed deciduous type have degenerated into scrub forests. Perusal of Table-3.1 would reveal that the extents of dry deciduous forests in the districts are: Dharwar (296.63 km^2), Haveri (138.21 km^2), and Gadag (0.77 km^2). The extents of scrub forests in the districts are: Dharwar (8.79 km^2), Haveri (106.9 km^2), and Gadag (290.00 km^2). The proportion of land under agricultural (cereal) crop in the districts is very high: Dharwar (84.96%), Haveri (81.66%) and Gadag (87.69%). This clearly shows that expansion of agriculture in the districts has been very high. This resulted in severe pressure on the forests resulting in their fragmentation and contraction. The ever increasing human and cattle population continued to put tremendous pressure on these sparse patches of forests resulting in their further degradation and decimation.

Smelting of iron in various parts of the district adjacent to iron ore mines had also adversely affected the forests, as charcoal prepared from firewood was required in large quantities in the iron forges. With regard to iron ore mining in the areas of the erstwhile Dharwar district, the Gazetteer of the Bombay Presidency (Volume XXII), 1884, gives the following information:

"----In former times when fuel was plentiful in the Kappatgudd hills and English iron was dear, much iron was smelted at Doni and other places in these hills. Iron is still (1883) smelted at Tegur on the Poona-Harihar road fifteen miles north of Dharwar, and at Gulgi at Kalghatgi. The ore is of a darkish-brown and has a specific gravity of 3.60. It is found on a hill to the south-west of the village of Tegur in small pebbles and in large masses, both on and below the surface.----."

KAPPATAGUDDA FORESTS

The Kappatagudda forests of the erstwhile Dharwar district (now in Gadag district) were once clothed with very good vegetation. The forests of Kappat hills were well-known as favorite abode of the saints for meditation. These forests were also famous for varieties of medicinal plants with special healing powers. The local medical practitioners (*nati vaidyas*) were once totally dependent on the Kappat hills for procurement of medicinal plants. Many of the medicinal plants have now become extinct, although a few of them are still available in pockets.

The forests of Gadag district are under tremendous biotic pressure mainly due to over grazing and repeated fires. As a result, most of the forests including the Kappatagudda forests are now of the scrub type. In order to protect the remnant biodiversity of the Kappatagudda forests from complete extinction, the 'Kappatagudda Conservation Reserve' covering an area of 17,872 hectares was declared in 2017 under the Wildlife (Protection) Act, 1972. In 2019, the status of the protected area was raised to that of a wildlife sanctuary.

The Kappat hills had some quantities of iron ore and traces of gold. In the past, iron ore mining had been permitted in certain portions of the forests. These mining leases have since expired. The practice of collecting gold spangles from the sands of a number of streams such as Doni, Sortur, etc. by a community of people known as *Jalgars* was also in vogue. Survey conducted by the British did confirm the presence of gold but availability was considered inadequate for viable production. Eventually, however, gold mining was carried out for eight years at the turn of the previous century by a company called 'Dharwad Gold Mines Limited', which wound up in 1912 due to poor recovery of gold.

In the recent years, there have been reports about initiatives taken to restart gold mining in the Kappatagudda forests. There are also reports about lobbying to downgrade the status of the wildlife sanctuary in order to facilitate extraction of a few tons of gold. The Kappatagudda forests provide the only hope of sustaining some greenery in the entire Gadag district. The opportunity cost of this greenery is worth tons of gold.

NORTH KANARA DISTRICT
(present Uttara Kannada district)

The North Kanara district was the most forested district of the Bombay Presidency. According to the Gazetteer of the Bombay Presidency (Volume XV) compiled and edited by Mr. James M. Campbell (printed in 1883), the extents of the reserved and protected forests in the district as on 1882 were 683.67 and 2864.98 square miles totaling 3,548.65 square miles (about 9,191 square kilometers), which represented about 90 per cent of the geographical area of the entire district (3,910 square miles). [Eventually, most of these forests were brought under the domain of reserved forests.]

A brief description of the forests of North Kanara has been brought out in the Gazetteer of the Bombay Presidency (Volume XV) in the following words

"The forest area may conveniently be divided into three sections: the tableland above the Sahayadris, the main range of the Sahyadris, and the western spurs of the Sahyadris. In the tableland above the Sahyadris the commonest rocks are clay-slate and quartzite. On the lower lands the soil is mostly black with an underlayer of red, which crops up where the surface is wavy. Where teak prevails the soil is lighter in colour, loose, and mixed with quartz. Except in open tilled spaces and where the surface is rock, and along the more thickly peopled eastern frontier where they have been cleared away, the whole country is covered with trees. West from the eastern frontier towards the Sahyadri hills, tillage becomes rare, and there are splendid forests of teak, blackwood, terminalias, and other trees eighty to 150 feet high, and with fine clean stems sixty to ninety feet high and five to twelve feet in girth. Nearer the Sahyadris the country roughens into uplands and hills seamed by water-courses and valleys with rich rice lands and spice gardens. There are also patches of evergreen forest with splendid trees not generally found in the leaf-shedding forests further east.

"The central Sahydri forest belt, though it includes some large iron-clay plateaus with nothing but scrub and grass, has some of the finest forests in the district. The chief of these, in hills of clay-slate and quartz, are the magnificent teak forests of the Kalinadi and Kaneri rivers which run through Supa and Yellapur and of the Bedthihalla and Gangavali rivers which divide Yellapur from Sirsi.

"In the western or coast belt the lowlands are under tillage, and most of the forests are found on the spurs that run west from the Sahyadris, in some cases to the sea. The soil is red and gravelly, ill suited for teak, which when found is stunted and insignificant. Bamboos of several valuable kinds grow over the whole of Kanara, sometimes mixed and sometimes alone."

The present recorded forest area of the district is 8,296.46 km² which constitutes about 80% of the geographical area (10,291 km²) of the district. The forest cover of the district as per the India State of Forest Report (ISFR) 2019 is 8,123.75 km² which is more or less the same as the recorded forest area. This indicates that the forest area of the district has reduced by about 10% since 1882. A substantial portion of the reduction of forest area of the district has taken place due to expansion of agriculture in the post-Independence era in the eastern taluks of Haliyal, Yellapur and Mundgod which harbor all the dry deciduous forests of the district. [The other region where some reduction of forest took place was in the highly populated coastal region. Hydro-electric projects and related activities, including rehabilitation of the displaced families, also took away considerable forest areas of the district.]

The total extent of dry deciduous forests of the district is about 279.41 km² (Table-3.1). These forests occur in Haliyal range and parts of Sambrani and Bhagavathi ranges of Haliyal taluk and parts of Kirwatti, Mundgod and Katur ranges of Yellapur and Mundgod taluks. These forests occur in the eastern fringes of the Western Ghats region and continue beyond the eastern boundary of the Uttara Kannada district into the western parts of the present Dharwar and Haveri districts. These are primarily teak-bearing forests and are popularly known as Teak pole forests. Although these forests represent the best formation of the dry deciduous forests of Karnataka, the effects of severe biotic interferences in the form of illicit withdrawal, encroachment, over-grazing, fire, etc. are quite discernible in these forests which are interspersed with many villages. The population of the adjoining districts of Dharwar and Haveri also puts some pressure on these forests. The degradation of the forests is conspicuous near the habitations. Gradual disappearance of *Dendrocalamus strictus* (medri bamboo), once abundant in these forests, is a matter of serious concern.

BELLARY DISTRICT
(present Ballari district, also includes Adoni, Alur and Rayadurg taluks of Andhra Pradesh)

In Bellary district, which was a part of the Madras Presidency, forest management in the past was said to have been very simple. Graziers were allowed freely and they used to cut the tree growth for agricultural implements and for dwelling. Dr. Dietrich Brandis, Inspector-General of Forests, inspected the forests of Bellary in 1881 and suggested lines of future management. He gave importance to the protection of forests and suggested for reservation of forests under the Madras Forest Act that was on the anvil. He also suggested that kamara (*Hardwickia binata*), teak (*Tectona grandis*) and sandalwood (*Santalum album*) should be reserved. Real and systematic conservancy of forest in Bellary district started with the passing of the Madras Forest Act of 1882. Most of the major reserves of the district were constituted during the last quarter of the nineteenth century and the first quarter of the twentieth century. The total extent of reserved forests and reserved lands in the Bellary district as on 1904 was 624 square miles constituting 11 per cent of the geographical area of the district.

The Bellary district was one of the driest districts of the Madras Presidency. It appeared to have been devoid of tree growth since a very long time. Expansion of agriculture coupled with use and abuse of whatever trees grew in the vicinity of cultivations and settlements must have resulted in such a condition. In the Manual of Bellary district compiled and edited by John Kelsall (printed in 1872), the general barrenness of the topography of the Bellary district has been described as follows:

"To the centre of the district the surface of the plain presents a monotonous and almost treeless extent, bounded by the horizon, and unbroken, save by a few rocky elevations that stand forth abruptly from the sheet of black soil like rocks from the ocean. Of this tract, Sir T. MUNRO wrote, 'These districts are more destitute of trees than any part of Scotland I ever saw; the traveller scarcely meets with one in twenty miles and nowhere with a clump of fifty.' Since this was written large sums of money have been spent planting topes and trees and some success has been attained. It has however been found almost impossible to get trees to grow in the soil, and those that do take root are stunted miserable-looking objects. Water is very scarce, and what there is, is brackish and highly impregnated with lime."

In the Gazetteer of Bellary district compiled and edited by Mr. W. Francis (printed in 1904), the characteristics of the forests of the district have been described as follows:

"This growth, as was only to be expected in so arid a tract, is nowhere luxuriant and in no part of the district is there any continuous area of large timber. Popular tradition says that much of the forest which used to exist has been recklessly felled, and it is at least very noticeable how much rarer thick growth is in the neighborhood of towns and villages than in wilder parts. At present, the areas which have been constituted reserved forests contain little but scrub and grass, and their protection is undertaken less in the hope that they will eventually produce timber than with the desire to provide a reserve of fuel for the ryots and of grazing for their cattle. Of the annual forest revenue of the district only about one-seventh is derived from the sale of timber and bamboos (and much even of this represents money paid for trees standing on land newly taken on patta), while more than four-fifths are obtained from grazing fees, the sale of firewood and charcoal and such minor sources as fees for tapping date-trees, fruit (especially tamarind and custard-apples), tanning barks (especially tangedu, *Cassia auriculata*), and so forth."

In spite of the general dismal condition of the forests as indicated above, Mr. Francis has provided a vivid account of the diversity of whatever vegetation the Bellary district had harbored during those days in the following words:

"The forests of the district, like its crops, naturally differ with the soil in which they grow and the rainfall they receive.

"In the dry black-cotton soil areas the growth consists chiefly of babul, which rapidly sows itself in tank-beds or wherever land of any depth is left waste. Many of the fields which remained untilled after the great famine of 1877 speedily became covered with a thick growth of it. The areas of shallower soil produce *prosopis* and *balanites.*

"On the granite hills there is usually little depth of earth except in scattered pockets, but in these tamarind, custard-apple, babul, *cassia fistula* ('the Indian laburnum') and *acacia planifrons* ('the umbrella tree' which is so noticeable on the Fort hill of Bellary) grow with sufficient freedom.

"On the moorland plains of red and mixed soils formed by the disintegration of the granitic rocks, the growth, even in damper western taluks, is usually poor, consisting largely of *dodonaea, prosopis* and *carissa,* but where the country consists of continuous stretches of hill and valley – as in the parts of Hospet and Kudligi which adjoin the Sandur range – it is more varied and more valuable, containing *wrightia, vitis, zizyphus, nim,* tamarind, a little coppice teak and some *anogeissus* and *Hardwickia,* while the valleys are often fringed with thick groves of date. This *Hardwickia binata* (yepi) is one of the most characteristic trees of Bellary. Its growth round Anekallu, at the tri-junction of the Hadagalli, Hospet and Kudligi taluks, where it has been specially cared for by the head of the village for many years, and that in the Chiribi reserve, through which the Kotturu-Kudligi road passes (which was specially respected by the villagers at the request of former Collector) is remarkable, but usually this tree is greatly persecuted, as it makes excellent fuel for iron-smelting, etc., produces a hard wood, and supplies (from the inner bark of its young branches) a fibre which is of much value for ropes. Moreover, for reasons which are not yet clear, it reproduces itself slowly and unwillingly, very few of the numerous self-sown seedlings which spring up after rain ever surviving to grow into saplings.

The present forests of Ballari district also include the forests of the erstwhile Sandur State, a princely state that was surrounded on all sides by the Ballari district of the Madras Presidency. The extent of forests of the Sandur State was about 87,000 acres, or about 136 square miles. Of this area, 40,000 acres had been leased to the British Government for 25 years from 1882 at an annual rental of Rs. 10,000 and were administered by the Forest Department of Bellary district. This arrangement was made as per the advice of the Inspector-General of Forests, Sir Dietrich Brandis, who had visited Bellary district in 1881. The leased forests comprised the growth on the whole of the Ramandrug and North-eastern ranges from the Narihalla river westwards and also that on the Donimalai plateau. The remaining 47,000 acres consisted of the forest round the foot of the above three ranges and that on the Kummataravu and Kumarasvami plateaus. [Even before portions of Sandur forest had been leased to the Madras Presidency, the British Government had set up a sanatorium for the Army at a small town called Ramandurg situated at the top of one of the hill ranges of Sandur State known as Ramandurg range. The town was well known for its salubrious climate.]

The growth and general characteristics of the leased forest areas and the forests retained in the Sandur State were similar. The Gazetteer of Bellary district compiled and edited by Mr. W. Francis (printed in 1904), provides information about the status and condition of the Sandur forests in the beginning of the twentieth century (1903-04) as follows:

"On the soil produced from the Dharwar rocks the forest growth is the most diversified of all. The Sandur hills are of this formation, and on them are found very numerous varieties of trees, some of which do not occur anywhere else for 100 miles around. Among the more valuable are teak, *Hardwickia, anogeissus* and some sandal. The Copper Mountain range is also of Dharwar rock, but here the rainfall is more scanty and the former depredations of the wood-cutters of Bellary town have prevented the existence of any thick growth. On the west side of it, however, is a block of Hardwickia, called the Malappanagudi block, which shows the capabilities of the soil. But in both these ranges the depth of earth is usually small, the rock lying very near the surface, and, though in the damper hollows in Sandur the growth is dense, the trees seldom attain to any size. These Sandur hills contain, nevertheless, the only real forest to be found in Bellary, Anantapur or the western part of Kurnool."

The richness of the Sandur forests can also be gauged from the fact that during that period the forests harbored not only the tiger but also the sambar deer (*Cervus unicolor*), which is generally associated with relatively dense and moist vegetation with assured availability of perennial water sources. In the Manual of Bellary district compiled by John Kelsall (printed in 1872), the presence of tiger and sambar has been described as follows:

> "Tigers are rare but are still to be met with in the Sandur hills. ......
> The Sandur hills is, I believe, the only place where sambhur can be
> found. ...."

Iron-smelting had considerably affected the forests of Bellary district and Sandur State, as charcoal prepared from firewood obtained from these forests was used in the forges. The following information has been provided in the Gazetteer of Bellary district (1904):

> "Until twelve or fifteen years ago, iron used to be smelted by the
> usual primitive native processes at Kanivehalli in Sandur State, at
> Kamalapuram and Chilkanahatti in Hospet taluk and at Shidegallu
> and Mallapuram in Kudligi taluk, the ore being all of it mined in
> the Sandur hills.----."

In order to protect the forest from complete decimation due to iron-smelting, the Sandur State had attempted some preventive measures:

> "The seigniorage fee for the iron ore used to be two annas per cart-
> load, and portions of the State Forests were sold to the smelters for
> charcoal-making on condition that they left a certain percentage of
> the trees standing to allow reproduction."

Although, as depicted above in the Gazetteer of 1904, the forests of Sandur were the best forests of the Bellary region towards the end of the nineteenth century, they appear to have been much more luxuriant and very dense in the distant past. Apparently the forests had gone through a rough phase for some decades. The condition of the forests was reported to have been excellent till the 1860s. The deterioration of the forests of Sandur around Ramandurg since then has been described by Mr. Berthold Ribbentrop, Inspector-General of Forests in his book 'Forestry in British India (1900)' in which he has provided a vivid description about how the climate in general and rainfall in particular in the terrain were affected by the destruction of forests. Mr. Ribbentrop writes as follows:

"With regard to the actual decrease of rainfall consequent on the destruction of forests, Major General Fisher, R.E., an old resident of Bellary and Ramandrug, supplies the most interesting information in the following note:

'*I arrived in the Bellary district in June 1856 and visited the Ramandrug at once; the hills were then covered with a good strong jungle; there was always a heavy cloud during the night resting on the hills and for the greater part of the day: rain fell during the south-west monsoon constantly and frequently; during the north-east monsoon it was much lighter; in the months of March, April and May, the mango showers were usually very heavy and accompanied with much thunder and lightning. The average rainfall we calculated was then 45 inches in the year; all the springs about the hills ran abundantly throughout the year, and the Nareehulla, the main feeder of Darojee tank, with all its tributaries, had water running in them all through the year. The climate of the Drug during the monsoons and the cold weather was quite cold enough to make fires very necessary, although its elevation is not more than 3,300 feet above sea-level. The water-supply was most abundant during the whole of the hot weather, and the tank was almost always full, surplusing very largely during the south-west monsoon.*

'*These observations refer to the years 1856 up to 1864 inclusive, when I left Bellary District and did not visit the Drug again till 1879. I found everything changed; the jungle has been almost entirely destroyed; the rainfall is most precarious and certainly not so much as 24 inches in the year; the tank has not filled for the last three years, and is generally 10 or 12 feet below full tank level; the springs are almost always dry, dribbling only at the best; the climate is so changed that in the cold weather it is hardly necessary to shut the doors and windows; except for the high wind and the slight mists of the south-west monsoon, it would not be necessary to close the house at all. The main feeder of the Darojee tank dries up altogether by the end of February, and all its tributaries have no water in them.'*

"Mr. Macartney, the Agent of the Sandur State in the Bellary District, Madras Presidency, also maintains that the rainfall within the last ten years has become lighter and more irregular with the increased destruction of forests by wood-cutters and charcoal-burners and the indiscriminate grazing of cattle, sheep and goats. Mr. Macartney speaks from an experience extending over 22 years, and supports his observations by the following facts:

'In the first decade of my residence here, the tank near my house used to be regularly filled every year and to be running over for several weeks at a time. Latterly, though, it has accumulated an immense amount of silt, and is now consequently of diminished capacity; it rarely fills. The same remarks apply equally to the Ramandrug tank and to the Singankeri.'"

The above details provided by Ribbentrop give an indication that the forests of Sandur which once were very luxuriant had been destroyed over a period of about 20 years. It is not clear as to what had triggered such a large-scale destruction of the forests. Removal of firewood must have been the primary cause. Such high demand for firewood appears to have come from the growing city of Bellary which also had a large army establishment. The Sandur forests were the only potential source of firewood in the vicinity of the city which could have catered to such a demand; the remaining forests of the Bellary district, being of inferior quality, were incapable of meeting such a demand.

Exploitation of the forests which were leased to the Forest Department of Bellary district in 1882 must have also contributed to their degradation. However, the protection measures adopted by the Forest Department of Bellary district would have helped in their restoration to some extent. Strict protection measures adopted by the Sandur Government after the expiry of the lease period must also have facilitated quick recovery of the forests. Fortunately, the present condition of the Sandur forests is not as degraded as they were reduced to in the latter half of the nineteenth century as alluded to by Ribbentrop. As a matter of fact, the Sandur forests now represent the best tropical dry deciduous forests in the eastern plains of Karnataka, perhaps one of the best in the entire peninsular India. The excellent recovery of the forests may be attributed to the proactive action taken by the Sandur administration that enforced strict protection to almost all the public lands in the state by notifying these as State Forests under the Sandur Forest Act, 1937 and its amendment of 1943.

The unique and vibrant diversity of the Sandur forests in the midst of the otherwise dreary-looking forests of Bellary district is an indication of the high quality of patronage and protection afforded by the erstwhile Ghorpade rulers, who were known for their admiration for wildlife and forest. Significantly, the royal insignia of the kingdom was a monitor lizard. Mahatma Gandhi, the Father of the Nation, who had visited Sandur before the Independence, was so enchanted by the beauty of the forests of Sandur that he had left an advice for the future nature lovers: "See Sandur in September".

The present extent of recorded forest area of Ballari district is 1,378.52 km^2 (Table-3.1). The forest cover of the district as per the India State of Forest Report (ISFR) 2019 is 739.22 km^2. This figure is somewhat better than the forest cover of the district as interpreted by KSRSAC, Bengaluru (2006) on the basis of 1999-2000 satellite imageries, comprising 305.60 km^2 of dry deciduous forest, 72.00 km^2 of forest plantations, and about 21.00 km^2 of agricultural plantations. The extent of scrub forest of the district as per ISFR 2019 is 466.00 km^2, whereas this extent as per the KSRSAC (2006) report was 1,138.59 km^2. Apparently, considerable improvement has taken place in the forest cover of the district during the intervening years, thanks primarily to the initiatives of the Forest Department in raising plantations and protecting the forests.

[**Note:** Sandur forests are rich in iron ore. Out of about 32,000 hectares of forest, about 8,000 hectares have been leased out for mining, out of which about 2,000 hectares have actually been opened up. Considering the richness and diversity of the Sandur forests, it is necessary that the remaining forests are given complete protection without diverting any more forest area for mining. The best way to achieve this objective is to bring the Sandur forests under the fold of the protected area (PA) network by declaring as a sanctuary under the Wild Life (Protection) Act, 1972.]

BIDAR, GULBARGA AND RAICHUR DISTRICTS (now includes Koppal and Yadgiri districts also)

The erstwhile districts of Bidar, Gulbarga and Raichur were included in the Hyderabad Kingdom, a princely state ruled by the Nizam of Hyderabad. Records are not available to show the exact extent and nature of forests that originally existed in the Hyderabad Kingdom. Considering that the entire peninsular India had thick forest cover in the distant past, the kingdom also would have harbored fairly good vegetation a few centuries ago. Indications are available that barring the rocky outcrops and shallow soils with underlying sheet rock, the land was fertile in the Godavari and Krishna basins and supported good forests and wildlife. The early and medieval history of the region is replete with a series of wars fought amongst various dynasties and sultanates for gaining supremacy of power and authority. It is reported that the ravages of frequent wars and continuous trampling by men and animals besides dumping of huge quantities of ammunitions and poisonous materials have depleted the biodiversity of the region. The exploitative policies of the earlier rulers who had allowed liberal diversion of land in favor of agriculture, the persistent efforts of the people to clear the land for cultivation, and heavy grazing had resulted in depletion and degradation of forest resources. Acute land hunger for growing agricultural crops resulted in large-scale destruction of the forested areas in the region. As a result, barring the areas with difficult terrain and inhospitable sites, most of the forests were cleared and brought under the plough. Besides extension of agriculture and over-grazing by cattle, removal of trees for firewood and small timber for *bona fide* domestic uses kept a mounting pressure on whatever few patches of forests were spared of the plough, never allowing them to rejuvenate. The forests of the region which are primarily of dry deciduous and thorn types have always been prone to recurring fires, another important factor contributing to their shrinkage. The best forests of the kingdom in the Godavari basin were located on its northern and north-eastern sides bordering Berar and Central Provinces, and the princely state of Bastar. The erstwhile districts harboring fairly good patches of forest in this region were Adilabad, Warangal and Karimnagar. In the Krishna basin, forests were restricted mainly to the south-eastern part of the erstwhile Mahboobnagar district (presently in the Nagarkurnool district) and to some extent in Nalgonda district. During 1940-41, about 11.7% of the geographical area of the Hyderabad State was forest; the southern part of the state including the districts of Gulbarga, Raichur and Bidar was very thinly forested.

Prior to the establishment of a regular Forest Department, the forests in the Hyderabad State were administered by the Revenue Department. At that time a 'darkhast' or application system was in vogue. Under this system permit holders were allowed to cut trees wherever they liked in the forests. Since no special staff was employed to supervise the work, control was only nominal and vast tracts of forests covered with valuable tree growth were recklessly destroyed through this system of working. Besides, since forests were considered subservient to agriculture, clearance of forest land for extension of agriculture was the norm of the day. Even after the establishment of the Forest Department in 1867, the Department was manned by non-professionals for about 20 years and their work was mainly to protect and sell thirteen valuable tree species designated as '*Irsali*' or 'reserved' under a set of simple rules, while the rest of the tree species designated as '*Gairi*' continued to remain in the hands of the Revenue Department. As a consequence, there was dual control over the management of forests and it adversely affected the forests. Vast expanses of forest lands were cleared for extension of agriculture without any regard for environmental concerns. However, in 1887 the Government secured the services of a trained European Imperial Forest Service officer, Mr. Ballantine, from Berar. He served in the dominion of Nizam till 1893 during which period he was able to arrest forest abuses of unrestricted felling under 'darkhast' (application) system and selected several tracts of forest for reservation. Later in the year 1893 the Government declared vast tracts of forest as protected forests and placed them under the charge of the Forest Department. The Government issued specific circulars for the administration of these protected areas. The Forest Act was enacted to obtain legal control over the forests in 1899 (1309-*Fasli*) in conformity with the instructions contained in these circulars. The number of reserved timber species was increased in the non-protected areas. The efforts of the Department were directed mainly towards survey and reservation of forest areas, introduction of felling schemes and works of improvement, systematic exploitation of forest produce, development of sustained revenue and consolidation and conservation of vast and valuable forest areas. The Forest Act of 1899 (1309-*Fasli*) was found inadequate for the growing requirements of the Forest Department. It was, therefore superseded by a revised Forest Act of 1916 (1326-*Fasli*), which laid the foundation for the establishment of a more effective forest administration. The Forest Act of 1916 provides for constitution, rules and conditions to demarcate and declare forests as reserved, protected, open and village forests. This Act was again superseded by the Hyderabad Forest Act of 1945 (1355-*Fasli*), which was modeled on the lines of the Indian Forest Act, 1927.

Specific information about the status of the forests of Bidar, Gulbarga and Raichur districts in the earlier days is not available. However, the overall status of the vegetation including forests in the Hyderabad State as given in the Imperial Gazetteer of India Provincial Series Hyderabad State (1909) is reproduced below:

> "**Botany** – Much of the land in the Hyderabad State is level, and a large portion of it is under cultivation, though there are tracts where arable soil has never been broken or cultivated, or where cultivation has lapsed. But wherever the ground is left uncultivated for a year or two, it becomes covered with a low jungle, consisting chiefly of *Cassia auriculata* and *Zizyphus microphylla*. Other level tracts also exist where the ground is quite unfit for cultivation. The forests contain, among the larger species, *Tectona grandis*, *Diospyros tomentosa*, *Boswellia serrata*, *Anogeissus latifolia*, *Terminalia tomentosa*, *Dalbergia latifolia*, *Ougenia dalbergioides*, *Schrebera swietenioides*, *Pterocarpus marsupium*, and *Adina cordifolia*, with smaller species like *Bridelia retusa*, *Lagerstroemia*

parviflora, Woodfordia floribunda, Zizyphus, Morinda, Gardenia, Butea, Acacia, Bauhinia, Cochlospermum, Grewia and *Phyllanthus.* When ground once occupied is allowed to go out of cultivation for a short time, a similar forest speedily asserts itself, containing, besides the trees already mentioned, a considerable number of the semi-spontaneous shrubs and trees that are frequently found in the neighborhood of Indian dwellings such as *Bombax, Erythrina, Moringa, Cassia fistula, Anona reticulata, Melia azadirachta, Crataeva roxburghii, Feronia elephantum, Aegle marmelos,* and various species of *Acacia* and *Ficus.*

"In the hilly tracts the hills are often covered with forests; not as a rule containing much larger timber, leading constituent species being the same as those that grow in the level tracts and arable lands, but stunted and deformed. Throughout the whole State scattered trees of *Acacia arabica* and *Acacia catechu* and toddy-palms (*Borassus flabellifer* and *Phoenix sylvestris*) are common; the latter two are extensively cultivated on account of their sap, which, when drawn and allowed to ferment, produces an intoxicating beverage largely consumed in the Telingana tract. The soils of this area are also favourable to the growth of coco-nut, which cannot be grown even in the greatest cave in the Maratha region. Around villages, groves of mango (*Mangifera*), tamarind, Bombax, *Ficus bengalensis, Ficus religiosa,* and *Ficus infectoria,* and similar species exist. The tamarind does not flourish in the Maratha region to the same extent as in Telingana."

"**Forests** - A total area of nearly 18,000 square miles is under forests, which are divided into three classes: the 'reserved' (5,184 square miles), the protected (4,408 square miles), and the open or unprotected (8,387 square miles). In the 'reserved' and protected forests, trees are under the control of the Forest department; but in the open forests only sixteen species are 'reserved': namely, sandal (*Santalum album*), teak (*Tectona grandis*), shisham (*Dalbergia latifolia*), Ebony (*Diospyros melanoxylon*), satin-wood (*Chloroxylon swietenia*), eppa (*Hardwickia binata*), nallamadi (*Terminalia tomentosa*), bijasal (*Pterocarpus marsupium*), battagunam (*Stephegyne parvifolia*), some (*Soymida febrifuga*), dhaura or tirmani (*Anogeissus latifolia*), kodsha (*Cleistanthus collinus*), sandra (*Acacia catechu*), bhandara (*Adina cordifolia*), mokab (*Schrebera swietenioides*), and chinnangi (*Lagerstroemia parviflora*). The forests form six divisions – Warangal, Indur, Nirmal, Mahbubnagar, Aurangabad, and Gulbarga – the two last being in Marathwara, and the remainder in Telingana.-----"

From the above description of the forests and vegetation of the Hyderabad State it is apparent that the state primarily harbored dry deciduous forests. There are indications that the soil profile of the tract, including the hilly areas, was by and large favorable for tree growth. It has also been indicated that the status of natural regeneration of the vegetation was quite satisfactory, so much so that abandoned or fallow lands had shown signs of reverting back to forest.

The areas of Hyderabad State which were merged with Karnataka after reorganization in 1956 are the present districts of Bidar, Gulbarga, Raichur, Koppal and Yadgiri. At that time, all these areas were included in one forest division, namely, Gulbarga forest division with very vast jurisdiction that extended over three Revenue districts, namely, Gulbarga, Raichur and Bidar. (Raichur, Bidar, Koppal and Yadgiri forest divisions came into being with effect from 1961, 1974, 1997 and 2009 respectively.) As most of the forests were of inferior type and were in fairly degraded condition, there was no scope of large-scale extraction for timber or fuel wood. During 1915 there were simple working schemes for small forest areas such as Chincholi where coupes were auctioned and the purchasers were supposed to coppice everything except the standards. During 1920, a provisional working plan was prepared for a few forest reserves which were worked on simple coppice system with a rotation of 30 years. The rest of the blocks of the division were not covered by the plan. Fuel coupes were worked tentatively on simple coppice method. These coupes were marked on the map and after obtaining sanction of Inspector-General of Forests, they were auctioned. Since no provision was made for protection and restocking of felled areas, the density of forests decreased and soil became much degraded. Coppice shoots became congested producing crooked and malformed stems for want of proper tending operations. Such irregular working led to the deterioration in the condition of the forests rather than improving the same. The forests of the three districts of Gulbarga, Raichur and Bidar continued to be managed in such an unplanned manner without a regular working plan for a long time up to 1955.

The progress of reservation of forests in the three erstwhile districts of Gulbarga, Raichur and Bidar during the Nizam's rule was very slow. This was perhaps because the best forests situated on the northern and south-eastern parts of the State were given primacy and the relatively inferior forests of the Gulbarga region had attracted lesser attention. The total extent of notified forests (RF) in the three districts during the Nizam's administration was only about 340 km^2 constituting less than one per cent of the combined geographical area of the districts (35,688 km^2). This consisted of about 188 km^2 in Gulbarga district and about 152 km^2 in Raichur district, with no forest having been reserved in Bidar district during that period. Interestingly, the best forests of Gulbarga district, namely, the Chincholi forests were notified as reserved forests much later, after the merger of the states. The reserved forests of Raichur district were notified towards the fag-end of the Nizam's rule, during 1947-48. The reserved forests of Bidar district were subsequently notified during 1962 and onwards. The present extent of reserved forests in the above districts (including Koppal and Yadgiri) is about 670 km^2 which constitute about 1.88% of the combined geographical area of the districts.

The present forest cover of the districts as per the ISFR 2019 is as follows: Bidar (88.42 km^2), Gulbarga (195.05 km^2), Koppal (33.32 km^2), Raichur (44.23 km^2), and Yadgiri (147.64 km^2). These figures are somewhat different from the forest cover of the districts comprising natural (dry deciduous) forest, forest plantations and agricultural plantations as interpreted by KSRSAC, Bengaluru (2006) on the basis of 1999-2000 satellite imageries: Bidar (10.34+33.83+70.35=114.52km^2), Gulbarga (94.03+32.56+4.90=131.49km^2), Koppal (0+4.71+10.82=15.53km^2), Raichur (18.16+20.70+4.46=43.32km^2), and Yadgiri (2.10+20.80+5.70=28.60km^2). Apparently during the intervening years (i.e., after 1999-2000) there has been improvement in the forest cover in Gulbarga, Koppal and Yadgiri districts and reduction in Bidar district, whereas it has remained more or less the same in Raichur district.

The above figures broadly indicate that, notwithstanding some improvement in the forest cover in a few districts during the recent years, the condition of the natural forests in the districts is very poor. Perusal of Table-3.1 would reveal that there is hardly any natural (dry deciduous) forest left in the districts. Gulbarga (present Kalaburagi) is the only district that has a reasonably large patch of Dry deciduous forest in the form of the Chincholi forest. Bidar district has a few small patches of dry deciduous vegetation in the forests such as Changler, Shahapur, Honnekeri, etc. Similarly, Raichur district has a few sporadic patches of poorly developed dry deciduous vegetation in the reserved forests of Bunkaldoddi, Galaga, Jalahalli, Kavital, Kumarkhed, Deodurga, etc. Koppal district no longer harbors any dry deciduous forest of significance, the reserved forest blocks of Agoli and Benakal of Gangavathi range still retaining some natural vegetation, mostly of the scrub type. Yadgiri district also does not harbor any significant extent of dry deciduous vegetation except in a few forests like Ashnal, Minaspur, Yeragola, Motanalli, Horancha, etc. As per the KSRSAC report of 2006, all the five districts have fairly extensive scrub forests: Bidar (62.79 km²), Kalaburagi (92.73 km²), Koppal (175.84 km²), Raichur (256.75 km²), and Yadgiri (129.52 km²). As per ISFR 2019, these figures are somewhat better in Bidar, Kalaburagi and Raichur districts and have remained more or less the same in Koppal and Yadgiri districts: Bidar (37.00 km²), Kalaburagi (29.00 km²), Koppal (172.00 km²), Raichur (149.00 km²), and Yadgiri (131.00 km²).

CHINCHOLI WILDLIFE SANCTUARY AND KARPAKAPALLI MPCA

In the Eastern Plains, with the sole exception of the Sandur forests of Ballari district, reasonable extent of climax dry deciduous vegetation is met with only in the Chincholi forests of Kalaburagi district. The Chincholi forests stand out as an oasis of greenery surrounded all around by barren agricultural lands. The forests are rich in both flora and fauna. Certain patches of the forests have trees with stocking comparable with that of the dry deciduous forests of the Western Ghats. Tree species occurring in the Chincholi forests include *Anogeissus latifolia* (dindal), *Terminalia tomentosa* (matti, *Chloroxylon swietenia* (mashawal), *Hardwickia binata* (anjan/kamara), *Boswellia serrata* (dhupa), *Soymida febrifuga* (some), *Tectona grandis* (teak), *Terminalia chebula* (harda/alale), *Dalbergia paniculata* (padre/pachali), *Albizia amara* (tugli), *Wrightia tinctoria* (hale), *Lagerstroemia parviflora* (channangi), *Diospyros melanoxylon* (tupra/tumri), *Premna tomentosa* (ije/narave), *Acacia catechu* (khair/tered), *Butea monosperma* (muthuga/muttal), *Madhuca indica* (hippe), *Gardenia gummifera* (bikke), *Zizyphus* species (bore), *Azadirachta indica* (bevu/neem), *Santalum album* (shrigandha/sandal), *Pterocarpus marsupium* (honne), *Cassia fistula* (kakke), etc. The undergrowth consists of *Dodonaea viscosa* (bandarki), *Cassia auriculata* (turwad), *Lantana camara* (chaduranga), etc.

Besides the occasional Panther, wild animals found in the forests of Chincholi include wolf, wild boar, wild cat, jackal, spotted deer, black buck, etc. and varieties of birds including the peacock. It is said that elephants inhabited the Chincholi forests in the distant past. Reference is made to a place called *Anepagadi* where operations similar to '*Khedda*' were held to capture, tame and train wild elephants.

Considering the uniqueness of the Chincholi forests in the midst of an expansive arid landscape, a proposal was submitted during 1977-78 to constitute these as a wildlife sanctuary under the provisions of the Wild Life (Protection) Act, 1972 (Annual Report of the Karnataka Forest Department, 1977-78). However, the proposal of the Forest department did not receive immediate approval of the Government. Eventually, **Chincholi Wildlife Sanctuary** covering an area of 134.88 sq km was notified on 28-11-2011.

A few reasonably good but relatively smaller patches of climax dry deciduous forest are met with in the Bidar district also; prominent among these are Changler, Shahapur, etc. The composition of tree species in these forests is more or less similar to that of the Chincholi forests mentioned above. Some of the forests such as Changler are of the teak-bearing type with predominance of the species.

The Changler forest located in Humnabad range is rich not only from the point of tree diversity but also for the abundance of medicinal plants. The Forest department, with the help of the Foundation for Revitalization of Local Health Traditions (FRLHT), Bengaluru, has established (1993) one **Medicinal Plant Conservation Area (MPCA)** in **Changler forest near Karpakapalli** village. This MPCA is spread over approximately 150 hectares of dry deciduous and scrub vegetation. The number of medicinal plant species recorded is 176.

Chapter 4

DISTRIBUTION OF TREE SPECIES ACROSS THE DRY DECIDUOUS FORESTS OF KARNATAKA

In a preceding chapter (*Chapter 2*) while describing various types and sub-types of dry deciduous and thorn forests of Karnataka, we have named a few important tree/shrub species that commonly occur in these forests. These have been taken from the examples of forest types/sub-types from Karnataka that Champion and Seth have given in their book titled 'Revised Survey of the Forest Types of India (1968)'. We have also mentioned in the introductory chapter that, broadly speaking three types of dry deciduous forest are met with in the state: (a) an association of *Tectona-Anogeissus-Terminalia* along the eastern fringes of the Western Ghats or *malnad* region; (b) an association of *Anogeissus-Chloroxylon-Albizia amara* in the Eastern Plains or *maidan* region; and (c) an admixture of the above two associations in the interior Karnataka region. However, there is a fairly wide diversity of species across the dry deciduous and thorn forests of Karnataka which occur in patches distributed sporadically over a vast landscape that covers more than three fourths of the state's geographical area. In the following paragraphs, an attempt will be made to discuss in some more detail the occurrence of various tree/shrub species across the dry deciduous and thorn forests of the state. It may however be added that there is no distinct line of demarcation about the presence or absence of the species in various regions within the vast landscape, and quite often some species dominant in one region are found to spill over to other regions as well. Some species do exhibit certain discernible characteristics regarding their presence or absence in a region. Such characteristics will also be discussed in brief.

Dry deciduous forests in the eastern fringes of the Western Ghats region

In an earlier chapter, we had mentioned that in the Western Ghats region there is practically no difference between a moist deciduous forest and a dry deciduous forest in terms of species composition, but the growth is very poor in the latter type, the trees generally not attaining a girth of more than 1.2 m (4 feet). Such dry deciduous forest is a climax formation represented in Karnataka by two forest types, namely, Southern tropical dry teak bearing forest (5A/C1) and Southern dry mixed deciduous forest (5A/C3), and occurs as a linear strip along the eastern rim of the Western Ghats; it encloses the eastern part of the *malnad* region and the western part of the semi-*malnad* region covering portions of the districts of Belagavi, Uttara Kannada, Dharwar, Haveri, Shivamogga, Davanagere, Chikkamagaluru, Chamarajanagar and Mysuru. Tree species occurring in this strip of forest include the following: *Tectona grandis* (teak/thyega), *Dalbergia latifolia* (beete), *Terminalia tomentosa* (matti), *Terminalia paniculata* (kindal/hunal), *Terminalia bellirica* (tare/ghoting), *Terminalia chebula* (harda), *Lagerstroemia lanceolata* (nandi/nana), *Pterocarpus marsupium* (honne), *Adina cordifolia* (heddi/yethega), *Mitragyna parvifolia* (kalam/kongu), *Anogeissus latifolia* (dindiga/dindal), *Dillenia pentagyna* (kanagal), *Schleichera oleosa* (sagadi/kusum), *Grewia tiliifolia* (tadasalu/dhaman), *Xylia xylocarpa* (jamba), *Kydia calycina* (bhende), *Sapindus emarginatus* (antawala), *Cordia macleodii* (hadaga), *Saccopetalum tomentosum* (omb), *Albizia procera* (bellate), *Albizia odoratissima* (goddahunase), *Albizia lebbeck* (bage), *Bombax ceiba* (buruga), *Gmelina arborea* (shivani), *Terminalia arjuna* (holematti), *Lannea coromandelica* (gojjal/godda), *Hymenodictyon excelsum* (doddi/doddatope), *Hymenodictyon obovatum* (bhoga), *Stereospermum xylocarpum* (kharsing), *Stereospermum chelonoides* (padre/mukarti), *Stereospermum suaveolens* (billa), *Melia dubia* (hebbevu), *Emblica officinalis* (nelli), *Ficus* species, *Madhuca longifolia* (ippe/sanna ippe/mahua), *Spondias pinnata* (ambate), *Syzygium cumini* (neral), *Diospyros montana* (jagalaganti), *Diospyros melanoxylon* (tupra/tumri), *Strychnos nux-vomica* (kasarka/kasan), *Madhuca indica/latifolia* (Ippe/hal-tumri/alippe), *Careya arborea* (kavalu), *Cassia fistula* (kakke), *Bauhinia malabarica* (basavanapada), *Acacia ferruginea* (banni), *Bauhinia racemosa* (Basavanapada), *Santalum album* (shrigandha/sandal), *Holoptelia integrifolia* (tapasi), *Bridelia retusa* (asana), *Pongamia pinnata* (honge), *Butea monosperma* (muthuga), *Wrightia tinctoria* (hale), *Cordia myxa* (salle/challe), *Buchanania lanzan* (char/nurkal), *Semecarpus anacardium* (kadgeru), *Lagerstroemia parviflora* (channangi), *Dalbergia paniculata* (padre/pachali), *Morinda tinctoria* (maddi), *Schrebera swietenioides* (ganthihuvu), *Gardenia gummifera* (bike/dicky), *Premna tomentosa* (ije/narave), *Feronia elephantum* (bela), *Aegle marmelos* (patri), etc.

Some of the above-mentioned species primarily restrict themselves in the western part of the forest adjoining the moist deciduous zone where rainfall is relatively higher, while some others gain prominence in the eastern part where rainfall is lower. The remaining species have their presence in varying proportions throughout the forest. The moisture loving tree species occurring in the western part include *Lagerstroemia lanceolata* (nandi/nana), *Dillenia pentagyna* (kanagal), *Schleichera oleosa* (sagadi/kusum), *Grewia tiliifolia* (tadasalu/dhaman), *Xylia xylocarpa* (jamba), *Kydia calycina* (bhende), *Sapindus emarginatus* (antawala), *Spondias pinnata* (ambate), *Saccopetalum tomentosum* (omb), *Madhuca longifolia* (sanna ippe/mahua), *Melia dubia* (hebbevu), *Hymenodictyon excelsum* (doddi/doddatope), *Strychnos nux-vomica* (kasarka/kasan), etc. Their presence in the drier part of the forest towards the east is occasional or sporadic, except in areas with better soil where they continue to thrive even with lesser rainfall. The presence of *Xylia xylocarpa* (jamba), primarily a species of moist deciduous and semi-evergreen forests, is less common in the dry deciduous forest, being restricted to some lateritic areas as well as repeatedly burnt patches.

In the eastern part of the forest which receives less rainfall, moisture loving tree species gradually disappear or become rarer, and species tolerant of dry conditions gain prominence. The species gaining predominance in this part of the forest include *Lagerstroemia parviflora* (channangi), *Dalbergia paniculata* (padre/pachali), *Semecarpus anacardium* (kadgeru), *Diospyros melanoxylon* (tupra/tumri), *Madhuca indica/latifolia* (Ippe/hal-tumri/alippe), *Cassia fistula* (kakke), *Butea monosperma* (muthuga), *Emblica officinalis* (nelli), *Wrightia tinctoria* (hale), *Buchanania lanzan* (char/nurkal), *Morinda tinctoria* (maddi), *Gardenia gummifera* (bike/dicky), *Schrebera swietenioides* (ganthihuvu), *Feronia elephantum* (bela), *Aegle marmelos* (patri), *Acacia ferruginea* (banni), etc. *Santalum album* (shrigandha/sandal) starts appearing in this part of the forest although it occasionally occurs in the moister parts of the forest also, especially in opened up areas.

Tectona grandis (teak/thyega), *Anogeissus latifolia* (dindiga) and the *Terminalias* such as *Terminalia tomentosa* (matti), *Terminalia paniculata* (kindal/hunal), *Terminalia bellirica* (tare/ghoting) and *Terminalia chebula* (harda/alalekai) occur throughout the dry deciduous forest under discussion. Their other prominent associates are *Dalbergia latifolia* (beete), *Pterocarpus marsupium* (honne), *Adina cordifolia* (heddi/yethega), *Cordia macleodii* (hadaga), *Albizia odoratissima* (goddahunase), *Albizia lebbeck* (bage), *Bombax ceiba* (buruga), *Gmelina arborea* (shivani), *Lannea coromandelica* (gojjal/godda), *Hymenodictyon obovatum* (bhoga), *Stereospermum xylocarpum* (kharsing), *Stereospermum chelonoides* (padre/mukarti), *Stereospermum suaveolens* (billa), etc. *Anogeissus latifolia* (dindiga), which starts appearing in the drier end of the moist deciduous forest where it attains good girth, becomes more conspicuous in the dry deciduous zone, increasing in numbers towards the east but with gradual reduction in size.

A few species commonly occur along river and stream banks. These are: *Terminalia arjuna* (holematti), *Albizia procera* (bellate), *Syzygium cumini* (neral), *Bridelia retusa* (asana), *Pongamia pinnata* (honge), *Holoptelia integrifolia* (tapasi), *Mitragyna parvifolia* (kalam/kongu), *Mangifera indica* (mavu/mango), *Salix tetrasperma* (neeranji), *Vitex negundo* (lakki), etc.

As regards *Tectona grandis* (teak/tega), though it is present almost throughout the climax dry deciduous forest mentioned above, it is dominant in certain parts, at times constituting about 10-20% of the tree crop, sometimes even more. These forests, known as Dry teak bearing forests (5A/C1), are met with primarily in Uttara Kannada district, and in parts of Belagavi, Dharwar, Haveri, Davanagere, Shivamogga, Chikkamagaluru and Mysuru districts. Because of the preponderance of pole-sized teak trees, these forests are also known as Teak pole forests. As we know, Dry teak bearing forests (5A/C1) have two sub-types: Very dry teak forest (5A/

C1a) and Dry teak forest (5A/C1b). The dry teak bearing forests occurring in the eastern fringes of the Western Ghats region belong to the sub-type 'Dry teak forest (5A/C1b)'. [The other sub-type, namely, 'Very dry teak forest (5A/C1a)' occurs in certain patches of the Eastern Plains.)

There are considerable extents of climax dry deciduous forest in the eastern fringes of the Western Ghats region where teak may be present but is not dominant. These forests belong to the type Southern dry mixed deciduous forest (5A/C3). The floristic composition of both 5A/C1 and 5A/C3 is similar except for the dominance or otherwise of teak. For obvious reasons, the teak-bearing forests (5A/C1), which were well-known for hardwood yielding trees of small to medium size, have been subjected to heavy felling in the past, especially for teak; as a result, the proportion of teak has come down considerably in substantial extents of these forests and such areas no longer exhibit the predominance of teak as in the past. These forests now virtually appear similar to the adjoining dry mixed deciduous forest (5A/C3) where teak may be present but is not dominant. Most of the dry deciduous forests occurring in the eastern fringes of the Western Ghats now primarily belong to the type 5A/C3 with patches of 5A/C1 in relatively less disturbed portions of the forests. Larger patches of 5A/C1 are now mostly confined to Uttara Kannada and Dharwar districts. Smaller patches of 5A/C1 are occasionally met with in the remaining districts such as Belagavi, Haveri, Davanagere, Shivamogga, Chikkamagaluru and Mysuru.

As regards bamboos, both *Dendrocalamus strictus* (medri bamboo) and *Bambusa bambos* (dowga bamboo) are present. Between the two, the former is commonly met with throughout the forest. *Bambusa bambos* is restricted in moister areas only, such as stream banks and depressions. *Dendrocalamus strictus* occurring in these forests are of medium to small size, becoming stunted in drier areas. (The best growth of *Dendrocalamus strictus* is attained in the drier end of the adjoining moist deciduous forest.)

The undergrowth of a dry deciduous forest includes many small trees, shrubs and herbs. These include *Abelmoschus* species (kadubende), *Abutilon* species (tutti), *Adatoda vasica* (adusoge/adasal), *Baliospermum montanum* (danti/hastidanti), *Calotropis* species (ekka), *Carissa carandas* (kawli), *Cassia auriculata* (tarwad), *Cassia tora* (senna), *Clerodendrum* species (ibbane/bhandira/taggi), *Crotalaria* species (gejjegida), *Curcuma* species (kadu arisina), *Desmodium* species (murelehonne/salparni), *Dodonaea viscosa* (bandurki), *Erythroxylon monogynum* (devadari), *Eupatorium, Flemingia* species (kumalu/nari baalada honne/kanphuti), *Euphorbia* species (kalli), *Gardenia turgida* (bongeri), *Gardenia gummifera* (dickemali/bikkegida), *Gardenia latifolia* (kambi/kalkambi), *Gardenia resinifera* (dickemali), *Gymnosporia montana* (yekkadi/tandarsi), *Holarrhena antidysenterica* (kodasa/kuda), *Helicteres isora* (yedmuri/murud sheng), *Ixora parviflora* (goravi/kepla), *Lantana camara* (chadurangi/ghanerdi), *Lasiosiphon eriocephalus* (rami), *Opuntia* (pappasukalli/nagatali), *Osbeckia* species, *Phoenix* species (ichalu), *Randia dumetorum* (kare), *Randia uliginosa* (kare/pandri/adkale), *Solanum* species (sonde), *Strobilanthes* species (karvi), *Securinega virosa* (bilisuli), *Sida* species (atibala/bala), *Vangueria spinosa* (kare/gunda kare/mullu kare), *Zizyphus jujuba* (bore), *Zizyphus xylopyrus* (chotte), etc. Needless to say, the above list is only indicative and is not exhaustive.

Commonly found climbers are *Abrus precatorius* (gulaganji), *Acacia concinna* (seege balli), *Acacia pennata/intsia* (kaadseege), *Calicopteris floribunda* (enjarigekubsa/marasadaboli), *Celastrus paniculatus* (bhavamga/malkanguni), *Clematis gouriana* (talejadari/vadiyambu/gometi), *Dalbergia volubilis* (mardi balli), *Smilax zeylanica* (ghotuce/kaadu hambu), *Jasminum* species (mallige), *Pterolobium indicum* (badabakka), *Zizyphus oenoplia* (pargi/barige/burgi), etc.

The dry deciduous forests occurring in the eastern fringes of the Western Ghats have suffered severe degradation due to biotic interferences such as heavy withdrawal of biomass, encroachments, over-grazing and recurring fires. Such degradation is quite conspicuous in the forests that are located adjacent to villages and townships. The condition of these forests has deteriorated alarmingly causing degradation of the climax dry deciduous forests (5A/C1 & 5A/C3) into **Dry deciduous scrub forests (5/DS1).** The floristic composition of these forests has changed with preponderance of hardier species and gradual emergence of thorny species. Most of the trees are multi-stemmed due to repeated felling in the past. Trees are shorter, there being not much distinction between trees and shrubs. The species include: *Lagerstroemia parviflora* (channangi), *Semecarpus anacardium* (kadgeru), *Diospyros melanoxylon* (tupra), *Emblica officinalis* (nelli), *Butea* *monosperma* (muthuga), *Cassia fistula* (kakke), *Dalbergia paniculata* (padre/pachali), *Santalum album* (srigandha), *Albizia amara* (tugli/chujjulu), *Cassia auriculata* (tarwad), *Randia dumetorum* (kare), *Gardenia gummifera* (dickemali/bikkegida), *Gardenia turgida* (bongeri), *Gardenia latifolia* (kambi/kalkambi), *Gardenia resinifera* (dickemali), *Morinda tinctoria* (maddi), *Aegle marmelos* (patri), *Limonia acidissima* (bela), *Zizyphus jujuba* (bore), *Zizyphus xylopyrus* (gotte), *Flacourtia montana* (chaperi), *Gymnosporia montana* (yekkadi/tandarsi), *Strychnos potatorum* (chilla), *Carissa carandus* (kawli), *Vangueria spinosa* (mullu kare), *Erythroxylon monogynum* (devadari), *Elaeodendron glaucum* (mukarki), *Acacia nilotica* (karijali), *Acacia catechu* (kutch), *Acacia latronum* (hottejali), *Acacia chundra* (kempujali), *Acacia leucophloea* (bilijali), etc. Residual coppice shoots of the original species such as *Tectona grandis* (teak), *Terminalia tomentosa* (matti), *Terminalia paniculata* (kindal/hunal), *Anogeissus latifolia* (dindiga), *Pterocarpus marsupium* (honne), *Albizia lebbeck* (bage), etc. are also found here and there. Signs of hacking and lopping are visible in most of the trees.

Further degradation of the scrub forest (5/DS1) leads to more and more open formations such as Dry savannah forest (5/DS2), *Euphorbia* scrub (5/DS3) and Dry grassland (5/DS4). In these formations, trees become rarer. While Dry savannah forest (5/DS2) is grassland interspersed with a few fire hardy trees (solitary or in groups), Dry grassland (5/DS4) is open grassland without any tree growth. The *Euphorbia* scrub (5/DS3) comes up on rocky areas or stony sites where mostly *Euphorbias* survive. These three formations are met with in severely ravaged dry deciduous forests. Such forests are more common in the Eastern Plains and the eastern portions of the interior Karnataka region.

Dry deciduous forests in the Eastern Plains

The dry deciduous forests occurring in the Eastern Plains or the *maidan* region of Karnataka are somewhat different from the dry deciduous forests of the Western Ghats region mentioned above primarily because of further reduction in rainfall. In addition, most of these forests, barring a few patches, are located in relatively hostile sites with shallow/poor soils, most of the areas with better soils having already been cleared of vegetation and brought under agriculture. As a result, composition of species in these forests is considerably different although some among the hardier species met with in the Western Ghats region such as *Anogeissus latifolia* (dindiga), *Terminalia tomentosa* (matti), *Terminalia bellirica* (tare), *Albizia lebbeck* (bage), *Pterocarpus marsupium* (honne), *Emblica officinalis* (nelli), *Cassia fistula* (kakke), etc. continue to thrive. There is also an increase in the number of thorny/spiny/prickly species. Some of the species appearing as shrubs or small/insignificant trees in the Western Ghats region gain prominence in the Eastern Plains and are often found to compete with the dominant trees for space and light.

Predominant species found in the dry deciduous forests in the Eastern Plains region include *Albizia amara* (tugli), *Anogeissus latifolia* (dindiga), *Terminalia tomentosa* (matti), *Chloroxylon swietenia* (mashval), *Hardwickia binata* (anjan/kamara), *Boswellia serrata* (dhupa), *Soymida febrifuga* (some), *Buchanania lanzan* (char/nurkal), *Pterocarpus marsupium* (honne), *Stereospermum chelonoides* (padre), *Madhuca indica/latifolia* (Ippe/haltumri/alippe), *Lannea coromandelica* (gojjal/godda), *Butea monosperma* (muthuga/muttal), *Albizia lebbeck* (bage), *Emblica officinalis* (nelli), *Acacia catechu* (kutch/tared), *Terminalia bellirica* (tare/ghoting), *Holoptelia integrifolia* (tapasi), *Ailanthus excelsa* (hebbevu/moosi mara), *Ficus glomerata* (atthi), *Semecarpus anacardium* (kadgeru), *Cassia fistula* (kakke), *Azadirachta indica* (bevu/neem), *Lagerstroemia parviflora* (channangi), *Dalbergia paniculata* (padre), *Alangium lamarckii* (ankole), *Wrightia tinctoria* (hale), *Diospyros melanoxylon* (tupra/tumri), *Diospyros montana* (jagalaganti), *Acacia latronum* (hirejali/godda jali), *Feronia elephantum* (bela), *Erythroxylon monogynum* (devadari/bastard sandal), *Dolichandrone crispa* (godmurki/belundare), *Santalum album* (shrigandha/sandal), *Acacia leucophloea* (bilijali), *Acacia sundra* (kempujali), *Erythrina* species (halivana/dadap), *Bauhinia* species (basavanapada), *Gardenia gummifera* (bikke/dicky), *Gardenia latifolia* (kambi/kalkambi), *Gardenia turgida* (bongeri), *Gardenia resinifera* (dickemali), *Morinda tinctoria* (maddi), *Givotia rottleriformis* (betta thavare/butala), *Strychnos potatorum* (chilla), *Capparis divaricata* (revdi/thottala), *Flacourtia indica* (mulluthotti), *Carissa carandas* (kawli), *Zizyphus jujuba* (bore), *Zizyphus xylopyrus* (gotte), *Grewia salvifolia* (ulpi), *Atalantia monophylla* (kadu nimbe), *Commiphora caudata* (konda mavu), *Annona squamosa* (seetaphal), *Dichrostachys cinerea* (wadu/odavinaha), *Mundulea suberosa* (bettahurali/purachali gida), *Schrebera swietenioides* (ganthihuvu),

Randia dumetorum (kare), *Cassia auriculata* (tangdi), etc. Species such as *Tectona grandis* (thyega/teak) and *Dalbergia latifolia* (beete/rosewood) also occur in certain favorable patches where teak is generally multi-stemmed or stag-headed and rosewood is of poor and lanky growth. Species occurring in rocky and stony areas include *Gyrocarpus jacquini* (kadu bende/thanaku), *Sterculia urens* (buthale/kempudale), *Cochlospermum religiosum* (kadu buruga/arasina buruga), *Commiphora caudata* (konda mavu/assuaru), *Givotia rottleriformis* (bilitale/butala/poliki), etc. Species found on banks of rivers and streams are *Pongamia pinnata* (honge), *Eugenia corymbosa* (nai-neral), *Alangium lamarckii* (ankole), *Terminalia arjuna* (holematti), *Butea monosperma* (muthuga), *Vitex negundo* (lekki), *Caesalpina bonduc* (gajag), etc. Bamboos are practically absent except in a few patches such as Sandur Hills of Ballari district where *Dendrocalamus strictus* (medri bamboo) occurs. *Bambusa bambos* (dowga bamboo) is met with in certain stretches along the banks of Tungabhadra, Krishna and other rivers. Euphorbia species are met with in the rocky patches.

As already mentioned, there is not much distinction between trees and shrubs in the dry deciduous forests of the Eastern Plains; as a matter of fact, in certain areas of these forests, it is the shrubs which hold the fort and protect the soil cover. Some of the common species of shrubs are: *Cassia auriculata* (tarwad/tangadi), *Randia dumetorum* (kare), *Dodonaea viscosa* (bandurgi), *Erythroxylon monogynum* (devadari), *Mundulea suberosa* (banditti), *Carissa carandas* (kavali), *Gymnosporia montana* (malkanguni/tandarsi), *Zizyphus jujuba* (bore), *Zizyphus xylopyrus* (gotte), *Baliospermum montanum* (damti/kadu haralu), *Lantana camara* (chadurangi), etc.

Climbers include *Pterolobium indicum* (badubukalu), *Zizyphus oenoplia* (pargi/sodli), etc.

As regards teak-growing dry deciduous forest in the Eastern Plains, one of the sub-types of Dry teak bearing forest (5A/C1), namely, Very dry teak forest (5A/C1a) is met with in some parts of Bidar district. Such forests occur in Changler, Karpakapalli and Karaknalli forests. In these forests, teak is found mixed with dry deciduous species such as *Chloroxylon swietenia, Buchanania lanzan, Terminalia tomentosa, Anogeissus latifolia, Albizia amara, Cassia fistula,* etc. In the past, such forests appear to have occurred in other regions of the Eastern Plains such as Ballari (Sandur),

Kalaburagi (Chincholi), Yadgiri (Ashanal, Yeragola), Kolar (Royalpad), etc. However, due to excessive felling of teak because of its prized wood, the present crop of teak in these areas is scattered or occasional; coppice shoots with no future prospects are visible here and there.

The dry deciduous forests of the Eastern Plains have been under severe biotic interferences since a long time because of high human and cattle population. As the forests are confined to many small patches spread over a vast landscape and as their total extent is abysmally small compared to the population of the region, their degradation has been very rapid; so much so that there are not many patches of forest in the region that now qualify to be included in the category of climax dry deciduous forest (5A/C3). Except for the forests of Sandur Hills in Ballari district and the Chincholi forests of Kalaburagi district, most of the forests of the Eastern Plains now belong to the category of Dry deciduous scrub (5/DS1). In terms of species composition, the dry deciduous scrub forests are not much different from the climax dry deciduous forest (5A/C3). However, the structure and appearance of the forest undergo considerable change. The forest becomes a more or less open layer of shrubby growth with odd trees scattered here and there. Most of the trees are multi-stemmed on account of repeated hacking. Thorny species make their appearance, becoming more and more visible as degradation becomes more severe. However, these forests are in a fluid state and may again progress into the dry deciduous forest type (5A/C3) if properly protected and nurtured with suitable soil and moisture conservation measures along with rigid protection, including fire protection. On the contrary, if continuously ravaged, they degrade further into thorny types and ultimately dry grass prevails. In extreme cases, soil is almost completely lost and bare boulders are exposed.

In the midst of the by and large dreary and drab dry deciduous and scrub forests of the Eastern Plains, the forests of Sandur Hills of Ballari district provide a welcome relief. The Sandur forests represent the best tropical dry deciduous forests in this part of Karnataka, perhaps one of the best in the entire peninsular India. As already mentioned, these forests had gone through a very rough phase due to heavy withdrawals and severe biotic interferences in the past including in the colonial period when a large portion of the Sandur forests had been taken on lease by the Madras

Presidency from the princely State of Sandur. The excellent recovery of the forests may be attributed to the proactive actions taken by the Sandur administration that enforced strict protection to almost all the public lands in the State by notifying these as State Forests under the Sandur Forest Act, 1937 and its amendment of 1943.

A brief narration of the floral composition of the forests of the Sandur Hills as provided in the recent working plans of Ballari forest division is given below:

> The Sandur forests comprise Sandur North and Sandur South ranges and small portions of Hosapete and Kudligi ranges, all in Ballari forest division (Ballari district). These forests are comparatively thickly wooded with a higher canopy density with an average tree height of about 8 meters as compared with the other forests of the district. The crop varies from small timber to poles and finally deteriorates into scrub type. *Anogeissus latifolia* (dindal) in association of *Terminalia tomentosa* (matti) is typical. Poor quality teak is found in patches but the limits are not clear. Teak is intermixed with a number of species that are typical of the dry deciduous forests of the Eastern Plains such as *Anogeissus latifolia* (dindal), *Hardwickia binata* (kamara/anjan), *Boswellia serrata* (dhupa), *Chloroxylon swietenia* (mashval), *Soymida febrifuga* (some), *Terminalia tomentosa* (matti), *Pterocarpus marsupium* (honne), *Stereospermum chelonoides* (padre), *Lagerstroemia parviflora* (channangi), *Dalbergia paniculata* (pachali), *Erythroxylon monogynum* (devadari), *Morinda tinctoria* (maddi), *Acacia leucophloea* (bilijali), *Acacia sundra* (kempujali), *Azadirachta indica* (bevu/neem), *Santalum album* (shrigandha/sandal), etc. Interestingly, a number of species of the moist deciduous and semi-evergreen forests of the Western Ghats are also met with in some proportion in these forests. These include *Dalbergia latifolia* (beete), *Dalbergia lanceolaria* (bilibeete/dandous), *Albizia procera* (bellate), *Albizia odoratissima* (goddahunase), *Terminalia bellirica* (tare), *Terminalia arjuna* (holematti), *Terminalia chebula* (harda), *Grewia tiliifolia* (tadasalu/dhaman), *Grewia abutifolia* (jani-gida), *Gmelina arborea* (shivani), *Mangifera indica* (mavu), *Michelia champaka*

(sampige), *Mitragyna parvifolia* (kadawal), *Mimusops elengi* (ranjal), *Shorea talura* (jalari), *Tetrameles nudiflora* (kaadubende/jarmal), etc. It is interesting to note that *Lagerstroemia lanceolata* (nandi), a species typical of very moist deciduous forests of the Western Ghats is found in some of the moist valleys of Sandur Hills (Shri S.G. Neginhal). *Chukrasia tabularis* (kempu davadari), a species found in the evergreen to very moist deciduous forests of the Western Ghats, was reported from the Sandur Hills (Gamble). Similarly, *Cedrela toona* (gandhagarike), another species of the evergreen and semi-evergreen forests of the Western Ghats is reported from the Ballari forests (Shri S.G. Neginhal). However, these three species have not been mentioned in the recent working plans of Ballari forest division. Though medri bamboo (*Dendrocalamus strictus*) occurs as occasional clusters, it is very prominent in areas surrounding the famous Kumaraswamy temple. Sandal usually is confined to undulating land between hill ranges, especially in Swamimalai Block, Donimalai Block, Ramanmalai Block and North-East Block. Excellent regeneration of sandal is noticed in the forest patches which have been retained as such within the iron ore mining leases granted in these forest blocks, as these patches are free from biotic interferences. By and large, good regeneration of sandal is noticed wherever protection from fire and grazing has been ensured. *Pterolobium indicum* (badubakka) is the chief climber species. The hill slopes are heavily infested with *Cymbopogan martinii* (bade grass) rendering the forests highly susceptible to fire during summer. *Strobilanthes kunthianus* (neelakurunji) occurring as undergrowth in some of the open patches of Sandur forests provides an excellent view when the species bloom, once in twelve years.

Medicinal plants

The Sandur forests are a potential source of medicinal plants. Many eternal springs locally known as **"Theerthas"** originate in Sandur hills. These theerthas are held in high esteem and are worshipped. The important ones are Agastya theertha, Gaja theertha, Koti theertha, Brahma theertha and Hari-Shankara theertha. Invaluable medicinal plants are found in the wild around these springs and the mineral springs are believed to be endowed with manifold healing properties. *Crotalaria sandurensis* is endemic to the Sandur forests.

The Forest Department has established a Medicinal Plant Conservation Area (MPCA) at Sandur with the help of the Foundation for Revitalization of Local Health Traditions (FRLHT), Bengaluru. This conservation area is spread over an area of approximately 350 hectares of southern dry mixed deciduous vegetation in Swamimalai forest block. The number of medicinal plant species recorded in this MPCA is 279.

Dry deciduous forests in the interior Karnataka region

As already mentioned, the dry deciduous forests of the interior Karnataka region comprise an admixture of species that are typical of the two types of dry deciduous forests mentioned above. The areas that are favored with relatively higher rainfall show affinity towards the former type (*Tectona-Anogeissus-Terminalia* association), and the drier areas show affinity towards the latter type (*Anogeissus-Chloroxylon-Albizia amara* association).

Due to population pressure and resultant biotic interferences, the fate of the forests of interior Karnataka has been more or less similar to that of the forests of the Eastern Plains. As a result, most of the forests have degraded to scrub formations with preponderance of hardy and thorny species. Fortunately, substantial extents of forests from this region, especially from the south interior Karnataka region*, have been included in the protected area (PA) network such as national parks and wildlife sanctuaries. These forests (mainly from Bengaluru Urban, Ramanagara and Mandya districts) have shown signs of rejuvenation as a result of continued protection measures carried out in the PAs. The Bannerghatta national park (BNP) in Bengaluru Urban district originally comprised about 10,000 hectares of forest area which have been under protection since the early 1970s when the national park was first notified. (Subsequently the national park was expanded by adding more forest areas from the adjoining Ramanagara district). A brief description of the floristic composition of the forests of the erstwhile BNP is given below:

The forest areas of Bengaluru Urban district included in the Bannerghatta national park (BNP) are: Ragihalli SF, Ragihalli South Extension SF, Gullahatti Kaval SF, Mahadeswara SF, Bannerghatta SF, Kalkere SF, Karadikal SF, Bantanal SF, Bannerghatta and Suddehalla Lack Reserves. The total extent of these forests is about 10,274 hectares.

Tree species found in the forests include *Tectona grandis* (teak), *Santalum album* (shrigandha), *Butea monosperma* (muthuga), *Azadirachta indica* (bevu), *Albizia amara* (chujjulu), *Emblica officinalis* (nelli), *Buchanania latifolia* (maradi), *Syzygium cumini* (neral), *Dalbergia latifolia* (beete), *Albizia odoratissima* (bilwara), *Gardenia gummifera* (bikke), *Acacia catechu* (kaggali), *Albizia lebbeck* (bage), *Pterocarpus marsupium* (honne), *Cassia fistula* (kakke), *Diospyros melanoxylon* (tupra), *Feronia elephantum* (bela/thondarsi), *Pongamia pinnata* (honge), *Wrightia tinctoria* (hale), *Hardwickia binata* (kamara/anjan), *Anogeissus latifolia* (dindiga), *Alangium lamarckii* (ankole), *Terminalia paniculata* (huluve/kindal), *Premna tomentosa* (ije), *Schrebera swietenioides* (ganthihuvu), *Garuga pinnata* (godda), *Chloroxylon swietenia* (hurugulu), *Bauhinia malabarica* (basavanapada), *Phoenix sylvestris* (ichalu), *Ficus* species, etc.

Dendrocalamus strictus (medri bamboo) occurs in a few forest blocks; *Bambusa bambos* (dowga bamboo) occurs sporadically in moister localities such as stream banks. The undergrowth comprises *Randia dumetorum* (kare), *Erythroxylon monogynum* (devadari), *Cassia auriculata* (tangdi), *Dodonaea viscosa* (hangarakaddi/bandurki), *Ixora parviflora* (goravi), *Pterolobium indicum* (badabakka), *Acacia concinna* (seege balli), *Lantana camara* (chadurangi), etc.

Dendrocalamus strictus (medri bamboo) occurs quite extensively, at times almost gregariously, on the slopes of Ragihalli and Mahadeswara state forests of Bannerghatta national park. It also occurs in other forests of the park with varying intensity. *Shorea talura* (jalari) comes up in markedly clayey patches in Kalkeri state forest, Bannerghatta Lac reserve, Sudduhalla Lac reserve, Ragihalli state forest and other forests within the park. There is fairly good growth of *Shorea talura* (jalari) in Doresanipalya state forest of Kaggalipura range.

[***Note**: In the north interior Karnataka region, some good quality dry deciduous forests are met with in the western parts of Dharwar, Haveri and Davanagere districts. These forests have been included in the dry deciduous forests occurring in the eastern fringes of the Western Ghats region.]

In the previous chapter (*Chapter 3*), we have referred to Dr. Buchanan's description of the Savanadurga forests of Magadi taluk (now in Ramanagara district) more than 200 years ago. During those days, these forests were definitely richer than what they are today, as exemplified by the presence of species such as *Chukrasia tabularis* (kalgarike). Although this moisture-loving species has not been reported now from the Savanadurga forests, by and large the forests of Ramanagara district (including those of Savanadurga) represent the best forests of the south interior Karnataka region. A brief description of the floristic composition of the forests of Ramanagara district is given below:

The forests of Ramanagara district exhibit a lot of diversity in terms of composition of species. Various tree species typical of deciduous forests occur in varying proportions in the forest blocks. These include *Anogeissus latifolia* (dindiga), *Acacia catechu* (kaggali/katha), *Azadirachta indica* (bevu), *Gardenia gummifera* (bikke), *Boswellia serrata* (maddi), *Alangium lamarckii* (ankole), *Chloroxylon swietenia* (hurugulu), *Feronia elephantum* (bela/thondarsi), *Albizia amara* (chujjulu), *Holoptelia integrifolia* (tapasi), *Wrightia tinctoria* (hale), *Gmelina arborea* (shivani), *Cassia fistula* (kakke), *Vitex altissima* (naviladi), *Emblica officinalis* (nelli), *Tectona grandis* (teak), *Santalum album* (shrigandha), *Annona squamosa* (seetaphal), *Mangifera indica* (mavu), *Tamarindus indica* (hunase), *Pongamia pinnata* (honge), *Melia dubia* (hebbevu), *Syzygium cumini* (neral), *Terminalia tomentosa* (matti), *Terminalia bellirica* (tare), *Acacia ferruginea* (banni), *Xylia xylocarpa* (jamba), *Terminalia paniculata* (huluve/ kindal), *Dalbergia paniculata* (pachali/padri), *Diospyros melanoxylon* (tupra), *Premna tomentosa* (ije), *Albizia odoratissima* (bilwara), *Dalbergia latifolia* (beete), *Saccopetalum tomentosum* (hesare/omb), *Bauhinia racemosa* (achalu), *Albizia lebbeck* (bage), *Semecarpus anacardium* (kadgeru), *Butea monosperma* (muthuga), *Shorea talura* (jalari), *Cordia myxa* (challe), *Schleichera trijuga* (kendala/chakota), *Garuga pinnata* (godda), *Sterculia villosa* (bilidale), *Bauhinia malabarica* (basavanapada), *Pterocarpus marsupium* (honne), *Acacia suma* (mugali), *Kydia calycina* (bhende), *Albizia procera* (bellate), *Bombax ceiba* (buruga), *Cochlospermum religiosum* (bettathavare), *Schrebera swietenioides* (ganthihuvu), *Hardwickia binata* (kamara), *Stereospermum suaveolens* (padre), *Diospyros montana* (jagalaganti), *Elaeodendron glauca* (mukarti), *Ailanthus excelsa* (dhupa), *Strychnos potatorum* (chilla), *Trema orientalis* (garakale), *Sapindus emarginatus* (antuvala), *Phoenix sylvestris* (ichalu), *Terminalia arjuna* (holematti), *Grewia tiliifolia* (tadasalu), *Buchanania latifolia* (maradi), *Ficus* species, etc. *Dendrocalamus strictus* (medri bamboo) occurs in many forest blocks. It is more prevalent than *Bambusa bambos* (dowga bamboo) which usually occurs sporadically in moister localities such as protected folds and stream banks. The undergrowth consists of *Randia dumetorum* (kare), *Erythroxylon monogynum* (devadari/bastard sandal), *Cassia auriculata* (tangdi), *Securinega virosa* (bilisuli), *Dodonaea viscosa* (hangarakaddi/bandurki), *Ixora parviflora* (goravi), *Pterolobium indicum* (badabakka), *Acacia concinna* (seege balli), *Lantana camara* (lantana), *Zizyphus jujuba* (bore), *Zizyphus xylopyrus* (gotte), etc.

Sandal occurs in profusion in the relatively drier localities in association with a wide range of dry deciduous and thorny species. Associations of *Hardwickia binata* (kamara) and *Boswellia serrata* (dhupa), sometimes the former dominating, are seen in the forests of Sathanur, Kanakapura and Ramanagara ranges, especially on hill tops of Basavanabetta state forest, Chilandvadi state forest, etc. Species such as *Terminalia arjuna* (holematti), *Pongamia pinnata* (honge), *Tamarindus indica* (hunase), *Mallotus philippensis* (kumkum), *Eugenia* species (neral), etc. are commonly met with in narrow strips along the hill sections of the larger streams in some forests of the district.

Medicinal plants

The Savanadurga forest located in Magadi range is rich not only from the point of tree diversity but also for harboring varieties of medicinal plants. The Forest department, with the help of the Foundation for Revitalization of Local Health Traditions (FRLHT), Bengaluru, has established one Medicinal Plant Conservation Area (MPCA) in this forest. The extent of the MPCA is 280 hectares and it is primarily a dry deciduous scrub forest. The FRLHT has identified 353 medicinal plant species in the MPCA.

Thorn forests of Karnataka

In Karnataka, Thorn forests are met with in the driest localities of the state, primarily in the districts of the Eastern Plains and in the eastern parts of the northern and central districts of interior Karnataka (Belagavi, Dharwar, Haveri, Gadag, Davanagere, Chitradurga and Tumkur). These forests belong to the type **Southern thorn forest (6A/C1)** and, as the name suggests, are characterized by the preponderance of thorny species. The most characteristic species of the thorn forests belong to the genus *Acacia*. Species belonging to the genera such as *Zizyphus* and *Capparis* are also common. Fleshy *Euphorbias* are often met with in very degraded and rocky patches.

The species occurring in the thorn forests are *Acacia arabica* (karijali), *Acacia catechu* (kaggali), *Acacia latronum* (hottejali/hirejali), *Acacia leucophloea* (bilijali), *Acacia chundra* (kempujali), *Acacia suma* (mugali), *Flacourtia indica* (bilehuli/mulluthare), *Capparis divaricata* (revdi/thottala), *Capparis sepiaria* (himsra/kathari mullu), *Capparis decidua* (karina/chippuri), *Dicrostachys cinerea* (waradu), *Aegle marmelos* (patri), *Carissa carandas* (kavali), *Randia dumetorum* (kare), *Zizyphus jujuba* (bore),

Zizyphus xylopyrus (chotte), etc. Stunted specimens of *Albizia amara* (tugli/chujjulu), *Chloroxylon swietenia* (mashawal), *Strychnos potatorum* (chilla), etc. are also occasionally met with scattered here and there. Sometimes, *Calotropis gigantea* (bili aekke), *Opuntia dillenii* (nagatali/paapasu kalli), *Cassia auriculata* (tangadi/tarwad), *Dodonaea viscosa* (bandurki), etc. are also met with. Various species found in the *Euphorbia* patches include *Euphorbia antiquorum* (kontekalli/jadekalli/mundukalli), *Euphorbia neriifolia* (malekalli), *Euphorbia nivulia* (dubbakalli/dundukalli/elegalli/gutagalli), *Euphorbia tirucalli* (bontakalli/bontekalli), etc.

The degraded variant of the thorn forest, namely, Southern thorn scrub (6A/DS1) comprises a few species drawn from the above list with the difference that, here the trees are of shrubby growth, often forming almost impenetrable thorny thickets and the scattered dry deciduous species become rarer. In the other variant, namely, Southern *Euphorbia* scrub (6A/DS2), which comes up in the shallowest and poorest sites with practically no soil, *Euphorbias* become the most important constituents.

It has already been mentioned in earlier chapters that thorn forest, dry deciduous scrub, and their degraded formations constitute a very large segment of the forest areas in the rain-deficient Eastern Plains and interior Karnataka regions. However, there are no distinct demarcation boundaries among these various forest types and they change from one type to another depending upon the prevailing soil conditions. Oftentimes, it becomes difficult to categorically indicate as to whether a particular scrub formation has degraded from a climax dry deciduous forest or from a climax thorn forest.

Edaphic (soil-related) forest types

In a forest ecosystem sometimes a particular species shows affinity to congregate or occur gregariously. Such congregation or gregarious occurrence is attributed to the ability of the species to adapt and thrive in an environment that is hostile or unfavorable to other species. In the moist deciduous and semi-evergreen forests, *Xylia xylocarpa* (jamba) shows signs of gregarious appearance in lateritic or repeatedly burnt forest areas. *Terminalia tomentosa* (matti) also tends to be gregarious in clayey or heavy soils. Gregarious formation of certain bamboo species in wet soil or that of *Calamus* species (cane/betha) in very wet soil is well known. Gregarious patches of *Butea monosperma* (muthuga) are often met with in flat and open areas with poor drainage, abandoned marshy cultivations, saline soils, etc. In the past, *Phoenix sylvestris* (ichalu) used to come up gregariously in the cultivated lands that were abandoned because of wars, famines, epidemics, etc. In Chapters 2 and 3 we have seen that *Hardwickia binata* (kamara/anjan/karachi), *Boswellia serrata* (dhupa/chitta) and *Shorea talura* (jalari/jala) exhibit the tendency to occur gregariously in the dry deciduous forests, especially in interior Karnataka as well as in the Eastern Plains. Although in a climatic climax forest these species grow normally along with other species of the tract, in certain patches with shallow and gravelly soil, *Hardwickia binata* or *Boswellia serrata* tends to be gregarious. Similarly, in certain areas with shallow, sandy or clayey and calcareous soil, *Shorea talura* tends to be gregarious. These forest patches are edaphic forests where the presence of a species with the exclusion of others is dictated primarily by soil related factors. The gregarious presence of certain species is also linked to their being extremely fire hardy. By and large most of the species which exhibit gregarious nature in dry deciduous forests are more resistant to fire than their normal associates. In certain forest tracts, *Anogeissus latifolia*, *Acacia catechu*, *Acacia chundra*, *Acacia latronum*, etc. also exhibit tendency to form gregarious stands. [**Note:** The gregarious nature of *Shorea talura* (jalari/jala) is also partly attributable to past forest management practices; this species was a very important host for the propagation of the *Lac* insects. The people in charge of *Lac* collection used to keep the areas harboring *jalari* trees free from other intruders including bamboos. This must have also assisted in the formation of pure or nearly pure patches of the species.]

In the Eastern Plains, especially on the upper slopes and hill tops with shallow and gravelly soil and on the sunny aspects, one sometimes comes across associations of fire hardy species such as *Dalbergia paniculata*, *Lannea coromandelica*, *Sterculia urens*, *Boswellia serrata*, *Anogeissus latifolia*, etc. Although these are difficult and hostile areas, the above-mentioned species with the exception of the multi-stemmed *Anogeissus latifolias* put on respectable girth and present an impressive look. It is also a coincidence that most of these trees have light or ash-colored bark, adding brightness to the otherwise dreary forest.

One interesting characteristic of *Shorea talura* (jalari/jala) is that it is rare in the moist deciduous forests of Karnataka but occurs sporadically in the semi-evergreen forests of the state (Sagar, Siddapur). As we have already seen, it is common in the south interior Karnataka region where it often occurs in gregarious patches. *Vitex altissima* (bharanige/naviladi) is another species which exhibits very wide adaptability. While it is common in the semi-evergreen, evergreen and very moist deciduous forests of the state, it also occurs in the dry deciduous and scrub forests, especially in south interior Karnataka.

Chapter 5

PRESENT STATUS OF THE DRY DECIDUOUS FORESTS OF KARNATAKA

In the preceding chapters we have seen that the extent of forests in Karnataka, more particularly in the Eastern Plains and in the interior Karnataka region has undergone considerable reduction over the years due to increasing demand on land for cultivation and settlements triggered primarily by increase in human population. We have also seen that the pressure of population in these two regions is so intense that vast extents of forests have been not only decimated but whatever forests had been spared for being unsuitable for the plough or for living have also degraded due to continuous use, overuse and abuse; so much so that the extent of dry deciduous forests belonging to the types 5A/C1 and 5A/C3 is negligibly small in these two regions. Barring a few patches of these climax forest types that are met with in a few districts such as Dharwar, Haveri, Davanagere, Ramanagara, Mandya, Kalaburagi and Ballari, the remaining forests that are met with are primarily of the scrub types (5/DS1, 5/DS2, 5/DS3, 5/DS4), at times sporadically mixed with patches of thorn forest (6A/C1) and its degraded or scrub formations (6A/DS1 and 6A/DS2).

Impact of population on forest

That population has a very strong bearing on the occurrence as well as quality of forest is generally not well appreciated. However, for effective management of the remaining forests that we are now left with in the Eastern Plains and in interior Karnataka, it is necessary to more objectively assess the human footprint on the forest ecosystem so that ways and means of protecting and developing the remaining forests can be found out. This is necessary as these remnant forests are the last vestiges of natural vegetation in the midst of expansive dry lands of Karnataka which constitute the second largest arid region in India, next to the dry lands of Rajasthan.

We have already seen in Table 3.1 that the distribution of forests in Karnataka is highly skewed. A very large portion of the state's forests including all the evergreen, semi-evergreen and moist deciduous forests is confined to the *malnad* region which constitutes about 25% of the state's geographical area. As a matter of fact, about 75% of the state's forests occur in this region. The remaining 25% of the state's forests are distributed sporadically in numerous patches in the interior Karnataka and the Eastern Plains which together constitute the balance 75% of the state's geographical area. It will be of some interest to understand as to how human populations have influenced the forests of the regions and transformed them to their present condition and status. For this purpose, it will be necessary to know as to how the state's population is distributed between the *malnad* region and the remaining part of the state. This will be discussed in some detail in the following paragraphs:

The distribution of recorded forest area (as per the Annual Report of KFD for 2017-18), forest cover as per the India State of Forest Report (ISFR) 2019, and population density (as per 2011 Census) in respect of the districts of Karnataka are indicated in the following table (Table - 5.1):

Table – 5.1   District-wise details of recorded forest area, forest cover, and population density in Karnataka

(Area in km²)

District	Geographical area (GA)	Recorded forest area (RFA) as per Annual Report of KFD	Forest Cover as per ISFR 2019	Population density as per 2011 Census (persons/km²)
(1)	(2)	(3)	(4)	(5)
MALNAD REGION				
Belagavi	13,415	2,063.20 (15.38)	1,141.60 (8.51)	357
Chamarajnagar	5,676	2,791.46 (49.18)	2,724.19 (47.99)	180
Chikkamagaluru	7,201	2,767.80 (38.44)	3,951.78 (54.88)	158
Dakshina Kannada	4,560	2,012.18 (44.13)	3,064.66 (67.21)	457
Hassan	6,814	880.60 (12.92)	1,478.44 (21.70)	261
Kodagu	4,102	2,870.99 (69.99)	3,263.38 (79.56)	136
Mysuru	6,307	1,449.87 (22.99)	1,052.83 (16.69)	475
Shivamogga	8,477	6,642.55 (78.36)	4,270.78 (50.38)	207
Udupi	3,880	1,720.57 (44.34)	2,283.38 (58.85)	304
Uttara Kannada	10,291	8,296.46 (80.62)	8,123.75 (78.94)	140
	70,723	**31,495.68 (44.53)**	**31,354.79 (44.33)**	
INTERIOR KARNATAKA REGION				
Dharwar	4,260	468.54 (11.00)	374.42 (8.79)	434
Gadag	4,656	333.37 (7.16)	141.62 (3.04)	229
Haveri	4,823	432.80 (8.97)	343.25 (7.12)	332
Davanagere	5,924	544.98 (9.20)	709.57 (11.98)	329
Chitradurga	8,440	1,287.18 (15.25)	576.61 (6.84)	197
Tumkur	10,597	1,291.67 (12.19)	1,284.04 (12.12)	254
Bengaluru (Urban)	2,190	122.25 (5.58)	287.43 (13.09)	438
Bengaluru (Rural)	2,259	186.43 (8.25)	162.75 (7.08)	430

Contd.

Ramanagara	3,556	978.42 (27.51)	664.69 (18.90)	308
Mandya	4,961	664.61 (13.40)	499.32 (10.06)	365
	51,666	**6,310.25 (12.21)**	**5,043.70 (9.76)**	
EASTERN PLAINS REGION				
Bagalkote	6,575	838.93 (12.76)	252.97 (3.86)	288
Vijayapura	10,494	81.11 (0.77)	25.05 (0.24)	208
Bidar	5,448	456.16 (8.37)	88.42 (1.62)	312
Kalaburagi	10,954	480.93 (4.39)	195.05 (1.78)	234
Yadgiri	5,270	516.83 (9.81)	147.64 (2.80)	223
Raichur	8,386	327.47 (3.90)	44.23 (0.52)	230
Koppal	5,630	430.66 (7.64)	33.32 (0.60)	248
Ballari	8,450	1,378.52 (16.31)	739.22 (8.74)	290
Kolar	3,979	508.34 (12.78)	381.39 (9.59)	387
Chikkaballapur	4,244	557.88 (13.15)	269.70 (6.35)	296
	69,430	**5,576.83 (8.03)**	**2,176.99 (3.14)**	
	1,91,819	**43,382.76 (22.62)**	**38,575.48 (20.10)**	

[**Note:** figures within brackets indicate the percentage (%) with respect to the geographical area (GA) of the concerned district.]

Perusal of Table-5.1 indicates that among the six districts of the state that are located fully within the *malnad* region, four districts, namely, Kodagu (136), Uttara Kannada (140), Chamarajanagar (180) and Shivamogga (207), have low population density, while Dakshina Kannada (457) and Udupi (304) have fairly high population density. The Chikkamagaluru district, a major part of which is located within the *malnad* region, also has low population density (158). In fact, if the population of the portion of this district that falls outside the *malnad* region (i.e., Kadur taluk and parts of Chikkamagaluru and Tarikere taluks) is excluded, the population density of the portion of the district included in the *malnad* region will be even lower. As regards the other three districts that are located partly inside and partly outside the *malnad* region, Belagavi district has high population density (357). However, Khanapur taluk and a small portion of Belagavi taluk that are included in the *malnad* region have low population density (about 150). Similarly, among the taluks of Hassan district with a fairly high overall population density (261), the Sakleshpur taluk located in the *malnad* region has very low population density (125). As regards Mysuru district, although the overall population density of the district is very high (475), the population density of the district in the portion included in the *malnad* region (i.e., HD Kote, Sargur, Hunsur and Periyapatna taluks) is relatively low (239).

As per the Census of 2011, Karnataka's population was 6.1 crore. This works out to an average population density of about 319 persons/km^2. The population of the *malnad* region comprising six districts in full and four districts in parts has been computed to be about 99 lakh, or say, about one crore. As the geographical area of this region is about 48,000 km^2, the average population density in the region is about 208 persons/ km^2. The remaining part of the state covering about 144,000 km^2 harbors a population of about 5.1 crore. Thus the average population density in the region comprising interior Karnataka and the Eastern Plains is about 354 persons/km^2.

The above analysis reveals that by and large population has played an important role in determining the quality and extent of forest in Karnataka. Relative abundance and richness of forest in the *malnad* region is largely attributable to the low population density in the region. On the other hand, most of the districts of interior Karnataka and the Eastern Plains which are highly populated have limited extents of forest with poorer stocking. Although some districts in these two regions such as Chitradurga (197), Vijayapura (208), Yadgiri (223), etc. are not very highly populated, there is immense pressure on the natural forests due to very high livestock population, which never allows the ravaged forests to recuperate.

Although population pressure results in general degradation of forests, the problem is not insurmountable. The districts of Dakshina Kannada and Udupi are very good examples to demonstrate that it is possible to retain good forest cover even with high population pressure. Although these districts have high population density of 457 persons/km^2 and 304 persons/km^2, respectively, the districts have fairly high forest cover - 3,064.66 km^2 and 2,283.38 km^2 which constitute 67.21% and 58.85% of their respective geographical areas. Interestingly, the extent of forest cover of both the districts is higher than their respective recorded forest areas. This has been possible due to ideal land management practices being adopted in the districts. The districts have limited areas under cereal crop (mainly paddy) (16% and 21.63%, respectively); however, substantial areas are under plantation crops such as areca nut, coconut, rubber, cocoa, cashew, etc. Horticultural and agro-forestry plantations cover about 15% and 36% of the respective geographical areas of the districts. In addition to the reserved forests managed by the Forest department, there are substantial extents of fairly well-wooded revenue forests known as *kumki* lands which abut the agricultural lands. One remarkable feature of both the districts is the very limited presence of scrub forests: Dakshina Kannada (4.66 km²) and Udupi (14.53 km²); these figures are further lower in the ISFR 2019: Dakshina Kannada (3 km²) and Udupi (0 km²). Thus scrub forests in Dakshina Kannada and Udupi districts are negligible when compared with the extensive scrub forests that are met with in most of the districts of Karnataka (Table–3.1). Evidently, people have been able to procure substantial quantities of biomass needed by them from outside the traditional forest areas. This has considerably reduced the biotic pressure on the natural forests and enabled the districts to have fairly respectable forest cover in spite of having high population density.

Dendrocalamus strictus (medri bamboo) – Barometer of Dry Deciduous Forest

In a preceding chapter we had mentioned that *Bambusa bambos/arundinacea* (dowga bamboo) is a characteristic species of the moist deciduous forest and *Dendrocalamus strictus* (medri bamboo) is a characteristic species of the dry deciduous forest, although both species occur in both forest types. In the moist deciduous forest, *Bambusa bambos/arundinacea* is ubiquitous, at times dominant; however, in the dry deciduous forest, it is restricted to very moist localities such as depressions and stream banks. On the other hand, *Dendrocalamus strictus* is more common and sometimes abundant in dry deciduous forest where its growth varies from medium to small depending upon the soil-depth and dryness of the tract. *Dendrocalamus strictus* also occurs in the drier end of the moist deciduous forest where it attains its best possible growth; in relatively moister areas of the moist deciduous forest, *Dendrocalamus strictus* occurs only at higher elevations and in slopes where drainage is very good.

However, the present-day occurrence of *Dendrocalamus strictus* in Karnataka's forests is not according to how it is described in a text book. Its availability and abundance have undergone drastic reduction in the forests of the state. In the Eastern Plains it is very rare and sporadic, concentrated patches of the species being restricted to a few pockets of forest such as Sandur Hills, although in the distant past it is reported to have occurred even in the drier tracts such as the Narasimha Devara Betta forests (NDB) of Chikkaballapur district, Royalpadu forests of Kolar district, etc. It is now difficult to believe that, about a hundred years ago, forests of the erstwhile Bijapur district had harbored medri bamboo, and considering its threatened status, retention of the species was prescribed along with that of sandal and karanj (honge) at the time of felling of the fuel wood coupes. The presence of medri bamboo in the forests of interior Karnataka has also become limited, being restricted to some of the better forests of the districts such as Dharwar, Haveri, Davanagere, Bengaluru Urban, Ramanagara, Mandya, etc. Dr. Buchanan who had in 1800 travelled from Bangalore to Seringapatna had come across extensive bamboo forests (medri bamboo) around Channapatna and other areas on the way. These bamboo forests have practically vanished except a small patch, now included in the Ramadevarabetta Vulture sanctuary, near Ramanagara. The Gazetteer of Mysore State (1897) by Sir Benjamin Lewis Rice mentions about the presence of 'a few bamboos' in the Jogimatti forests of Chitradurga district. In the *malnad* region, although it is present, its abundance has come down considerably. Extensive forest areas in this region which were known in the past to be rich in medri bamboos either do not have any trace of the species now or have very scattered presence. The forests of the Chamarajanagar district, once well-known for medri bamboos, do not harbor the species with the same abundance. The species almost vanished from the forest areas of Haliyal range in Uttara Kannada district in the 1970s although it had very prolific presence in the adjoining forest areas of Sambrani and Bhagavathi ranges. However, after the last flowering in the early 2000s, the species appears to have become sparse in the Sambrani-Bhagavathi areas also although these areas were famous for high quality medri bamboos and used to cater to the needs of green bamboos required by the Medars and Buruds of Hubli-Dharwar areas.

Gradual depletion and eventual disappearance of medri bamboo (*Dendrocalamus strictus*) in our dry deciduous forests is a matter of grave concern. After every flowering season, some of the traditional medri bamboo growing areas do not harbor the species as they did before the flowering. The species by nature grows in dry localities. These areas, being generally located near habitations, are very prone to repeated fires, over-grazing and human interferences. They also have poorer soil with shallow profile. Such forests provide a rather hostile environment for the propagation and nurturing of the young bamboo seedlings. If such areas are not adequately protected from fire and grazing after the flowering season, the natural regeneration of bamboo gets wiped out and the species fails to make a comeback. By comparison, the moist deciduous forests are relatively less prone to fire hazards, have better soil profile and are less severely affected by damages due to grazing. As a result, natural regeneration of dowga bamboo is by and large quite satisfactory throughout the moist deciduous forests of the state. Fire and over-grazing appear to be the chief causes for depletion and eventual decimation of medri bamboo from some of our dry deciduous forests. The only solution to this problem is to re-introduce the species in all the traditional medri bamboo growing areas from where it has been wiped out. It is also of utmost importance to provide rigid protection to the areas which at present harbor the species. Special protection measures from fire and all other forms of biotic interferences should be strictly enforced in these areas, more particularly as and when signs of bamboo-flowering become visible. Natural regeneration of medri bamboo responds very positively to rigid protection. How the species has bounced back on its own after the last flowering (1990s) in the protected environments of the Bannerghatta national park in Bengaluru Urban district is to be seen to be believed.

Occurrence of medri bamboo in a dry deciduous forest is a pointer to the health and well-being of the forest. Depletion of the species itself is an indication that the forest is under stress. Its disappearance is indicative of the severe degradation of the forest that has set in, eventually transforming the climax forest into a scrub.

Impact of Eucalyptus on the dry deciduous forests of Karnataka

Systematic attempts to raise plantations in Karnataka (then Mysore State) had started in the latter half of the nineteenth century with the sowing/planting of indigenous species such as sandal, teak, cardamom, etc. Around the same time, interest was evinced in introducing a number of exotic species such as casuarina, eucalyptus, rain tree, sissoo, mahogany, etc. The first eucalyptus plantation was raised in 1877 at Malabavi (Devarayanadurga), Tumkur district. Eucalyptus was introduced in the dry deciduous forests of Tumkur, Kolar and Bengaluru districts since the early 1900s in order to recoup some of the forests which were harvested under coppice with standards system for the purpose of supplying fuel wood and small timber to Bangalore and other urban centers. There was huge demand for fuel wood from the Railways also. The decision to introduce the species was perhaps due to the fact that the coppice regeneration from the natural tree species was not satisfactory on account of various biotic factors and there was an urgency to restock the forests to meet future demand. During the period immediately before and after the Independence, Eucalyptus hybrid (then known as 'Chikkaballapur' variety) was gradually introduced in fuel wood plantations along with casuarina.

Although eucalyptus was introduced in Karnataka many decades ago, its planting was moderate in the beginning. The working plans written for the post Independence period for the forest divisions of the Eastern Plains and interior Karnataka regions had prescribed planting of eucalyptus under various working circles such as Plantation working circle, Fuel wood working circle, Afforestation working circle, etc. The areas covered under these working circles generally receive moderate to scanty rainfall. The main objectives of these working circles were to improve the vegetation of the highly degraded and refractory forest areas to prevent their further degradation and to meet the increasing demand for fuel wood from a growing population. The introduction of this species was considered inevitable at that time in view of its phenomenal rate of growth, its capability to adapt to highly degraded sites and also due to non-availability of planting technique of any alternative species of native origin capable of effectively tackling difficult areas under harsh conditions. Planting was done mainly by trench-mound method, the trenches being aligned along the contours; pit planting method was also adopted in the beginning but was later given up, as it was found to be unsatisfactory. Sowing of seeds of local species on the mounds was prescribed.

The tempo of planting eucalyptus in Karnataka picked up during the period between 1960 and 1980. During this period, in addition to the dry and degraded forests of the state, some of the high forests receiving moderate to heavy rainfall were also brought under eucalyptus plantation after clear felling the existing tree growth. After 1980, planting was restricted only to areas receiving moderate to low rainfall. However, the extent of planting in such areas increased due to the World Bank aided Social Forestry project which had afforestation of degraded areas as one of its project components. About 1,31,411 hectares of eucalyptus plantations had been raised by the Forest department until 1992-93. Since then, there was gradual reduction in the extent of forest area brought under eucalyptus plantations by the Forest department. The total extent of eucalyptus plantation raised so far by the Forest department is about 1, 52,000 hectares.

In the initial years of large-scale introduction of eucalyptus in the 1960s, a number of plantations were raised in the very high rainfall areas of the state mostly in Uttara Kannada, Belgaum, Dakshina Kannada, Shimoga, Kodagu and Chickmagalur districts. These plantations were soon found to be not doing well because of heavy rain and Pink disease (caused by a fungus *Corticium salmonicolor*). The practice of raising eucalyptus in areas receiving very high rainfall was discontinued in view of its failure. Secondary growth had come back in some of these plantations, while some areas had degraded due to laterisation. Most of these degraded areas were subsequently afforested, mainly with *Acacia auriculiformis* and to some extent with Cashew, and further degradation has been halted. These areas now give the look of near natural forest with patches of *Acacia auriculiformis* and lonely Eucalyptus trees standing here and there.

During 1960-1980, considerable extents of eucalyptus plantations were raised in the moist deciduous high forests, mainly in the districts of Uttara Kannada, Shimoga, Chickmagalur, Mysore and Kodagu. These areas receive moderate to heavy rainfall and also have good to very good soil cover. The earlier forestry practice adopted in these areas was clear felling and planting with teak. This practice was replaced in some forests by new models of planting, some with eucalyptus as a pure crop, and some with teak and eucalyptus mixed in various combinations. Eucalyptus by and large did well in these plantations due to favorable and conducive conditions. Most of these plantations have been harvested for eucalyptus as per prescribed rotation periods of 8/9 years. One redeeming feature about these plantations is the resilience shown by the original forest crop. While eucalyptus grew in these plantations, some of the hardy coppicing species such as matti (*Terminalia tomentosa*), beete (*Dalbergia latifolia*), kindal/hunal (*Terminalia paniculata*), honne (*Pterocarpus marsupium*), nandi/nana (*Lagerstroemia lanceolata*), dindiga/dindal (*Anogeissus latifolia*), jamba (*Xylia xylocarpa*), etc. were able to coppice and survive in the available inter-spaces among the fast growing eucalyptus poles. As eucalyptus poles were successively harvested in intervals of 8/9 years, these saplings of indigenous species grew from strength to strength and were able to establish despite competition from the vigorous coppice shoots of eucalyptus. It has been observed that in these plantations, the productivity of eucalyptus slowed down considerably after subsequent rotations due to resurgence of the indigenous miscellaneous species. These areas now look like regular moist deciduous forest with all the representative species including teak along with remnant eucalyptus trees here and there. It may be worthwhile to mention here that the growth of miscellaneous species in some of the eucalyptus plantations belonging to the Karnataka Forest Development Corporation (KFDC) in Shimoga district was so vigorous that these areas were eventually surrendered to the Forest department for maintaining as natural forest. The forest area included in the Tyavarekoppa Tiger and Lion Safari located by the side of Shimoga-Ayanur-Sagar Road is an example of how a series of eucalyptus plantations has transformed into a regular forest of *Terminalia tomentosa* (matti) and *Anogeissus latifolia* (dindiga) in a span of about thirty years.

Thus most of the eucalyptus plantations raised in the moist deciduous forests have been restored to a state of natural forest, thanks mainly to the coppicing vigor of the original crop. Wherever there were larger gaps, these have been planted up in subsequent afforestation programs. These areas now do not require intensive silvicultural intervention except for rigid protection from fire and other biotic interferences. The eucalyptus trees scattered here and there are of little consequence and their retention should not be hindrance to the existing forest. However, these can be removed, if considered necessary, after proper planning and obtaining approvals from competent authorities.

A vast majority of eucalyptus plantations of the Forest department were raised in the dry deciduous forests of the state, mainly in the districts of Bangalore, Mysore, Mandya, Tumkur, Kolar, Hassan, Chickmagalur, Shimoga, Dharwar, etc. These areas receiving moderate to low rainfall and having average soil were considered ideal for eucalyptus because the existing vegetation was in degraded condition due to biotic pressures and, keeping the enormous demand of fuel wood from the nearby villages and towns in mind, it was considered necessary to increase the productivity of the forest lands by introducing fast growing species. Plantations were raised mainly through trench-mound method. The plantations had by and large succeeded and contributed to the supply of fuel wood and small timber besides industrial raw material. However, unlike in the moist deciduous forests, the original species of the terrain could not make a comeback in these areas. This was primarily because the native species, due to continuous hacking and lopping in the past, were in highly degraded condition and had lost the vigor of coppicing. The soil and moisture conditions were also not adequately supportive of the native species. On the other hand, these conditions were just adequate for eucalyptus. As a result, the planted eucalyptus seedlings came up well and virtually suppressed any other vegetation in the area. Most of the older plantations have been harvested as per the rotation of 8/9 years. However, remnants of old eucalyptus trees continue to dominate the terrain. Substantial portions of these areas have been replanted mostly with native species after completion of the final harvest of eucalyptus. However, the results have been mixed. While the newly introduced plants have established well in areas free from old eucalyptus trees or stumps, they have suffered in the areas still dominated by eucalyptus. In these areas, the newly planted seedlings have not performed well both in terms of survival rate and growth. The stumps of old eucalyptus trees tend to send out multiple coppice shoots immediately after closure of the area. The established root system of eucalyptus appropriates most of the benefits of cultural operations as well as soil and moisture conservation measures carried out as a part of replanting activity. In addition to facing severe root competition, the planted seedlings have to compete for light with the vigorous coppice shoots of eucalyptus. In spite of these difficulties, it is absolutely necessary to find ways to raise successful plantations with native species in these vast stretches of forest lands so that these areas in the long run can be restored to their original status.

The earliest plantations developed in the very dry deciduous and dry thorny forests in the districts of Gulbarga, Raichur, Bidar, Koppal and Yadgiri were primarily eucalyptus plantations. The working plan written by Mr. Munawar Hussain for the period 1955-1965 for the management of these forest areas had recommended trench-mound plantations with planting of eucalyptus seedlings in the trenches and sowing of seeds of local miscellaneous species on the mounds. Eucalyptus continued to remain the principal species for planting in the subsequent years, although various other species such as *Gliricidia, Cassia siamea, Azadirachta indica* (bevu/neem) and *Hardwickia binata* (anjan/kamara) have also become popular. The eucalyptus plantations in these areas were subjected to severe biotic pressure and their growth was not encouraging except in some patches. As the extent of natural forest in this region is very low, these plantations were not subjected to rotational felling with the intention of retaining some vegetation. Even when the working plans prescribe some limited felling of eucalyptus trees, the field officers prefer to defer the felling in order to retain modicum of greenery in an otherwise almost barren and drab tract. Felling of over-mature road-side eucalyptus tree is also avoided unless there is a complaint or request from the adjoining farmer regarding damage to his crop. Evidently the focus in these tree-starved areas is to retain as many trees as possible irrespective of the species. As the distribution of the remnant eucalyptus trees in these areas is thin, introduction of other native species has not been a problem provided adequate care is taken regarding choice of species, quality of seedlings, preparatory soil working, timely planting and after care, soil and moisture conservation measures and above all, rigid protection. Extensive areas in the districts with residual eucalyptus population have already been tackled under various afforestation programs by trench-mound planting or ripping and planting method. Species such as *Azadirachta indica* (bevu/neem), *Hardwickia binata* (anjan/kamara), *Pongamia pinnata* (honge), etc. have been introduced in these plantations with encouraging results. Extensive soil and moisture conservation (SMC) measures adopted in the plantations have also contributed to their success.

The dominance of eucalyptus in the forests of Karnataka, especially in the interior Karnataka (semi-*malnad*) region, is depicted in the following table (Table-5.2), data for which have been culled out from the land use-land cover statistics provided by the Karnataka State Remote Sensing Application Center (KSRSAC), Bengaluru in their Report of 2006 that was based on interpretation of satellite imageries pertaining to the period 1999-2000.

Table-5.2 District-wise distribution of natural forest (crown density above 10%) and Eucalyptus plantations in Karnataka as per Land use-Land cover classification by KSRSAC (2006)

Sl. No.	District.	Geographical area (km^2)	Forest area (ha)	Natural forest with crown density above 10% (ha)	Eucalyptus plantations (ha)
			Malnad Region		
1	Belagavi	13,415	2,06,320	88,974.91	4,437.94
2	Uttara Kannada	10,291	8,29,646	5,98,091.56	314.36
3	Shivamogga	8,477	6,64,255	2,79,039.89	13,414.79
4	Udupi	3,880	1,72,057	96,917.13	101.13
5	Chikkamagaluru	7,201	2,76,780	1,79,692.49	12,663.17
6	Dakshina Kannada	4,560	2,01,218	2,22,933.48	101.13
7	Hassan	6,814	88,060	23,125.35	8,033.58
8	Kodagu	4,102	2,87,099	1,44,302.26	489.32
9	Mysuru	6,307	1,44,987	81,096.90	1,898.52
10	Chamarajanagar	5,676	2,79,146	2,54,038.23	728.62
		70,723	**31,49,568**	**19,68,212.19**	**42,182.56**
			Interior Karnataka /Semi-Malnad Region		
11	Dharwar	4,260	46,854	26,100.97	5,913.16
12	Gadag	4,656	33,337	77.05	2,904.13

13	**Haveri**	4,823	43,280	12,184.19	12,646.84
14	**Davanagere**	5,924	54,434	15,555.31	9,881.03
15	**Chitradurga**	8,440	1,28,718	588.97	4,482.38
16	**Tumkur**	10,597	1,29,167	1,939.02	21,303.20
17	**Bengaluru (Urban)**	2,190	12,225	1,597.73	14,884.94
18	**Bengaluru (Rural)**	2,259	18,643	0	26,380.66
19	**Ramanagara**	3,556	97,842	43,252.14	3,584.82
20	**Mandya**	4,961	66,461	11,190.5	13,416.74
		51,666	**6,31,025**	**1,12,485.88**	**1,15,397.9**
	Eastern Plains/Maidan Region				
21	**Bagalkote**	6,575	83,893	0	2,792.85
22	**Vijayapura**	10,494	8,111	0	296.35
23	**Bidar**	5,448	45,616	1,034.33	1,380.72
24	**Kalaburagi**	10,954	48,093	9,402.70	0.34
25	**Yadgiri**	5,250	51,683	210.39	0
26	**Raichur**	8,386	32,747	386.41	1,512.24
27	**Koppal**	5,630	43,066	0	460.15
28	**Ballari**	8,450	1,37,852	24,768.26	6,045.26
29	**Kolar**	3,979	50,834	0	22,545.94
30	**Chikkaballapur**	4,244	55,788	992.10	19,344.53
		69,430	**5,57,683**	**36,794.19**	**54,378.38**
	Grand Total	**1,91,819**	**43,38,276**	**21,17,492.26**	**2,11,958.84**

[**Note:** Some of the eucalyptus plantations, especially in Bengaluru (Rural), Bengaluru (Urban), Tumkur, Kolar and Chikkaballapur districts, are private plantations. Some plantations in forest areas had been raised and managed by the Karnataka Forest Development Corporation Limited and Mysore Paper Mills Limited.]

Perusal of Table-5.2 indicates that, although the tempo of planting of eucalyptus came down since the mid 1980s and most of the plantations have been harvested repeatedly, the species is quite visible in the forest areas because of its tenacity and coppicing vigor. In the *malnad* districts, its presence is mainly in the drier taluks of Belagavi, Shivamogga, Chikkamagaluru, Hassan and Mysuru districts where agro-climatic conditions are quite favorable for eucalyptus. It had been planted quite extensively in the semi-*malnad* districts such as Dharwar, Haveri, Davanagere, Bengaluru Urban, Bengaluru Rural, Ramanagara, Mandya, and parts of Tumkur and Chitradurga where similar agro-climatic conditions prevail and these plantations are visible even now. In the *maidan* districts, although eucalyptus was planted widely, its presence does not appear to be very dominating now partly because of hostile climatic conditions, which inhibited vigorous growth of the species, and partly because of high biotic pressure which resulted in frequent removal of whatever had grown. It became a popular species for planting in farmlands in a number of districts around Bangalore.

The large-scale plantations of eucalyptus raised by the Forest department, mostly in degraded forest areas, met the fuel wood and small timber requirements of the people to a considerable extent and for a fairly long time extending over a few decades. Besides, a number of wood-based industries were able to meet their pulp wood requirements from these plantations. More importantly, these plantations acted as buffer or cushion and reduced pressure on our natural forests from biotic onslaught. But for these plantations, which were criticized and maligned by many as being ecologically undesirable, vast extents of our natural forest would have vanished during the last fifty years.

To sum up, the performance of eucalyptus in the forests of Karnataka has been mixed: it has failed in the high rainfall zone and has been virtually suppressed by indigenous species in the moist deciduous forests. In dry deciduous forests, it has suppressed almost all the local species. The success of eucalyptus in dry deciduous forests has come at a heavy price – the basic composition of the forests has changed due to the suppression of the indigenous species, and the road to recovery has been slow and difficult. It is true that eucalyptus has served the specific purpose of meeting the biomass needs of the population for a considerable length of time and, as a result, vast extents of natural forests have been saved from degradation or decimation. However, considering that much progress has been made in the agroforestry and farm forestry fronts in the intervening period, and also that the Forest department has been able to successfully introduce many indigenous species in the degraded forests, it is necessary to forge ahead, away from eucalyptus, and strive towards revival of the pristine composition of the dry deciduous and thorn forests with appropriate indigenous species.

Encroachment of forests

Protection of forest from encroachment has always been a challenging task of the Forest department. Although population pressure is an important reason behind forest encroachment, non availability of alternative opportunity or avenue of employment/income often drives people to resort to encroachment of public land including forest land. The general policy of the government to distribute land for cultivation to one and all also results in a false perception that everyone, whether a traditional cultivator or not, should own and till a piece of land for a living. This leads to more hunger for land and puts additional pressure on forest land, which already is under severe strain.

While all types of forest land are prone to encroachment, dry deciduous and scrub forests are more vulnerable and become the easiest targets, as these forests are generally located in areas adjacent to habitations. Besides, due to gentle terrain and scattered growth of small trees and shrubs, conversion of these forests to agricultural land can be accomplished very easily and quickly.

Officers of the Forest department are empowered under Sections 24 and 64A of the Karnataka Forest Act, 1963 to take appropriate action against forest encroachers and retrieve the forest lands. It must however be conceded that in spite of the legal provisions in Acts and Rules, the Forest department has not been able to contain the menace of forest encroachment. Encroachment is a continuous process, and every year, during the onset of the rains, attempts are made by people to clear and occupy forest land. However, for various reasons, the pace of eviction of forest encroachments has been rather slow. As of now, about 80,000 hectares of forest land are under encroachment in the state. Attempt to evict encroachment is stiffly resisted by the encroachers who generally have the support, at times very vocal, of powerful people and political leaders with vested interests. Besides, there are many activist-groups who lend support to the encroachers in the garb of alleviating poverty and completely unmindful of the devastating consequences of their action on the environment. In the past, encroachments of all types of government lands for extension of cultivation and for dwelling were regularized by the governments from time to time. As a result, such an act was considered normal, and this had emboldened the people to encroach more and more lands, which they were hopeful of getting regularized sometime in the future. The practice of regularizing encroachment of non-forest (revenue) land is in vogue even today. As regards forest lands, the Karnataka Government in 1974 had amended Section 28 of the Karnataka Forest Act, 1963 and empowered only the two Houses of the State Legislature to de-reserve a reserved forest or any portion thereof (Act 23 of 1974). Earlier, it was possible to de-reserve any forest land by a simple government notification. The Act was further amended in 1978 (Act 15 of 1978) categorically stipulating that regularization of encroachment taking place after 27-04-1978 must have the approval of the State Legislature. This made the process of regularization of forest encroachments difficult. At the national level, the enactment of the Forest (Conservation) Act (FCA), 1980 and the promulgation of the National Forest Policy (NFP), 1988 put a brake to the earlier practice of regularizing forest encroachments. This was followed by issue of guidelines (18-09-1990) by the Ministry of Environment and Forests (MoEF) to regularize eligible encroachments and to expedite eviction of ineligible encroachments.

However, in spite of the stated policy objectives of both state and central governments to once and for all stop the menace of forest encroachment as indicated above, eviction of old encroachments continues to be a difficult task at the field level generally escalating into law-and-order situations. By and large, encroachers are overtly or covertly supported by politicians and many activist groups even though all of them are fully aware of the illegality of the encroachments as per FCA, 1980 and NFP, 1988. Sometimes, Forest department does not get support even from other government departments in evicting encroachment. At times the forest officials, especially the field-level functionaries, are harassed or trumped-up charges are filed against them on atrocities cases. For the exercise of eviction of forest encroachments to be successful, it is absolutely necessary that the field-level functionaries get unstinted and wholehearted support from the top. It is also necessary that in all cases involving eviction of forest encroachment, which are always very sensitive in nature, the Forest department, the government, the civil society, and the political leadership are all on the same page. Conflicting signals emanating from these quarters lead to demoralization of the staff and, in the long run, the entire mission becomes counterproductive.

However, the process of eviction of forest encroachments by the Forest department received a major setback from the 'Scheduled Tribes and Other Traditional Forest Dwellers (Recognition of Forest Rights) Act, 2006 (No 2 of 2007)', also known as the Forest Rights Act (FRA). This Act was followed up by the notification of the 'Scheduled Tribes and Other Traditional Forest Dwellers (Recognition of Forest Rights) Rules, 2008'. This Act and the Rules made there under have virtually created a pathway for the forest encroachers found ineligible under FCA and NFP to stake claims on the encroached forest lands. The guidelines that have been framed by the Ministry of Tribal Affairs (MoTA), the nodal agency for implementation of FRA, have also set forth very liberal conditions which have not only enabled the ineligible forest occupants to stay put in the forest lands till finalization of the claims, but have also put unreasonable pressure on the authorities scrutinizing the claims to regularize the claims by any means. Such developments have also encouraged other people to clear, burn and occupy forest land with the sole motive of claiming rights under the FRA. The Act has become a very convenient tool in the hands of politicians and activists, who, in the guise of removing historical injustice to the tribal and other forest dwellers, have actually helped illegal occupants of forest land to continue to enjoy the land almost perpetually. Although on paper the procedure for finalizing the rights under the FRA is quite rigorous, many ineligible claimants have reportedly been able to secure the rights through unholy means. Interestingly, the guidelines of MoTA are silent on the issue of reviewing the rights vested by illegal means but are doggedly insistent on exploring all possible means to confer rights to those whose claims have been rejected. (**Note:** An analytical write-up highlighting various aspects of forest encroachments is appended at **Annexure-III**).

Forests now occupy only about 20% of the geographical area of the state and most of the forests located in the vicinity of habitations have been dented by the scars of encroachment. The condition of the dry deciduous forests, which are mostly located adjacent to habitations, is even more dismal, having been the worst affected as a result of encroachment for extension of cultivation. It is necessary for one and all, including politicians and activists, to realize that it is no longer possible to play with the forest lands. Whatever forests we are now left with need to be protected by any means. All our efforts should focus on restoration and rejuvenation of these leftover forests so that the environmental benefits emanating from them can be enhanced and sustained for the common good of the society at large. It is also necessary for politicians and policy makers to believe that by providing alternative employment opportunities people can be assisted to make an equally happy and content living without having to take up cultivation in encroached forest land.

Chapter 6

RESTORATION AND REJUVENATION OF THE DRY DECIDUOUS FORESTS OF KARNATAKA

Dry deciduous forests, their edaphic variants, and various degraded formations, along with patches of thorn forests and thorn scrub in highly recalcitrant sites, constitute the principal forest ecosystem in interior Karnataka and in the Eastern Plains. Although these forests are distributed over a vast landscape in these two regions, their present cumulative extents are very limited. In interior Karnataka, they occur over about 12% of the geographical area of the region, whereas in the Eastern Plains they occupy about 8% of the geographical area of the corresponding region (Table-5.1). While the status of these forests in the above two regions is pathetic to say the least, the dry deciduous forests of the *malnad* region have also suffered from the onslaught of severe anthropogenic pressure. In this regard, the dry deciduous forests of Uttara Kannada district are somewhat better although signs of deterioration are clearly visible in the eastern fringes, more particularly in their easternmost limits adjoining the districts of Dharwar and Haveri which are dotted with many villages. In Shivamogga district, these forests have suffered heavily on account of encroachments and heavy withdrawals. Degradation of these forests is very conspicuous in Shikaripura, Soraba, Shivamogga and Bhadravathi taluks where large-scale deforestation has taken place in many reserved forests. A number of minor forests have just vanished. Parts of Chikkamagaluru and Tarikere taluks of Chikkamagaluru district have also suffered similarly, in varying degrees. Due mainly to their inclusion in the protected area (PA) network of the state, the condition of a bulk of the dry deciduous forests of Chamarajanagar, Mysuru and Mandya districts is relatively better, with visible signs of restoration and rejuvenation.

While population pressure is the primary cause of degradation and decimation of the dry deciduous forests, a number of other factors have also contributed to their present plight. Compared with the moist deciduous, semi-evergreen and evergreen forests which generally occur in precipitous terrain receiving high rainfall, the dry deciduous forests by and large occur in relatively less precipitous terrain receiving medium to low rainfall. After the removal of tree growth, such forests can be converted to agricultural land with relative ease. In the past, forest areas in the high rainfall zone were known for epidemics such as malaria, and people desisted from settling down in the vicinity of moist deciduous and evergreen forests. As a matter of fact, at times the entire village situated in the high rainfall zone shifted to low rainfall areas just to get rid of the wrath of malaria. Dry deciduous forests are more ideal for grazing by domestic cattle, as these open forests facilitate favorable light conditions on the forest floor resulting in abundant availability of grass and other fodder species. Due to limited availability of alternative grazing grounds and increasing number of cattle, grazing intensity has far exceeded the carrying capacity of these forests, resulting in their rapid deterioration. These forests also become very vulnerable to fire during the dry season when the forest floor becomes highly inflammable owing to the presence of dry grass and fallen leaves. Recurring fires, repeated year after year, render the dry deciduous forests very unproductive and the quality of the forests deteriorates very rapidly.

Attempts at restoration and rejuvenation of the shrinking deciduous forests of Karnataka will need a two-pronged approach. There is need to protect whatever forests we are left with from any further loss or shrinkage and to facilitate development of the forests to their pristine state. Secondly, there is need for augmenting biomass resources required by the people from areas outside these natural forests so as to reduce pressure on them thereby facilitating their restoration and rejuvenation.

Protection and development of existing forests

We have mentioned earlier that large extents of the dry deciduous forests of interior Karnataka and the Eastern Plains have undergone so much degradation that except for a few reasonably good patches of climax forest in the districts of Dharwar, Haveri, Davanagere, Ramanagara, Mandya, Ballari, Kalaburagi, etc., most of the districts in these two regions now harbor scrub forests. As a matter of fact, scrub forests constitute the principal forest ecosystem in most of the districts in these two regions. Therefore, any attempt at restoration and rejuvenation of forests will have to focus on these scrub forests also in addition to the available climax forests. [**Note:** As per the 2006 Report of the Karnataka State Remote Sensing Application Centre (KSRSAC), Bengaluru, the extent of scrub forests in the state is 7,655.73 km^2 (Table-3.1). However, as per India State of Forest Report (ISFR) 2019, this figure is 4,484.07 km^2. As these two reports are based on satellite imageries pertaining to two different periods separated by about 18 years (1999-2000 and 2017-18), the above difference is understandable and can perhaps be attributed to various conservation initiatives including plantations raised during the intervening period. The district-wise break-up of the scrub forests of Karnataka as per ISFR 2019 is as follows: Belagavi (688.00 km^2), Chitradurga (595.00 km^2), Ballari (466.00 km^2), Bagalkote (399.00 km^2), Tumkur (387.00 km^2), Davanagere (322.00 km^2), Chikkaballapur (181.00 km^2), Koppal (172.00 km^2), Ramanagara (170.09 km^2), Raichur (149.00 km^2), Yadgiri (131.00 km^2), Chamarajanagar (129.00 km^2), Gadag (117.00 km^2), Haveri (103.00 km^2), Mandya (96.70 km^2), Chikkamagaluru (74.00 km^2), Kolar (68.00 km^2), Hassan (68.00 km^2), Bidar (37 km^2), Mysuru (29.92 km^2), Kalaburagi (29.00 km^2), Bengaluru Rural (23.36 km^2), Shivamogga (23.00 km^2), Vijayapura (10.00 km^2), Bengaluru Urban (8.00 km^2), Dakshina Kannada (3.00 km^2), Dharwar (3.00 km^2), Uttara Kannada (2.00 km^2), Kodagu (2.00 km^2), and Udupi (0 km^2).]

It has been already mentioned that substantial forest areas of southern Karnataka comprising Chamarajanagar, Mysuru and Mandya districts have been included in the protected area (PA) network of the state comprising national parks, tiger reserves, wildlife sanctuaries, etc. and that visible changes have been noticed in these forest areas in terms of their stocking as well as diversity because of overall protection afforded.

As the condition of the natural forests in the semi-*malnad* and *maidan* regions of Karnataka is very poor and is fast deteriorating, it is necessary to include the remaining relatively better natural forests into the protected area (PA) network of the state. The objective is primarily to protect the remaining bio-diversity of flora and fauna existing in these forests. This will automatically help in conservation and development of the natural forests within the protected areas. This process has already begun with the notification of a number of protected areas such as Jogimatti wildlife sanctuary (Chitradurga district), Gudekote sloth bear sanctuary (Ballari district), Rangayyanadurga four-horned antelope wildlife sanctuary (Davanagere district), Ramadevarabetta vulture sanctuary (Ramanagara district), Yadahalli chinkara wildlife sanctuary (Bagalkote district), Chincholi wildlife sanctuary (Kalaburagi district), Thimlapura wildlife sanctuary (Tumkur district), Kappatagudda wildlife sanctuary (Gadag district), Bukkapatna chinkara wildlife sanctuary (Tumkur district), Kamasandra wildlife sanctuary (Kolar district), Thimlapura conservation reserve (Tumkur district), etc. Notification of Hirekalgudda state forest of Hassan district as a wildlife sanctuary is also on the anvil. In addition, a number of dry deciduous forests of Bengaluru (Rural), Ramanagara and Mandya districts have been added to the existing protected areas such as Bannerghatta national park and Cauvery wildlife sanctuary. It is necessary to continue this process and include more and more natural forests into the protected area (PA) network. Priority should be given to those districts from which natural forests have practically vanished. The Royalpadu forests of Kolar district, Narasimhadevarabetta and Ittikaldurga forest blocks (NDB and IDB) of Chikkaballapura district, forests of Manvi and Deodurga ranges in Raichur district, Agoli-Benakal forest blocks of Koppal district, Changler and Shahabad forests of Bidar district, Devarayanadurga and Siddarabetta forests of Tumkur district, etc. are examples of such forests which harbor some natural vegetation and which need urgent protection. The Savanadurga state forest of Ramanagara district needs to be given rigid protection in order to conserve its rich floral diversity including a wide range of medicinal plants. The Kukwada-Ubrani state forest (KUSF) of Shivamogga, Davanagere and Chikkamagaluru districts, which stands precariously as an oasis surrounded by typical barren areas of the Deccan Plains, also deserves to be included in the PA network before it is too late.

The forests of Sandur in Ballari district, which have been adversely affected by large-scale iron ore mining during recent years, also need to be given utmost protection. Sandur forests stand out as an important example of how a forest eco-system can retain its unique bio-diversity in spite of harsh climatic and soil conditions. The erstwhile rulers of Sandur state were successful in managing these forests ensuring the least biotic interference.

Most of the afforestation initiatives of the KFD in interior Karnataka and in the Eastern Plains take place in the scrub forests of the regions. While these efforts should be continued, focus should be more on overall protection of the landscape than on planting seedlings. The principal components of such eco-restoration initiatives should comprise activities such as dibbling of seeds of native species, soil and moisture conservation, protection from all forms of biotic interferences, and rigid fire protection. However, in limited areas with better soil, planting of indigenous species may be done with lesser number of seedlings, say, 100-200 per hectare. The seedlings should be hardy and must have spent at least nine months to one year in the nursery. Teak (*Tectona grandis*), medri bamboo (*Dendrocalamus strictus*) and sandal (*Santalum album*) should be encouraged in these areas wherever feasible. Seedlings of other hardy species which are typical of the tract should also be introduced. Seedlings of some of these species may not have been raised in forest nurseries so far, but a beginning must be made, as these species are more likely to thrive and grow in their native tract. Species for sowing and planting may be chosen from among the following: Bevu (*Azadirachta indica*), Honge (*Pongamia pinnata*), Kamara/Anjan (*Hardwickia binata*), Kakke (*Cassia fistula*), Muthuga (*Butea monosperma*), Hale/Beppale (*Wrightia tinctoria*), Tapasi (*Holoptelia integrifolia*), Ankole (*Alangium lamarckii*), Nelli (*Emblica officinalis*), Nerale (*Syzygium cumini*), Bage (*Albizia lebbeck*), Bilwara (*Albizia odoratissima*), Tugli/Chujjulu (*Albizia amara*), Doddabevu/Moosimara (*Ailanthus excelsa*), Some (*Soymida febrifuga*), Ippe (*Madhuca latifolia*), Kadgeru (*Semecarpus anacardium*), Char/Nurkal (*Buchanania lanzan*), Hurugalu/Mashawal (*Chloroxylon swietenia*), Dhupa (*Boswellia serrata*), Tupra/Tumri (*Diospyros melanoxylon*), Patri/Bilva (*Aegle marmelos*), Belaa (*Limonia acidissima*), Karijali (*Acacia nilotica*), Bilijali (*Acacia leucophloea*), Kutch/Kaggali (*Acacia catechu*), Kempujali (*Acacia chundra*), Banni (*Acacia ferruginea*), Hottejali/Hirejali (*Acacia latronum*), Seegeballi (*Acacia concinna*), Channangi (*Lagerstroemia parviflora*), Pachali

(*Dalbergia paniculata*), Godda/Gojjal/Moi (*Lannea coromandelica*), Padri/ Kharsing (*Stereospermum* species), Chilla/Chitta (*Strychnos potatorum*), Seetaphal (*Annona squamosa*), Godmurki/Oody (*Dolichandrone crispa*), Bilidale/Bettathavare/Ponkimara/Tella Poniki/Butala (*Givotia rottleriformis*), Kadburuga/Arishinaburuga (*Cochlospermum religiosum*), Halwan/Dadap (*Erythrina variegata*), Bettahurali (*Mundulea suberosa*), Bore/Elachi (*Zizyphus jujuba*), Kadunimbe (*Atalantia monophylla*), Ulpi (*Grewia salvifolia*), Kondamavu/Bettamavu (*Commiphora caudata*), Wadu (*Dichrostachys cinerea*), Bikke (*Gardenia* species), Maddi (*Morinda tinctoria*), Ghanthemara/Mogalingam/Weaver's Beam tree (*Schrebera swietenioides*), Buthale (*Sterculia urens*), Devadari (*Erythroxylon monogynum*), Revdi/ Himsra/Karina (*Capparis* species), Kadubende (*Gyrocarpus jacquini*), Kawli (*Carissa carandas*), Salle (*Cordia myxa/dichotoma*), etc. Species such as Mango (*Mangifera indica*), Honge (*Pongamia pinnata*), Holematti (*Terminalia arjuna*), Tapasi (*Holoptelia integrifolia*), Hunase (*Tamarindus indica*), Nerale (*Syzygium cumini*), Basavanapada (*Bauhinia* species), Holelakki/Neeranji (*Salix tetrasperma*), Lakki/Nocchi (*Vitex negundo*), etc. should be planted on stream banks.

Soil and moisture conservation (SMC) works should constitute an integral part of the eco-restoration initiatives aimed at restoration and rejuvenation of the dry deciduous forests and their various degraded formations. Such works play very significant role especially in the dry and rain deficient areas by conserving most of the precipitation received. These activities are particularly helpful in arresting the precipitation received from the early, late and stray showers. SMC works definitely help in ground water recharge thereby rejuvenating the surrounding vegetation. However, excavation of very large and deep trenches and ponds/tanks with the help of machines is not desirable and should be avoided. The percolation trenches/ponds should be of reasonable dimensions and should be distributed evenly so that the benefits of SMC works are shared equally in the entire treatment area. Staggered contour trenches of moderate dimensions can be considered in over-exposed and highly degraded open areas. Check dams or Gully plugs may be erected across stream and nala beds. The SMC works should be of low intensity and should be carried out with local manpower and as far as possible with locally available material.

In the preceding chapter, while discussing the impact of eucalyptus on the dry deciduous forests of Karnataka it was pointed out that large extents of dry deciduous forests of a number of districts such as Shivamogga, Chikkamagaluru, Hassan, Dharwar, Haveri, Davanagere, Tumkur, Bengaluru Rural, Bengaluru Urban, Kolar, Chikkaballapur, Mandya, etc. have lost their natural biodiversity due to aggressive dominance of eucalyptus; so much so that even after eucalyptus has been removed a number of times as per its normal coppice rotation period of 8/9 years, the species continues to dominate the landscape, not giving any room for the local species to make a comeback. Some of these districts now do not harbor any natural forest or have very limited presence of such forest. It will therefore be necessary to retrieve some of these areas under the strangle-hold of eucalyptus and help them revert to their original natural state by planting seedlings of indigenous species appropriate to the tract.

Raising successful plantation in areas having remnants of old eucalyptus trees has been a daunting task. In most of these areas planted seedlings have not performed well both in terms of survival rate and height growth. As already mentioned, the stumps of old eucalyptus trees tend to send out multiple coppice shoots which physically obstruct the growth of the planted seedlings. In addition to facing severe root competition from the well-entrenched root systems of the eucalyptus trees, the planted seedlings have to compete for space and light with these vigorous coppice shoots. The best way to raise successful plantation in such areas is to remove the eucalyptus trees and stumps along with their roots. However, it is a very difficult and expensive task. The next best option is to harvest all the standing eucalyptus trees for timber, pole, pulp wood and fuel wood and then prepare the area for planting after digging pits or trenches by mechanized devices. The pits or trenches should be dug judiciously, away from the eucalyptus stumps. Number of seedlings for planting should be kept limited in view of the existing vegetation, including possibly a few suppressed seedlings of hardy native species. After planting of tall and hardy seedlings of suitable species, the plantation should be maintained for at least five years by repeated weeding and soil working. Eucalyptus shoots found to interfere with planted seedlings should be removed. Good soil working, fertilizer application and effective soil and moisture conservation (SMC) works should be carried out. These initiatives will enable the planted seedlings to establish and grow side by side with some eucalyptus shoots here and there which should be removed as and when necessary. With the establishment and growth of the indigenous species, eucalyptus will gradually get suppressed.

Although the principal objective of protecting the remaining dry deciduous, thorn and scrub forests of Karnataka is to consolidate and stabilize these forests to prevent their further degradation/decimation and to facilitate their restoration and rejuvenation, these operations yield multifarious benefits. They provide a sanctuary to the entire plant kingdom comprising trees, shrubs, herbs, climbers, lianas, palms, ferns, orchids, grasses, mosses, etc. inhabiting these forests. The ones in the verge of extinction get an opportunity to bounce back. All the major, minor and minute constituents of a forest ecosystem have definite ecological roles to play, and all of them collectively help the forest ecosystem function effectively and efficiently (**Annexure-II**). These forests also serve as *in situ* conservation reserves of genetic resources of several plant species, including varieties of medicinal plants, for present and future use by humankind. In short, these forests serve not only as sanctuary for the flora and fauna to thrive and propagate but also as the sanctuary of hope and future.

The expansive dry deciduous forests of Karnataka, along with the scrub forests and the barren hills strewn with rocks and boulders, provide a safe haven to a large number of mammalian and other species of animals including many species of birds. The scrub forests of the state in particular are suitable for drought-resistant herbivores like the black buck (*Antilope cervicarpa*), chinkara (*Gazella bennettii*), four-horned antelope (*Tetracerus quadricornis*), hare (genus *Lepus*) and other smaller mammals. Some of these forests also support small groups of elephants and other herbivores such as spotted deer. These forests sustain some carnivores like leopard (panther) and wolf. The sloth bear is abundant in the scrub forests, mostly inhabiting the rocky and bouldery terrain interspersed with caves and crevices, and sharing the space with the occasional leopard.

Although leopards and sloth bears inhabit most of the forests of the state, a sizeable number of these two animal species are found in the scrub forests and rocky hillocks which are scattered all over the state. These areas are mostly situated nearer to habitations/settlements. The natural prey base or feed of these animals within the forest areas include small herbivores, monkeys, hares, wild boars, rodents and birds, in case of leopard, and fruits, roots and tubers, in case of sloth bear. Due to rapid degradation and decimation of the forests, the availability of prey base for leopards and that of feed for sloth bears has drastically reduced inside the forests thereby forcing these animals i.e., the leopards and the sloth bears to move out into habitations and agricultural lands in search of prey or feed. Leopards generally move at night into village and town limits looking for stray dogs that are usually abundant. They also prey upon sheep and goat, if easily accessible. In the absence of dogs, goat or sheep, leopards prey upon children or old persons, who come out to the open at night. Sloth bears move into agricultural or marginal lands looking for fruits, roots or tubers. Normally both these animals avoid human beings; however, when suddenly confronted with human beings, they behave aggressively and cause grievous injuries, or even death. Quite often the leopard runs helter-skelter and gets trapped in an open well or in a shed or a room. In earlier days, such a straying animal was collectively chased, surrounded and beaten to death by the people. However, because of increasing awareness regarding conservation of wildlife, such instances have come down. In the recent years, there have been increasing numbers of instances of human-animal conflict resulting in death and injuries to both humans and animals. The only way to reduce the occurrence of such unfortunate confrontations is to augment the availability of prey base or feed inside the forests so that these animals do not have the compulsion of straying out in search of food. Restoration and rejuvenation of the forests, as suggested in the preceding paragraphs, will automatically ensure increased availability of prey base and feed for leopards and sloth bears, respectively. This in the long run is expected to reduce the frequency of occurrence of human-animal conflicts in areas outside the forests.

Augmenting biomass resources from areas outside natural forests (Agroforestry)

Although Karnataka Forest Department (KFD) has been relentlessly engaged in large-scale tree planting programs in order to halt forest degradation and improve forest quality, such efforts have met with limited success. The forests and plantations continue to be under tremendous stress due to pressure from external biotic factors. Even the plantations which are provided with fencing for rigid protection are not safe from these external factors, as the fencing provides protection only for a few years. Most of the plantations raised by KFD, as revealed by evaluations carried out through independent/external agencies, show fairly good survival rates. It must however be admitted that these plantations, despite being excellent in the beginning, gradually thin out over a period of seven to eight years because of continuous biotic interferences. Past experiences have shown that it is physically impossible to protect the plantations raised by the Forest Department if these biotic interferences are allowed to continue unchecked. By and large, it has not been possible for the Forest Department to contain the external factors that are primarily responsible for forest degradation. It is apprehended that until and unless the primary causes of forest degradation are comprehensively addressed, any initiative at arresting forest degradation and improving forest quality will not succeed. Such initiative is akin to giving health tonic to a sick person without curing his sickness.

One of the most important factors responsible for degradation of our forests is excessive withdrawal (mostly unrecorded) of biomass in the form of firewood and small timber. Another important factor is uncontrolled grazing by very large numbers of unproductive cattle. Other factors such as fire, soil erosion, etc. are subsidiary to these two primary factors and will be under check once the primary factors are brought under control. The only way to reduce excessive removal of biomass from forest is to create abundant biomass resource outside the forest. This is possible only through very intensive and aggressive agroforestry. The notion that fuel wood should come from forest must go. Fuel wood required to cook food must also be grown along with food crops. Agroforestry not only reduces the pressure on forests but also helps in increasing the tree cover. Besides, it improves the income levels of the farmers.

As regards reducing or regulating grazing in forest areas by large numbers of unproductive cattle, it is necessary to discourage rearing of unproductive cattle, to encourage cattle improvement and stall feeding, and to ensure substantial increase in fodder production, preferably within the boundaries of agricultural lands. Farmers owning cattle can achieve these objectives by adopting sound animal-husbandry practices and integrating these with appropriate agroforestry practices.

As per the India State of Forest Report (ISFR) 2019 published by the Forest Survey of India (FSI), Dehradun, the forest cover and tree cover of Karnataka are 38,575 km² and 6,257 km² respectively. Thus the combined forest and tree cover of the state is 44,832 km² which is about 23.4% of Karnataka's geographical area of 1,91,819 km². In order to increase the state's forest and tree cover to 33%, an additional 9.6%, or say 10% of the state's geographical area has to be brought under tree plantations. The extent of land with the Forest Department is limited and this extent is not likely to increase significantly in the future. Besides, most of the forest areas with the Forest Department which are accessible and which are capable of growing trees have already been afforested. Although the Forest Department will continue to afforest the remaining tree-deficient areas under its custody in order to increase the forest cover, it will not be possible to bridge the existing gap of about 10% by the Department alone. Bulk of the increment in forest or tree cover to make up for the deficit has to take place on non-forest land. The scope of taking up large-scale tree planting on non-forest government land is also very limited. Some such areas have already been taken under tree planting by the Social Forestry (SF) wing of the Forest Department or other Government Departments such as the Watershed Development Department (WDD). Besides, vast extents of non-forest government lands are either in much degraded condition or are under unauthorized cultivation. Therefore, the only way to achieve the national goal of 33% forest or tree cover is to encourage massive tree planting in private land under agroforestry program. Agroforestry has a number of advantages over community or public forestry: (a) the benefits from agroforestry entirely accrue to the individual farmers thereby improving their livelihood condition and economic status; (b) agroforestry does not have some of the inherent problems associated with community/public forestry such as, multiple stake holders/users, clash of interest, problems of protection, etc.; (c) the level of protection and management of an agro-forest is far superior than that of a community or public forest due to undivided individual attention and interest from the owner of the land.

Agroforestry refers to growing trees as a complementary crop in agricultural lands. This farming system in some form or the other has been in practice in Karnataka since ages. The trees planted are usually multipurpose trees providing food, fodder, fuel, timber, oil, gum, resin, flower, manure, fiber, medicine, etc. Many of the trees are primarily horticultural crop. In the recent years, there has been increasing thrust in propagating agroforestry for a number of reasons: Agroforestry is a very practical system of increasing tree cover. Agricultural lands with poor quality respond better to tree crop than to agricultural crop. Agroforestry improves the soil profile by preventing soil erosion, improving moisture availability, and increasing soil fertility. People's dependence on fuel wood and timber from the natural forest is reduced considerably or is totally avoided; this reduces the pressure on our natural forests helping them to rejuvenate.

Although agroforestry is seen as a very practical step to increase tree cover and to increase farmers' incomes, its benefits go far beyond. Agroforestry has the potential of transforming the entire rural/ agrarian landscape in terms of economic, ecological and environmental development. Agroforestry through its mitigating effects enables agricultural lands to face the challenges posed by climate change. It plays a complementary but important role in providing climate-resilience to agricultural lands. In the coming years, agroforestry will hold the key to an overarching development in the agricultural sector, more particularly in the vast expanses of dry lands of interior Karnataka (semi-*malnad*) and the Eastern Plains (*maidan*). Agroforestry has the capability of restoring the ancient and organic relationships among forest, water and agriculture.

Land is the most important asset of the farmer. Conservation and improvement of this precious asset is of utmost importance for sustainable production of agricultural crops. For a number of reasons including natural calamities, large extents of our agricultural lands are in various stages of degradation. Severity of such degradation is more visible in the semi-*malnad* and *maidan* regions. Such degradation is generally triggered by the loss of soil due to water and wind erosion and because of the resultant reduction of water-holding capacity of the land. One principal cause for such degradation is the absence of adequate tree cover in and around the agricultural lands. Trees help in a number of ways in protecting and enriching the soil. These include, soil retention, moisture conservation, increase in the organic matter and fertility, improvement of soil structure, etc. However, in order to expand their agricultural activities farmers often resort to clearing of tree growth from their lands. Clearance of such tree growth especially on both sides of the natural water courses or drainage lines that run through the agricultural lands is found to be very harmful, as it leads to increased runoff of rain water and accelerated soil erosion. In order to prevent soil erosion and to control runoff to increase groundwater recharge, it will be beneficial to grow as many trees within the farmlands as possible. In particular, re-establishment of a pair of narrow belts of trees, shrubs, herbs and grasses along both sides of the natural water courses or drainage lines that run through the agricultural landscape is highly recommended. Trees in and around agricultural lands also provide a micro-climatic effect by bringing down the ambient temperature thereby creating an environment that is ameliorative and salubrious for both men and animals.

Although agroforestry aims at increasing tree cover and thereby at conserving soil and water and improving soil quality, the focus should be on ensuring a balanced and diverse mixture of tree species catering to various needs of the people including timber, firewood, food, fodder and other utilities. The choice of species in agroforestry primarily depends upon the preference and convenience of farmers. Focus on timber trees should be limited to a few species. At present, *Tectona grandis* (teak/thyaga), *Grevillea robusta* (Silver Oak) and *Melia dubia* (hebbevu) are very popular among the farmers of Karnataka. *Swietenia macrophylla/mahagoni* (mahogany), *Azadirachta indica* (bevu/neem) and *Acacia auriculiformis* (in the coastal districts) have also some popularity. Timber yielding trees are planted mostly by farmers owning large and medium land holdings. *Santalum album* (sandal/shrigandha) is also becoming increasingly popular among farmers because of its precious wood. It is however advisable that planting of sandal is taken up only by those farmers who can provide fortified protection to the trees from smuggling which is quite rampant.

Fruit yielding trees have a very wide outreach covering all types of farm holdings - small, medium and large. Farmers are generally more attracted towards planting of fruit yielding trees for various reasons including easy marketability of the produce. Karnataka has a very rich legacy of horticultural practices; as a matter of fact, plantations of horticultural species such as coconut, coffee, areca nut, tea, rubber, cashew and various fruit yielding species contribute to at least 25% of the forest and tree cover of the state. The principal focus of agroforestry should therefore be on fruit yielding trees (**see box**).

Planting of *Pongamia pinnata* (honge), *Azadirachta indica* (bevu/neem), *Alangium lamarckii* (ankole), *Gmelina arborea*

> ### PLANTING OF FRUIT YIELDING TREES IN AGROFORESTRY
>
> An important objective of agroforestry is to have adequate tree cover. Tree cover does not necessarily mean that only the tree species which are found in forest and which the Forest Department normally plants in the forest should be planted in agroforestry. The principal requirement is that the tree should be perennial and it should have a woody stem. Most of the fruit-bearing horticultural tree species (except banana and papaya) satisfy these two requirements. The species include, coconut (*Cocos nucifera*), areca nut (*Areca catechu*), cocoa (*Theobroma cacao*), nutmeg (*Myristica fragrans*), watehuli (*Artocarpus lakucha*), mango/mavu (*Mangifera indica*), halasu/jackfruit (*Artocarpus integrifolius*), hunase/tamarind (*Tamarindus indica*), nerle (*Syzygium cumini*), nelli (*Emblica officinalis*), perle/guava (*Psidium guajava*), dalimbe/pomegranate (*Punica granatum*), nimbe (*Citrus latifolia/aurantifolia*), pomelo (*Citrus maxima*), orange (*Citrus X sinensis*), chikoo/sapota (*Manilkara zapota*), seetaphal (*Annona squamosa*), ramphal (*Annona reticulata*), borehannu/jujube (*Zizyphus mauritiana*), avocado (*Persea americana*), star fruit/carambola (*Averrhoa carambola*), cashew/godambi (*Anacardium occidentale*), nugge/drumstick (*Moringa oleifera*), fig (*Ficus carica*), murugal/punarpuli (*Garcinia* species), kaulikai (*Carissa carandas*), salle/challe (*Cordia myxa/dichotoma*), bread fruit/neer phanas (*Artocarpus altilis*), bela (*Limonia acidissima*), bilva (*Aegle marmelos*), rose-apple (*Syzygium jambos*), gooseberry (*Phyllanthus acidus*), etc. Farmers may choose to plant some of the above tree species depending upon the extent and soil condition of their lands. Many of the fruit species mentioned above are ideal for very dry lands where agricultural crops may not be remunerative.

(shivani), *Wrightia tinctoria* (hale/beppale), *Givotia rottleriformis* (butala/polka), etc. should be encouraged in the boundaries of agricultural lands. While the first two are well-known oilseed bearing trees besides being important sources of organic manure (oil-cake and leaves), the last three are famous for their wood which is much in demand for making of handicraft articles (Kumta, Channapatna, Kinnal, etc.). *Alangium lamarckii* (ankole) is an ideal tree of small to medium size that provides good quality wood for agricultural implements and small household furniture. It would be ideal if the home- or kitchen-garden in every household has one plant each from among the following species of daily needs: *Moringa oleifera* (nugge), *Murraya koenigii* (karibevu), *Limonia* species (nimbe), *Cinnamonum* species (dalchinni), *Emblica officinalis* (nelli), *Psidium guajava* (perle) and, where possible, a clump of *Oxytenanthera stocksii* (seemegala/marihal bamboo) or *Dendrocalamus strictus* (medri bamboo). Planting of the above five-six species in every home-garden or kitchen-garden will bring a sea change in the state's tree-cover scenario.

Planting of fodder yielding trees is another area that needs focus so that the fodder needs of the domestic cattle are more or less fulfilled from within the farmlands (**see box**) thereby reducing the pressure of over-grazing on the natural forests.

Agroforestry provides a platform in which a number of productive and mutually beneficial activities such as agriculture, forestry, horticulture, floriculture, animal husbandry, sericulture, apiculture and pisciculture (fishery) can be pursued together. In other words, agroforestry provides an opening for integrated farming systems (IFS) that result in optimum utilization of resources, increased

---

PLANTING OF FODDER YIELDING TREES IN AGROFORESTRY

Many of the fodder yielding trees planted within the agricultural lands can be lopped judiciously and periodically to make green fodder available to the domestic cattle. Such tree species include, bevu (*Azadirachta indica*), karijali (*Acacia nilotica*), bilijali (*Acacia leucophloea*), nugge (*Moringa oleifera*), bore (*Zizyphus mauritiana*), ala (*Ficus benghalensis*), arali (*Ficus religiosa*), basavanapada (*Bauhinia* species), bage (*Albizia lebbeck*), kamara (*Hardwickia binata*), peenari (*Ailanthus excelsa*), neral (*Syzigium cumini*), agasthi/agase (*Sesbania grandiflora*), glrircidia (*Gliricidia sepium*), sissoo (*Dalbergia sissoo*), subabul (*Leucaena leucocephala*), seeme hunase (*Pithecellobium dulce*), *Calliandra calothrysus*, *Delonix regia*, etc. The Mulberry tree (*Morus alba*), the leaves of which are primarily used as feed for silk worms, is also a very good fodder tree. Various palatable shrubs, grasses and legumes may be introduced underneath the trees that are planted along the *bunds*, borders, windbreaks/shelterbelts, and the linear strips on either side of the water courses or drainage lines. Bamboos, wherever planted, are an excellent source of fodder. Some quantities of grass and legume will also be available from underneath the block plantations such as horticultural plantations, fuel wood and pulpwood plantations, and the plantations that have been raised on problematic soils.

---

levels of production and income, and at the same time, ensures sustainable conservation of the natural resources including land, air and water. Gandhiji's dream of a *Ramarajya*, which is another name for comprehensive rural development, can be realized through agroforestry. Agroforestry also has the potential of generating enormous employment opportunities. Expansion of this farming system in the country-side will result in stopping/reducing the present trend of people flocking to the urban centers. In fact, agroforestry has the potential of triggering a reverse migration, a phenomenon that will be beneficial to our highly-congested urban centers as well as to the far-flung rural areas. It will be a win-win situation for both our urban and rural landscapes.

Although there is need to propagate agroforestry throughout the length and breadth of Karnataka in order to relieve the natural forests from the severity of biotic pressures, it assumes special significance in the Eastern Plains and in the interior Karnataka region, as these regions are more or less bereft of natural forests, most of these forests having been cleared in the past for extending cultivation. Introduction of agroforestry in these regions will go a long way in restoring and rejuvenating whatever little natural vegetation in the form of dry deciduous and scrub forests we are still left with in these regions.

Conclusion

Air, water, soil and forest are four natural resources that are very important for growth and sustenance of human life as well as other life forms. Interestingly, forest plays a pivotal role as regulator or moderator for the overall well-being of the other three natural resources: forest purifies the air, conserves the water, and protects/enriches the soil. Conservation of forest is necessary for sustaining a healthy environment that provides pure air, adequate water and fertile soil. Former President of the United States of America Franklin Delano Roosevelt had said: "The nation that destroys its soil destroys itself." He had further said: "Forests are the lungs of our land, purifying the air and giving fresh strength to our people".

The above words of Franklin D. Roosevelt are as relevant today as they were when spoken about a century ago; and it is necessary to protect whatever forests that we are now left with and to grow more trees wherever possible. In the context of the dry deciduous forests, which for various reasons were considered dispensable and were subjected to centuries of use, over-use and abuse, and are therefore in very precarious state now, the above words are perhaps even more relevant. These forests are scattered sporadically as oases of some greenery in the midst of the ever-expanding agricultural lands and multitudes of villages and towns. Protection and development of these forests by any means and increasing the tree cover in and around villages and agricultural lands through agroforestry are the only options by which the specter of drought and desertification, already imminent in many parts of the peninsular India, can be contained.

FOREST

What is a forest? It is both easy and difficult to define a forest. The simplest definition perhaps is the one adopted by the Forest department, i.e., any land notified as 'forest' is a forest. This definition is helpful from the point of protecting the lands which the department is mandated to protect and manage. However, what conceptually constitutes a forest is missed out in such a sweeping definition. A simple definition of forest as per Oxford dictionary is: 'A large area covered chiefly with trees and undergrowth.' According to Cambridge dictionary, forest is 'a large area of land with trees and plants, usually larger than a wood, or the trees and plants themselves.' As per Merriam-Webster dictionary, forest is 'a dense growth of trees and underbrush covering a large tract'. The common elements in these definitions are: large area, trees, plants and undergrowth.

Ideally, a normal forest has the following attributes: it has many trees belonging to different genera and species; the trees are of different ages, i.e. each species is represented by seedlings, saplings, poles and trees. In addition to trees, there are other plants such as herbs, shrubs, climbers, lianas, palms, ferns, orchids, grasses, mosses, etc. The trees and other plants along with their root systems occupy different layers of the space above as well as below the ground. A distinct feature of an ideal forest is the forest-floor which is a layer of organic matter just above the soil surface. This layer is made up of fallen or shed vegetative parts like leaves, branches, twigs, bark, stems, flowers, fruits, etc. and left-over body parts of dead animals. These are in different stages of decomposition brought about by the soil-fauna and soil-flora present in the soil. Soil-fauna includes mice, moles, earthworms, ants, beetles, termites, spiders, nematodes, mites, centipedes, springtails, mollusks, protozoa, etc. Soil-flora includes bacteria, archae, fungi, algae, etc. The ultimate product of decomposition of the organic matter is called humus, a protective cushion over the soil surface - a very important component that provides sustainability to a forest ecosystem. A forest is not complete without its terrestrial as well as arboreal inhabitants including mammals, reptiles, amphibians, birds and a very large variety of insects such as bees, beetles, butterflies, cicadas, crickets, dragonflies, grasshoppers, moths, etc.

The type of forest occurring naturally in a given tract of land is dictated primarily by the general climate and soil in the tract. The treatment to which the forest was subjected in the past also influences its present composition as well as status. A number of factors such as rainfall intensity, rainfall distribution, temperature, humidity, incident radiation, wind, altitude, topography, aspect, etc. determine the overall climate of a place. The soil conditions of a locality depend upon a set of factors such as geology, soil formation (*in situ* or *ex situ*), soil maturity, soil structure, soil moisture, etc. Soil-related factors are commonly known as edaphic factors. Past treatment of the forest includes past forest management practices as well as other biotic factors such as shifting cultivation, withdrawals, recurring fires, grazing, etc. All these climatic, edaphic and biotic factors are collectively known as locality factors. The relative dominance of the locality factors varies from place to place. Depending upon the interplay of the prevailing locality factors, different types of forests occur in different areas.

The formation and development of a particular type of forest in a given landscape is however the result of a dynamic evolutionary process called **Succession (see Box)** in which the composition of the plant community keeps

---

SUCCESSION

Forest is a dynamic ecosystem which undergoes constant change as the trees/plants compete with one another for sunlight, water and nutrients. As a result of such competition, one type of plant is replaced by others, and the process continues. This process of replacement of one type of plant by another is called succession. Each stage of succession creates a set of environmental conditions which make it ideal for the establishment of the next stage, and so on. During succession, with the progress of time and change in the environmental conditions, different species of trees/plants become dominant.

Natural succession of forest in the earth, known as primary succession, began after the ice age ended, when ice began to melt in certain parts of the planet and conditions there became warmer. Primary succession usually begins on bare soil or sand where no plants grew before. When the sunlight, moisture and air temperature are just adequate, seeds begin to germinate and grow. The plants which appear first are often made up of mosses, grasses and herbs. They continue to grow and eventually form grasslands. Over

on changing until it attains a stage of stable equilibrium for that specific locality with given climatic and soil conditions. This stage of equilibrium is known as climax stage. In a **climax forest**, trees growing within a particular geographic region essentially remain unchanged in terms of species composition for as long as the site remains undisturbed. When a climax forest is disturbed by external / biotic factors such as shifting cultivation, repeated fires, over grazing, excessive felling, etc., the composition of the forest undergoes change. The resultant forest is known as **secondary forest**. When the composition of a forest is determined mainly by the soil factors or soil conditions, such forest is known as **edaphic forest**. Bamboo brakes (wet soils), Cane brakes (very wet soils), lateritic semi-evergreen forest (lateritic soils), *Hardwickia* forests (shallow hard gravelly soils), *Terminalia tomentosa* forests (heavy soils), etc. are examples of edaphic forests.

India's tropical region, of which Karnataka is a part,

time, and as environmental conditions change and become favorable, other plants such as shrubs and trees begin to grow. These plants become dominant and replace or take over where mosses, grasses or herbs originally grew.

As primary succession continues, pioneer trees begin to thrive. The pioneer trees are light demanding or sun-loving and are intolerant of shade. They quickly take over the grasslands. They change the environment by providing shade. This allows trees with broader leaves that prefer some protection from the sun to take root and establish. These are also called shade-tolerant or shade-bearer trees as they tolerate or bear some shade. If conditions are favorable, a mixed forest of light-demanding and shade-tolerant trees may continue for many years before more changes occur.

Climax forest

Seedlings from pioneer trees do not grow well in shade; therefore, new pioneer trees do not grow. As the mature trees start dying and falling from old age, disease and other causes, the broad leaved shade-tolerant trees become dominant. The shade from these broadleaved trees can also be too dense for their own seedlings. As a result, seedlings from trees which are more and more tolerant of shade begin to thrive and dominate the forest. These trees produce such deep shade that only those trees or plants that can survive in complete shade will succeed. When this happens, the result is a climax forest - one in which certain species of trees characteristic of the ecological conditions of the area are dominant.

Few true climax forests actually exist because forests are dynamic ecosystems and changes take place that interfere with a forest's stability. A climax forest may get destroyed or damaged because of natural or man-made causes such as glacier movements, floods, high winds, volcanic activities, fires, excessive grazing, shifting cultivation, heavy felling, etc. Then the process of succession starts all over again. Such succession is called secondary succession.

Secondary succession

If a climax forest destroyed or damaged due to natural or man-made causes as mentioned above is left alone, it will eventually be covered with trees again. This is called secondary succession. Secondary succession normally takes place more quickly than primary succession. Seeds from neighboring forests are carried to the site due to wind or rain, or through animals. Soon, the seeds take root and seedlings sprout, and the process begins again.

harbors two principal types of forest: **Deciduous forest** and **Evergreen forest**. Before discussing further about these two types of forest, it is necessary to know about the characteristics of deciduous trees and evergreen trees, which respectively constitute the major components of these two types of forest.

Deciduous trees: The word 'deciduous' means 'falling off at maturity' or 'tending to fall off', and it is typically used in order to refer to trees or shrubs that lose their leaves seasonally. In forestry, deciduous trees are those that lose all of their leaves for part of the year. This process is called 'abscission'. Abscission is the shedding of various parts of an organism, such as a plant dropping a leaf, fruit, flower, or seed. It is a natural process of detachment of parts of a plant, typically dead leaves and ripe fruit. In some cases, such as in temperate or polar climates, leaf fall coincides with autumn or winter season. In other parts of the world, including tropical, subtropical and arid regions, plants lose their leaves during dry seasons or other seasons, depending on variations in rainfall. Deciduous trees are predominantly broad-leaved trees. The act of shedding leaves by deciduous trees is usually an adaptation to a cold or dry season. Trees shed leaves in order to conserve water and energy. The period of leaflessness is dependent on the period and degree of dryness in the soil; it also varies from species to species. Certain species shed leaves early whereas in certain species the leaves hold on to trees much longer. Under drought conditions, trees tend to shed leaves earlier than usual.

Evergreen trees: Evergreen trees or plants have leaves throughout the year, and therefore they always remain green. This contrasts with deciduous plants, which completely lose their foliage during the winter or dry season. It however does not mean that evergreen trees do not shed their leaves at all. Evergreen trees do lose leaves, but each tree sheds its leaves gradually and not all at once. In other words, unlike deciduous trees, evergreen trees do not have a distinct period of leaflessness. Evergreens include most species of conifers, most angiosperms from frost-free climates, such as eucalyptus and rain forest trees.

As the names suggest, deciduous forests have preponderance of deciduous trees and evergreen forests are dominated by evergreen trees. However, it is not necessary that all the trees of an evergreen forest are evergreen trees. There are a number of deciduous tree species which are found in evergreen forests. These include *Ailanthus malabarica* (halmaddi), *Cedrela toona* (gandhagarike), *Acrocarpus fraxinifolius* (balanji), *Antiaris toxicaria* (ajjanapatte/karvat), *Xanthoxylum rhetsa* (jummanakai), *Spondias acuminata* (amtekai), *Tetrameles nudiflora* (jarmal), *Bischofia javanica* (neelimara), *Trewia nudiflora* (kat-kumbala/petari), etc. Similarly, there are a number of evergreen trees which are found in deciduous forests. *Santalum album* (sandal/shrigandha) is a typical example of an evergreen tree found in deciduous forests. Evergreen tree species such as *Azadirachta indica* (neem/bevu), *Tamarindus indica* (hunase), *Ixora arborea* (lokhandi), *Pithecellobium dulce* (vilayati hunase), *Thespesia populnea* (bugari/ hoovarasi), *Morinda tinctoria* (maddi), *Erythroxylon monogynum* (devadari/ jivadali/jeemthali), *Mangifera indica* (mavu), *Prosopis juliflora* (Ballari jali), *Trema orientalis* (charcoal tree/kiruhale), *Salvadora persica* (khakhin/ karigoni mara), *Mallotus philippensis* (kumkuma/sinduri), *Syzigium cumini* (neral), *Ficus* species (atthi, ala, goni and others), etc. are quite common in deciduous forests. *Pongamia pinnata* (honge) is an almost evergreen tree found in stream banks of both evergreen and deciduous forests. It is in reality a deciduous tree with a very short period of leaflessness, sometimes just a day or two. Among the *Artocarpus* species which are common in evergreen forests, *Artocarpus lakucha/gomezianus* (watehuli) is deciduous, whereas the other species such as *Artocarpus hirsutus* (hebbalsu) and *Artocarpus heterophyllus* (halasu) are evergreen. In the *Sterculiaceae* family, *Pterygota alata* (kolugida/anathondi/poola) and *Sterculia guttata* (happu savage/kuhimdar) are evergreen species, whereas *Sterculia villosa* (bilidale/savaya/anenar) and *Sterculia foetida* (patala mara/peenari) are deciduous, although all these four species mostly occur in the semi-evergreen and evergreen forests in Karnataka. There are certain species such as *Chukrasia tabularis* (kalgarike/kempudevadar), *Strychnos nux-vomica* (kajra/kaasarka), etc. which are deciduous or evergreen depending upon the environment in which they grow. Some common tree species of deciduous forests such as *Dalbergia latifolia* (beete/sissum), *Saccopetalum tomentosum* (omb), *Acacia nilotica* (jali), *Terminalia arjuna* (holematti), *Buchanania lanzan* (char/nurkal), *Madhuca longifolia* (sanna ippe/hal-tumri), etc. exhibit characteristics of nearly evergreen trees with a very short, or almost negligible, period of leaflessness. Many herbs and shrubs of deciduous forests are evergreen in nature. Similarly, deciduous shrubs are found in evergreen forest also.

Being evergreen or deciduous is an intrinsic quality of a species. However, the natural occurrence of a tree species either in an evergreen forest or in a deciduous forest is not very rigid; it is determined by the interplay of various factors such as rainfall intensity, rainfall distribution, temperature, soil profile, etc. Depending upon these factors, the distribution pattern may change from region to region. It is quite often found that a number of tree species generally associated with evergreen forest in peninsular India are commonly found in the deciduous forests of the North East. *Sterculia villosa, Alstonia scholaris, Tetrameles nudiflora, Aphanamixis polystachya* (*Amoora rohituka*), *Cedrela toona, Chukrasia tabularis*, etc. are examples of such tree species.

Availability of soil moisture (mostly through rainfall) is the primary factor deciding the evergreen or deciduous character of tropical forests. As we move from moister areas to drier areas, evergreen forests give way to deciduous forests. In deciduous forests too, marked change in composition is noticed as we move from dry to drier areas; the proportion of trees with thorny elements (thorns,

> ### *THORNS, SPINES AND PRICKLES*
>
> **Thorn** *is a sharp pointed modified stem;*
>
> **Spine** *is a sharp pointed structure that is a modified leaf or a stipule;*
>
> **Prickle** *is a sharp outgrowth from the epidermis or bark.*
>
> *Thorns and Spines emerge at the nodes of a plant whereas Prickles arise in locations other than the nodes. Prickles can also grow on surface of leaves or fruits.*

spines and prickles) increases. They provide protection from herbivorous intruders thereby ensuring survival and prolonged life of the trees and the forests. They help in conservation of water and energy by reducing evapo-transpiration from trees. **Thorn forests** are important forests in the arid region (*bailuseeme/maidan*) of Karnataka. Many of these forests are remnants of erstwhile deciduous forests which in the past had been subjected to maltreatment due to heavy felling, over-grazing and recurring fires. Such forests in defence tend to throw up more and more thorny species during the secondary succession. These forests have preponderance of species such as *Acacia nilotica* (babul/karijali/gobli), *Acacia catechu* (khair/cutch/kaggli), *Acacia latronum* (hottejali), *Acacia leucophloea* (bilijali), *Acacia ferruginea* (banni), *Acacia chundra* (kempujali), *Zizyphus jujuba* (bore), *Zizyphus xylopyrus* (gotte), *Randia dumetorum* (kare), *Dichrostachys cinerea* (wadu), *Capparis divaricata* (thottala/mullippi), *Capparis decidua* (karina), *Pterolobium hexapetalum* (baadubakka/kabala mullu), *Gymnosporia spinosa* (tandrasi), *Euphorbia* species (kalli), etc. *Opuntia* species (cacti) has naturalized in some of the highly degraded sites.

In view of certain discernible characteristics including floristic composition, rainfall and soil quality, the three types of forest mentioned above, namely, the evergreen, deciduous and thorn forests are re-classified into five categories: The deciduous forest is bifurcated into **moist deciduous forest** and **dry deciduous forest**. An intermediate zone between the evergreen forest and the moist deciduous forest is identified as **semi-evergreen forest**.

The upper storey of a **semi-evergreen forest** comprises an intimate mixture of species drawn from both evergreen and deciduous forests. The lower storey is generally dominated by evergreen species. An upper storey of a typical semi-evergreen forest will have trees such as *Terminalia paniculata, Lagerstroemia lanceolata, Dalbergia latifolia, Xylia xylocarpa,* etc. (drawn from deciduous forest) intermixed with trees such as *Hopea parviflora, Artocarpus hirsutus, Machilus macrantha, Cinnamomum* species, etc. (drawn from evergreen forest.) A semi-evergreen forest normally comes up in an area where the rainfall is somewhat intermediate between the rainfall received in an evergreen forest and the rainfall received in a deciduous forest.

The categorization of the deciduous forest into **moist deciduous forest** and **dry deciduous forest** is primarily because of difference in rainfall received and prevailing soil conditions. In the Western Ghats region, the species composition of both moist and dry deciduous forests is more or less the same, although predominance or rarity of certain species may be noticeable. By and large, the trees of a moist deciduous forest attain fairly large size; some of the characteristic species of these forests such as *Tectona grandis, Dalbergia latifolia, Pterocarpus marsupium, Adina cordifolia,* etc. attain girth up to about 5 m (15 feet). Other characteristic species such as

Terminalia paniculata, Terminalia tomentosa, Lagerstroemia lanceolata, etc. attain girth up to about 2.5 - 4 m (8-12 feet). In a dry deciduous forest, the same tree species normally do not attain a girth beyond 1.2 m (4 feet).

The floristic composition of a dry deciduous forest met with in the Eastern Plains of Karnataka (*maidan* region) is somewhat different from that of the dry deciduous forest of the Western Ghats region, although some species such as *Terminalia tomentosa, Anogeissus latifolia*, etc. are found in both these regions. Species such as *Hardwickia binata, Chloroxylon swietenia, Albizia amara*, etc. are more predominant in the dry deciduous forests of the *maidan* region.

The most important factor responsible for the occurrence of a particular type of climatic climax forest in a given area is the average annual rainfall received by the area. The typical rainfall limits indicated by Champion and Seth for the occurrence of the five principal climatic climax forest types are: Evergreen forest (above 300 cm); Semi-evergreen forest (200 cm - 300 cm); Moist deciduous forest (150 cm – 200 cm); Dry deciduous forest (100 cm – 130 cm); and Thorn forest (50 cm – 85 cm). However, the above limits of rainfall are not sacrosanct. Two other factors also have some bearing on the formation of these forests: (a) Distribution of rainfall; and (b) Quality of soil. In case the rainfall is uniformly distributed throughout the rainy season, the lower rainfall limit can go further down to sustain a particular type of forest. For example, with well distributed rainfall, an area receiving 75 cm can harbor a dry deciduous forest. An area with very good soil may harbor a moister forest even with a lower rainfall limit. For example, under excellent soil conditions evergreen forest can occur even with a rainfall of 150 cm. In case of poor soil, the upper rainfall limit for sustaining a particular forest type may go up. For example, in highly degraded soil, dry deciduous forest may occur in areas receiving as high rainfall as, say 190 cm.

In certain situations, altitude (temperature) also plays a decisive role in the formation of a particular type of climax forest. For example, at an altitude of about 1,000 m and above in the Western Ghats region, the climax evergreen forest changes to a special type of climax forest popularly known as *Shola* forest, also referred to as 'stunted rain forest' - a dense, close-canopy evergreen forest with trees of relatively smaller size.

Such forest harbors a large number of tree species drawn mainly from the tropical evergreen forests with a few species drawn from the temperate forests of the Himalayan region.

The southernmost district of the state, namely, Chamarajanagar presents itself as an interesting example of how altitude influences the occurrence of a climax forest. This district, where the Western Ghats converge with the Eastern Ghats, receives fairly low rainfall as compared with the Western Ghats region proper that receives high to very high rainfall of 200 to 300 cm and above. The annual average rainfall in Chamarajanagar district is about 80 cm; at higher elevations, precipitation is more but does not exceed about 150 cm. The district mostly harbors dry deciduous forests with some scrub forests in the eastern part. However, other climax formations also start appearing at higher elevations: moist deciduous forests at an altitude above 900 m, climax evergreen forests between 1200 m and 1400 m, and *Shola* evergreen forests above 1,400 m. It may be noted that, while in the Western Ghats region proper the *Shola* vegetation starts appearing from 1,000 m and above, its occurrence in the Chamarajanagar district situated in the eastern edge of the Western Ghats begins from an elevation of about 1,400 m upward.

Evergreen forest versus Semi-evergreen forest

We have earlier mentioned that an evergreen forest primarily harbors evergreen trees along with some deciduous trees. We have also mentioned that a semi-evergreen forest harbors both evergreen and deciduous trees. However, there is some difference between the deciduous trees of an evergreen forest and the deciduous trees of a semi-evergreen forest. The deciduous trees of a semi-evergreen forest are primarily drawn from the adjoining deciduous forest, e.g. *Terminalia paniculata* (kindal/hunal), *Lagerstroemia lanceolata* (nandi/nana), *Dalbergia latifolia* (beete/sissum), *Xylia xylocarpa* (jamba), etc. On the other hand, the deciduous trees of an evergreen forest are naturally growing trees of the tract, e.g. *Ailanthus malabarica* (halmaddi), *Cedrela toona* (gandhagarike), *Acrocarpus fraxinifolius* (balanji/havalgi), *Antiaris toxicaria* (ajjanapatte/karvat), etc. Some of the deciduous trees of the evergreen forest may occur in the semi-evergreen forest also; but the deciduous trees occurring in the semi-evergreen forest that are drawn from a deciduous forest are usually not met with in the evergreen forest. The proportion of deciduous trees in an evergreen forest is rather small, say, about 5-10%. The proportion of deciduous trees in a semi-evergreen forest is relatively higher, say 30-40%, or even more.

Light demander trees and Shade tolerant or Shade bearer trees

In forestry, the terms 'light demander' and 'shade tolerant' or 'shade bearer' are often used to indicate the preferences of trees/plants in terms of their light requirement. As sunlight is the principal source of energy for growth, trees/plants necessarily need sunlight. However, during the initial stage of their lives, certain species may show preference for sheltered light or tolerance to shade. By and large, most of the evergreen tree species in their younger stage prefer sheltered light or tolerate partial shade. As a matter of fact, these species exhibit extremely high degree of shade tolerance. In the evergreen zone, the density of seedlings or saplings is quite high; they occupy substantial portions of the ground floor. As and when an opening is created in the forest due to tree fall, snapping of a branch, or the neighboring deciduous tree shedding its leaves, there is intense competition among the seedlings/saplings growing underneath, and some of them gain height to occupy the vacant vertical space. The unsuccessful ones wait for another opportunity. In this way, the dynamic growth process of the forest is continued.

In deciduous forest, most of the tree species are usually strong or moderate light demanders, although there are some species which in the seedling or sapling stage prefer sheltered light or tolerate partial shade. *Dalbergia latifolia* (beete/sissum/rosewood), *Lagerstroemia lanceolata* (nandi/nana), *Xylia xylocarpa* (jamba), *Terminalia paniculata* (kindal/hunal), *Santalum album* (shrigandha/sandal), etc. are examples of tree species of the deciduous zone which show some degree of preference for, or tolerance to, partial shade during their initial phase of growth. However, they generally require full overhead light beyond sapling or pole stage. The tree species occurring in the thorn forests are usually strong light demanders.

Most of the evergreen tree species regenerate from seeds. The seeds usually remain viable for shorter periods. For effective germination and initial growth, the seeds prefer a forest floor which is rich in humus. As already mentioned, seedlings and saplings in the evergreen forest either prefer sheltered light or tolerate partial shade, and they have tremendous patience and tenacity to wait for their turn to grow up. These conditions are generally met with in a normal evergreen forest thereby ensuring regeneration and growth of the existing forest in perpetuity. The moment such a forest is opened up and exposed to biotic disturbances, the local conditions of the opened-up area change drastically due to over-exposure to light and heat; the soil surface rich in humus soon gets drained and impoverished as a result of heavy rainfall, which is common in these areas. Removal of forest cover is soon followed by permanent drop in fertility. The conditions obtaining in such exposed and disturbed areas are not conducive to regeneration of the existing tree species. Such areas are quickly invaded by light demanding weeds and shrubs. Colonizing tree species such as *Macaranga peltata* (uptige/chandoda), *Macaranga indica* (bettadavare/holenekki), *Trema orientalis* (kiruhale/home/charcoal tree), *Mallotus philippensis* (kumkuma), *Mallotus tetracoccus* (kukbuta), *Debregeasia longifoila* (kurigele), *Callicarpa tomentosa* (towdatti/mardi/kanphulia), etc. often appear in such cleared and disturbed evergreen forests.

A large number of tree species from the deciduous zone coppice well, some of them very vigorously. Coppicing refers to the phenomenon of production of new shoots from the stump of a tree after the tree is felled. In the deciduous zone, coppicing is an additional means of propagation of many tree species, notably the hardwood species. Besides, the seeds of tree species of deciduous forest generally remain viable for a relatively longer period compared with the seeds of tree species of evergreen forest. As a result, in a deciduous forest the tenacity of the trees to perpetuate is higher. On the other hand, most of the evergreen species do not coppice at all, or they coppice poorly. Besides, as already mentioned seeds of evergreen species remain viable for short periods and they have difficulty in germinating and growing up in sunny positions and exposed or disturbed environment. These adverse conditions make the evergreen forest extremely vulnerable to human intervention and interference. Once an evergreen forest is disturbed or opened up, it is very difficult, at times almost impossible, to restore its original status.

Although deciduous forests have the tenacity and resilience to perpetuate on account of a number of favorable factors such as coppicing vigor of many of their constituent species, relatively longer viability of their seeds, and light demanding nature of most of the species, these forests face challenges of a different kind. They have been subjected to higher degree of interventions and interferences because of their proximity to habitations, and the economic importance of their constituent trees as source of valuable timber, including teak, rosewood and many other hardwood species, and excellent fuel wood. More often than not, these forests are subjected to heavy withdrawals; they also suffer from excessive grazing, recurring fires, and large-scale encroachments for extension of cultivation and settlements. Repeated onslaughts on our deciduous forests for many years have resulted in their decimation or, where they have been spared, in the formation of what are collectively known as **scrub forests** that harbor some stunted and malformed specimens of the original forest with an increasing preponderance of thorny elements.

HEALTH OF A FOREST

Forests are one of the most complex ecosystems in the world. In the previous article (**Annexure-I**) we have discussed various components of a forest, briefly highlighting the main types of forest met with in the tropical region. We have seen that a forest ecosystem comprises both plants and animals which occupy different layers of the ecosystem. In addition to trees belonging to different genera and species, the plant community of a forest ecosystem comprises varieties of shrubs, herbs, climbers, lianas, palms, ferns, orchids, grasses, mosses, etc. In some forests trees themselves occupy two or three layers below which there is a layer of shrubs. Underneath the shrubs, there is a layer of herbs and ferns, and then a ground layer covered with grasses, lichens, mosses, etc. We have also mentioned about humus, a layer of organic matter overlying mineral soil that functions as a protective cushion over the soil surface, providing sustainability to a forest ecosystem. The faunal diversity of a forest ecosystem is also very wide comprising mammals, reptiles, amphibians, birds, nematodes, centipedes, mites, mollusks, springtails, and a very large variety of insects such as ants, bees, beetles, butterflies, cicadas, crickets, dragonflies, grasshoppers, moths, spiders, termites, etc.

Each constituent of a forest ecosystem plays definite role to keep the ecosystem healthy or robust. In this article, we will highlight the characteristics of a healthy forest ecosystem.

Trees belonging to various genera and species constitute the largest segment of a forest. They together with their root systems occupy the maximum space above as well as below the ground. In a healthy forest, there is a distinct pattern in which trees of different age-classes are distributed: the number of trees with the highest age class (or diameter class) is the least and the number of trees with the lowest age class (seedlings) is the highest. With increase in age, the number of trees decreases, as depicted in the following graph:

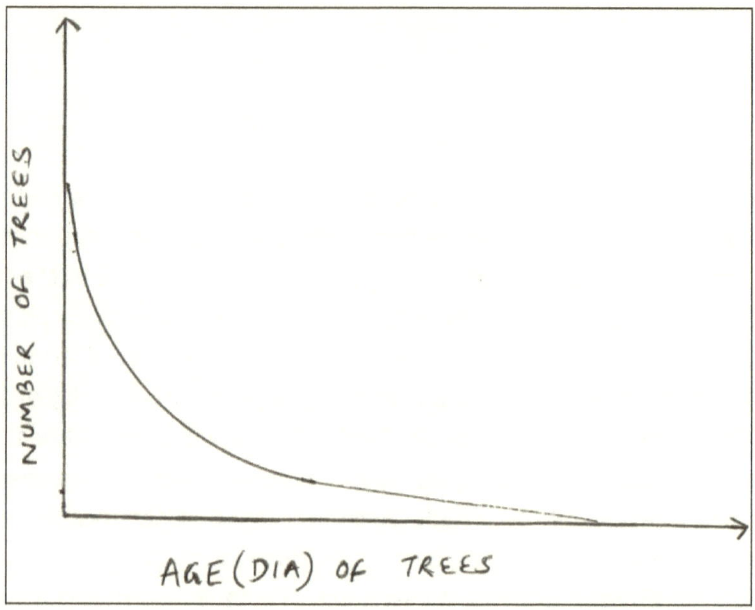

The presence of trees of difference age classes makes it possible to accommodate more number of trees in a given area. In such a scenario, trees of different age classes (along with their root systems) occupy different levels both above and below the ground and a state of dynamic equilibrium is achieved with optimum utilization of available resources (light, water and nutrition). The number of trees per unit area in such a forest depends upon factors such as rainfall, soil, drainage, etc. The number is high in the evergreen forest which has high carrying capacity, being favored with high rainfall and good quality soil. This number gradually comes down as we move to relatively drier forests such as semi-evergreen, moist deciduous, dry deciduous, thorn forest, etc., in that sequence.

The tendency of every tree species to have more members in the younger age classes is a tendency dictated by nature in order to ensure perpetuation of the species. This tendency of having more offspring is exhibited by all living organisms which are not favored with any artificial life-saving or life-enhancing means. Even human beings in the distant past had exhibited this inherent tendency. About a hundred years ago, it was quite common for a man and his wife to have about a dozen children; this figure came down to about half a dozen about 50 years ago, and has come down further to one or two children in the present days. In a community of trees, seedlings and younger trees, which occupy the lower levels of the forest starting from the ground floor, keep on competing with the seedlings and trees of similar age for gaining height and moving to the next higher level. Whenever an opening is created because of a tree fall or snapping of a branch or any other reason, a few of the vigorous younger trees and seedlings take advantage and shoot up to occupy the vacant spaces created overhead. In this way some of the more vigorous among the younger trees and seedlings keep on growing up in the forest. As the older trees start dying and falling, the younger ones keep on occupying the space vacated by them. By having progressively more number of trees in the younger age classes, nature ensures that the most vigorous among the competitors get promoted to the next higher level. This naturally induced competition results in the formation of a forest stand with healthy members at different age groups, leading to a healthy forest.

For a forest to remain perpetually healthy, it is necessary that the youngest members of the tree community, i.e. the seedlings should not only be numerous but they should also be safe and healthy. Any biotic activity that affects the life and health of the seedlings adversely affects the health of the forest. For example, when there is a fire in a forest, most of the seedlings get burnt; this is in addition to the burning of the humus along with the seeds on the forest floor. Poles and trees may survive the fire, although many among them get injured and impaired. If a forest is subjected to repeated fires, year after year, it not only becomes bereft of seedlings and saplings but is also populated by an increasing number of poorly grown and malformed poles and trees. Such a community of trees is like a community of human beings without any children and comprising only adult members many of whom are also sick. Such a community is destined to become extinct in due course of time. Similarly, a forest repeatedly ravaged by fire is doomed to extinction.

Over-grazing of forest by domestic animals also has a devastating impact on forest, as large numbers of seedlings get physically damaged by browsing, trampling (action of the hooves of the cattle) and also due to the compaction of soil. Degradation of a forest situated near a village or a town is mostly caused by fire and over-grazing. In addition, if there is excessive withdrawal of biomass from the forest, the degradation becomes more rapid.

Due to repeated fires, over-grazing by domestic cattle and heavy/ unregulated felling of trees, the over-exposed, scarred and battered forest floor loses substantial quantities of soil during the following monsoon. This leads to impoverishment of the soil mantle of the forest which is no longer in a position to sustain the original tree species of the terrain and these are replaced by a different set of hardier species that are capable of thriving on the degraded tract. A climax forest thus gets transformed into a secondary forest. If at this stage, the causes of degradation such as fire, grazing, heavy withdrawal, etc. are withdrawn or brought under control, the degradation stops or slows down and the forest may show signs of recovery/rejuvenation although it is normally difficult for the forest to revert to its pristine state, as recovery of the soil mantle to its original state is very unlikely. Such a forest is often said to have reached a stage of sub-climax. If, on the other hand, the causes responsible for degradation continue to affect the forest without any let up, further degradation takes place and the forest transforms into what is known as degradation stage (DS), also known as scrub forest. Further degradation of a scrub forest leads to formation of savannah (grassland dotted here and there with a few small and stunted trees), and then to pure grassland which is completely bereft of trees. At times, degradation can be so severe that the area may be fully stripped of its soil, exposing the underlying rocks and boulders.

Shrubs, herbs, climbers, lianas, ferns, etc. play a very important role in a forest eco-system. Shrubs, herbs, ferns, grasses, selaginella, mosses, etc. occupy certain areas of the forest floor that are not occupied or not required by trees and prevent such areas from exposure that may lead to loss of soil and fertility. Areas not accessible to or not suitable for tree species are occupied by such plants. A shrub or herb has an inherent tendency to quickly occupy vacant land, as is exemplified by invasion of such species the moment a forest is cleared or an opening is created within it. This is primarily the nature's defense response mechanism to protect the soil in order to perpetuate the forest eco-system. Shrubs, herbs and other smaller plants also help in the retention of moisture in the soil for longer duration. This improves the humidity of the forest; humidity helps in reducing evaporation and in raising temperature within the forest facilitating growth.

Climbers, lianas, etc. in their pursuit of light move up, leaf by leaf, with the support of the nearby trees, and fill up the vacant spaces in the forest canopy. As a result, the canopy becomes almost continuous and becomes more effective in moderating temperature and humidity of the forest, and in intercepting rainfall and in regulating stem-flow, thereby slowing down the force of rain water on the ground and enabling its better absorption into the soil. Climbers and lianas contribute substantially to canopy closure after tree fall and help to stabilize the microclimate underneath. They also provide connectivity among tree canopies facilitating arboreal animals to traverse the tree tops. Leaves, flowers, fruits and seeds of the herbs, shrubs, climbers, lianas, etc. provide food to animals including birds and insects, which also instinctively obtain natural remedies against ailments from these plants. Many herbs, shrubs, climbers and other plants provide medicines for human use as well.

In a forest ecosystem, the smaller plants like shrubs, herbs, climbers, lianas, ferns, orchids, grasses, mosses, etc. numerically constitute a much larger group than the trees. However, the trees because of their sheer size occupy a very large portion of the ecosystem; the other members of the plant community, being generally small or minute in size, occupy a small space in the ecosystem. In a normal undisturbed forest, there is a natural balance among its various constituents. The horizontal as well as vertical space of such a forest is naturally apportioned among these constituents in proportions determined mainly by climatic and soil factors. In general, the combined volume of the trees is much larger compared with the combined volume of the remaining plants. The ratio between the combined volume of trees to the combined volume of all other plants generally tapers down as we move from moister forest types to the drier forest types. This is primarily because the drier forests, being relatively more open than the moister forests, allow penetration of more sunlight to the forest floor which favors varieties of shrubs, herbs and other smaller plants to thrive and propagate. By and large, a typical wet evergreen forest has relatively fewer shrubs, herbs and climbers. In such a forest, substantial portion of the undergrowth consists of dense vegetation of seedlings and saplings of the existing tree species. It is mostly the natural openings such as banks of streams and edges of ponds within the evergreen forest that harbor some shrubs, herbs, climbers, etc. The number of herbs, shrubs, climbers, etc. rises in a disturbed evergreen forest, where species from the semi-evergreen forest or even from the deciduous forest start making inroads.

The number of herbs, shrubs and climbers is fairly high in a deciduous forest. In scrub forest, poor quality soil and deficient rainfall restrict the number of plants that a given area can sustain. In these forests, however, there is no distinct difference between a tree and a shrub. Many species which are considered as shrubs in a normal deciduous forest sometimes become the most important constituents in a scrub forest. Various species of shrubs or climbers such as *Cassia auriculata* (tangadi/tarwad), *Dodonaea viscosa* (bandurki), *Pterolobium indicum* (travelers' terror/badabakke), *Randia dumetorum* (kare), *Zizyphus xylopyrus* (gotte), *Lantana camara* (chadurangi/lantana), etc. zealously guard many of our degraded dry deciduous and scrub forests that are in the verge of extinction. It is primarily due to the tenacity of these hardy minor plants that the soil mantle of these forests has been saved from disappearance. In extreme cases, it is only the grasses that hold the fort and protect the soil.

Due to anthropogenic pressures, the natural balance of a forest ecosystem often gets upset resulting in skewed distribution of the constituents. Clearing of forest for agriculture and other purposes, logging and other forestry operations including plantations, illicit felling, over-grazing, fire, etc. are various forms of anthropogenic pressures that result in upsetting the natural balance of a forest ecosystem. Over-grazing and recurring fires have been the principal causes for the preponderance of invasive shrubs such as *Lantana* and *Eupatorium* in our forests. The widespread advent of *Lantana* in our deciduous forests is attributed to the system of early burning that was introduced during the last century in order to keep the menace of forest-fire under control. There is perceptible increase of *Randia* and *Zizyphus* in most of our relatively better deciduous forests including the protected areas which had been worked in the past but had not received adequate attention in terms of follow-up tending and cultural operations besides rigid protection from biotic pressures. *Perthenium* has made inroads into the tourism areas of a number of national parks and wildlife sanctuaries, besides the reserved forests. The *Shola* grasslands that are repeatedly run over by fire have been invaded by *Pteridium aquilinium*, a very hardy and invasive fern of disrepute (it is said to be carcinogenic) which is extremely difficult to get rid of.

In the technical documents of the Forest Department such as working plans, management plans, etc., except for making occasional references about the presence of a few shrubs, herbs, climbers, grasses, etc. sufficient information about the ecological aspects of these minor and minute plants is not provided unless these are economically or medicinally very important. Most of the forestry research and studies carried out under the oversight of the Department are primarily tree-centric or species-centric. There is need for increased focus on ecological research and studies of our forests. There is need for scientific and systematic documentation of the existing flora and fauna. Even now, we do not have complete details of all the species available in our forests. Our present method of documentation of a limited number of tree species for the entire forest division in the working plan should give way to comprehensive study of the floral diversity of each and every state forest. Such study should invariably encompass the ecological aspects of the smaller plants. Such scientific and systematic studies will form the basis of further studies on forest ecosystems and research on forest ecology.

FOREST ENCROACHMENT

People have been dependent on forest since ages. This dependence was perhaps total in the beginning when they obtained all their requirements including food from forest. As the need for more food grew, people started cultivating food crops on forest land on a temporary or cyclic basis – a system that continues even today in some pockets of forest and is known as shifting cultivation. With the introduction of settled agriculture, people's dependence on forest for food gradually came down; but it came at a heavy price – loss of forest land for cultivation. While forest was lost temporarily under shifting cultivation, it was lost forever under settled agriculture. For centuries, as human population increased, more and more forest lands were cleared for taking up agriculture and settlements. Clearance of forest land for cultivation was encouraged by the rulers too, as it provided avenues for collecting more land revenue. The British Indian administration encouraged clearance of forest for similar reasons. They also encouraged plantation crops in addition to cereal crops, which put more demand on forest land. They adopted a forest policy in which forest had no intrinsic right over land and agriculture was given precedence over forestry. The policy of encouraging agriculture over forestry continued even after India attained Independence. In view of severe shortages of food grains against a steadily rising population, the Government had no option but to take all necessary steps to maximize production of food grains for the people, and large chunks of forest lands were released for agriculture, under the "Grow More Food" campaign. Besides, diversion of forest land for other development purposes continued quite liberally until the enactment of the Forest (Conservation) Act in 1980, which slowed down the unabated loss of forest because of imposition of strict restrictions/regulations on diversion of forest land.

While pressure on forest land for being diverted for non forest purposes through official/legal channel has drastically come down with the enactment of the Forest (Conservation) Act, 1980, hunger for land continues and is reflected in acts of **forest encroachment** for cultivation, housing, etc. Such unauthorized acts are quite common in forest areas adjacent to habitations such as villages, townships, etc. Eviction of fresh forest encroachment is a relatively easy task, but if the encroachment is not detected immediately, its eviction at a later date becomes very cumbersome, as the encroacher progressively develops a stake in the land by making more and more investment. Encroachers, especially those extending cultivation, tend to garner support from various influential quarters and this makes the Forest department's task even more difficult. Encroachment of forest land near the limits of Bengaluru city for obvious real estate purpose is a matter of serious concern. While encroachment of forest land covered with tree growth is immediately detectable, the same is not true in respect of forest lands which have remained barren for a long time, unless the field level functionaries are quite conversant with the forest boundaries and are extremely vigilant. In many cases, revenue records do not properly reflect the forest status of the land which results in wrongful land grant and protracted litigation. Protection of forest land from permanent loss is the most important duty of any forest officer. While a degraded forest land can be restored to its original glory, it is very difficult to retrieve a parcel of forest land lost to encroachment or wrongful grant; at times it becomes a permanent loss. Officers of the Forest department of Karnataka are empowered under Sections 24 and 64A of the Karnataka Forest Act, 1963 to take appropriate legal action against forest encroachers.

It must however be conceded that in spite of the legal provisions in Acts and Rules, it has not always been possible for the Forest departments to control or evict forest encroachments. Although forest encroachment is an offence in the eyes of law, for a number of historical reasons, it was not treated on par with other criminal offences such as theft or robbery.

The general perception is that encroachment of forest is done by the poorest of the poor or the neediest of the needy out of dire necessity for cultivation to make a living or for the purpose of dwelling. As already mentioned, progress of human civilization from the nomadic phase to the phase of settled agriculture came about with the sacrifice of huge chunks of forest land. In the past, people were encouraged to open up forest areas so that more and more land could be brought under the plough. Not long ago, clearing forest area for the purpose of developing agriculture was considered a revolutionary or heroic act. Award-winning novels had been written eulogizing the act of clearing forest for agriculture for the poor and needy: the protagonist leads the villagers to clear the nearby forest and the DFO and the DSP confronting them are depicted as villains!

Since clearance of forest for agriculture is an ancient practice, and as the Acts and Rules framed for protecting forest from encroachment came much later, there has always been conflict between the rule of law and people's perception of forest-clearance for subsistence living, often perceived as birth-right. In view of this inherent conflict, attempt to evict encroachment by the authority is stiffly resisted by the encroachers who generally have the support and sympathy from various sections of the society, including political leaders with vested interests. In the past, encroachments of all types of government lands for dwelling and for extension of cultivation were regularized by the governments from time to time. As a result, such an act was considered normal and inoffensive, and this had emboldened the people to encroach more and more lands, hoping for regularization at a future date. The practice of regularizing encroachment of non-forest (revenue) land is in vogue even today. As regards forest lands, the Karnataka Government in 1974 had amended section 28 of the Karnataka Forest Act, 1963 and empowered only the two Houses of the State Legislature to de-reserve a reserved forest or any portion thereof (Act 23 of 1974). Earlier, it was possible to de-reserve any forest land by a simple government notification. The Act was further amended in 1978 (Act 15 of 1978) categorically stipulating that regularization of encroachment taking place after 27-04-1978 must have the approval of the State Legislature. This made the process of regularization of forest encroachments difficult. At the national level, the enactment of the Forest (Conservation) Act, 1980 and the promulgation of the National Forest Policy, 1988 put a brake to the earlier practice of regularizing forest encroachments.

According to information provided by the Ministry of Environment and Forests (MoEF), about 4.3 million hectares of forest land have been diverted for various purposes between 1951 and 1980, and more than half of it (2.623 million hectares) was diverted for agriculture. It has also been pointed out that 'the decisions of the State Governments to regularize encroachments from time to time seem to have acted as strong inducement for further encroachments in forest areas and the problem remained as elusive as ever for want of effective and concerted drive against this evil practice'.

The policy and legal position on encroachments is briefly stated below:

1. Encroachment of forest land is prohibited under Section 26 (h) of the Indian Forest Act, 1927. Similar provisions have been made in the state Forest Acts that have been formulated by some of the states in the country. As already mentioned, in Karnataka, Sections 24 and 64A of the Karnataka Forest Act, 1963 provide for legal action against forest encroachers.

2. The Forest (Conservation) Act, 1980 forbids regularisation of encroachments. The Act has provided for regularisation of pre-1980 encroachments and prohibited post-1980 encroachments. The regularisation of pre-1980 encroachments has been allowed under certain specific conditions.

3. The National Forest Policy, 1988 has stated that "4.8.1 Encroachment on forest lands has been on the increase. This trend has to be arrested and effective action taken to prevent its continuance. There should be no regularisation of existing encroachments."

Pursuant to the stated policy and legal position regarding encroachment of forest land, the Ministry of Environment and Forests, Government of India issued guidelines to the States/Union Territories vide communication No.13.1/90-FP.(1) dated 18-09-1990. Salient points of the guidelines are as follows:

All the cases of subsisting encroachments where the State Government stands committed to regularize on account of past commitments may be submitted to the Ministry of Environment and Forests for seeking prior approval under the Forest (Conservation) Act, 1980. Such proposal should invariably conform to the criteria given below:

Pre-1980 encroachments where the State Governments had taken a decision before enactment of the Forest (Conservation) Act, 1980, to regularize "ELIGIBLE" category of encroachments

Such cases are those where the State Governments had evolved certain eligible criteria in accordance with local needs and conditions and had taken a decision to regularize such encroachments but could not implement their decision either wholly or partially before the enactment of the Forest (Conservation) Act, on 25-10-1980; (b) all such cases should be individually reviewed. For this purpose the State Governments may appoint a joint team of the Revenue, Forest and Tribal Welfare for this work and complete it as a time-bound programme; (c) In cases where proposals are yet to be formulated, the final picture after taking into considerations all the stipulations specified here may be placed before the concerned Gaon Sabha with a view to avoid disputes in future; (d) All encroached lands proposed for regularization should be properly surveyed; (e) Encroachments proposed to be regularized must have taken place before 25-10-1980. This must be ascertained from the First Offence issued under the relevant Forest Act at that point of time; (f) Encroachments must subsist on the field and the encroached land must be under continuous possession; (g) The encroacher must be eligible to avail the benefits of regularization as per the eligibility criteria already fixed by the State; (h) As far as possible scattered encroachments proposed to be regularized should be consolidated/relocated near the outer boundaries of the forests; (i) The outer boundaries of the areas to be de-notified for regularization of encroachments should be demarcated on the ground with permanent boundary marks; (j) All the cases proposed to be regularized under this category should be covered in one proposal and it should give district-wise details; (k) All cases of proposed regularization of encroachments should be accompanied by a proposal for compensatory afforestation as per existing guidelines; (l) No agricultural operations should be allowed on certain specified slopes.

"INELIGIBLE" category of pre-1980 encroachments where the State Governments had taken a decision prior to the enactment of the Forest (Conservation) Act, 1980

Such cases should be treated at par with post 1980 encroachments and should not be regularized.

Encroachments that took place after 25-10-1980

In no case encroachments which have taken place after 24-01-1980 should be regularised. Immediate actions should be taken to evict the encroachments. The State/Union Territory Government may, however, provide alternate economic base to such persons by associating them collectively in afforestation activities in the manner suggested in letter No. 6-21/FP-89 dated 01-06-1990 of the Ministry of Environment and Forests, but such benefits should not extend to fresh encroachers.

Consequent upon the issue of the above guidelines from the Ministry of Environment and Forests, a number of State Governments, including Karnataka, submitted proposals of pre-1980 encroachments to the Ministry (MoEF) for approval of regularisation. In 1995, Karnataka submitted a proposal for regularization of 17,007.23 hectares of forest encroachment, stating that this was the extent of encroachment in 21,569 cases of diversion of forest land for non-forest purposes, and that the encroachments occurred prior to 27-04-1978. This date of 27-04-1978 had become the cut-off date in respect of Karnataka in view of the fact that the State had amended the Karnataka Forest Act in 1978 (Act 15 of 1978) categorically stipulating that regularization of encroachment taking place after 27-04-1978 must have the approval of the State Legislature. Out of the above 17,007.23 hectares of forest encroachment, the Union Government allowed regularization of 14,848.83 hectares, subject to certain conditions. Only land encroached by persons belonging to SC/STs, landless marginal farm laborers, and those with small holdings (less than 1.2 ha) could be regularized. It was also stipulated that encroachments in the midst of forest area, steep slopes, or in wildlife sanctuaries, and national parks would not be regularized. Similar proposals for regularization of forest encroachments had been received by the MoEF from other States such as Madhya Pradesh, Gujarat, Kerala, Andhra Pradesh and Andaman and Nicobar Islands, and approval for regularization of eligible cases had been accorded subject to certain conditions. As of November 15, 2002, MoEF had accorded approval of regularization of 2,58,171 hectares of forest encroachments.

However, the problem of forest encroachment continued to dog the country as the State Governments / Forest Departments have not been able to evict the encroachments which were found to be ineligible for regularization as per the 18-09-1990 guidelines issued by the MoEF. The general complaint against the State Governments / Forest Departments has been that while sending proposals for regularization of encroachments to the Government of India, many eligible / deserving cases had been left out and these need to be reviewed before any action could be taken to evict the ineligible encroachers. This view was by and large supported by various sections of the society who, for one reason or the other, were sympathetic to the encroachers and did not want them to be evicted.

The Hon'ble Supreme Court of India in their order dated 23-11-2001 on IA No. 703 in Writ Petition No. 202/95 had restrained the Central Government from regularization of encroachments on forest lands in the country without the leave of the Court. The Writ Petition had challenged the decimation of forests taking place on account of large-scale encroachments on forest lands. The petitioner had contended that such encroachments were rampant particularly in the States of Orissa, West Bengal, Karnataka, Tamil Nadu, Assam, Maharashtra, Madhya Pradesh, Chhattisgarh, Kerala and the union territory of Andaman and Nicobar Islands (A&N).

Subsequent to the above order of the Hon'ble Supreme Court, the Ministry of Environment and Forests issued a directive to the State Governments on 03-05-2002 to evict the ineligible encroachers and all post-1980 encroachers from forest lands in a time-bound manner. The letter to the State Governments also indicated that as per the information received from various States, approximately 12.50 lakh hectares of forest land were under encroachment. It was further added that there may be many more unrecorded instances which would add to the overall tally.

A number of reasons are attributed to the inability of the State Governments in evicting the ineligible encroachments. The grassroots and mass organisations are fully aware of the fact that vast majority of the people who have been found to be ineligible for regularisation of forest encroachments are small farmers and agriculturists and they will suffer the most in the eventuality of eviction. There is a groundswell of sympathy for these people not only from political leaders with vested interests but also from the intelligentsia, activists, press, media, etc. who look at the problem of forest encroachment as a social issue, and tend to ignore the adverse impact of ecological or environmental disaster arising from loss, degradation or honey-combing of forest. They also generally ignore or avoid highlighting the true and legal aspects of the problem; emotive issues are blown out of proportions.

However, the most important reason that came in the way of implementation of the MoEF guidelines dated 18-09-1990 and MoEF directive dated 03-05-2002 regarding eviction of ineligible pre-1980 and post-1980 forest encroachment cases has been the perception, that these guidelines/directive have not taken into account the traditional rights of the tribal people who have been living in the forests since ages, and whose traditional rights have not been settled in spite of the guidelines issued on 18-09-1990 by the MoEF regarding Forest-Tribal interface. It is true that on 18-09-1990, the Ministry of Environment and Forests had issued, in addition to the guidelines regarding eviction of forest encroachments, a set of separate guidelines involving Forest-Tribal Interface; one of these guidelines was with regard to settlement of disputed claims of tribals. It is also true that the MoEF, vide another letter dated 30-10-2002, had reiterated the Ministry's commitment to the settlement of tribal rights and requested the State Governments/UT Administrations to consider the settlement of disputed claims of tribals over forest lands and set up Commission/ Committees at the district levels involving the Revenue, Forest and Tribal Welfare Departments for the settlement of disputed claims of tribals and forest dwellers. The contention of various groups supporting the cause of the tribals, including the National Commission on Scheduled Castes and Scheduled Tribes, has been that the State Governments have not implemented the MoEF guidelines of 18-09-1990 which were supposed to provide a framework to resolve the problem of settlement of rights of tribals and other forest dwellers on forest land. On 05-02-2004, the MoEF issued a set of supplementary guidelines to encourage the State Governments/ UT Administrations to take up the matter of settlement of rights of tribals and other forest dwellers in the right earnest and perspective. However, these guidelines of 05-02-2004 were stayed by the Hon'ble Supreme Court of India on 23-02-2004. On 21-12-2004, the Ministry of Environment and Forests, without prejudice to Supreme Court's orders dated 23-11-2001 and 23-02-2004, requested the State Governments/UT Administrations that, as an interim measure, they should not resort to eviction of tribal and other forest dwellers other than ineligible encroachers, till a complete survey is done for the recognition of such people and their rights, after setting up of District Level Committees involving a Deputy Collector, a Sub-Divisional Forest Officer, and a representative of the Tribal Welfare Department, as reiterated in guidelines dated 18-09-1990 and 30-10-2002 of the Central Government.

The above letter dated 21-12-2004 of the MoEF requesting not to 'resort to eviction of tribal and other forest dwellers other than ineligible encroachers' virtually set at nought the entire process of eviction of forest encroachments, as although the 'tribals' constituted a distinct identifiable group, there was no distinct line of demarcation between the 'other forest dwellers' and the 'ineligible encroachers'. As a matter of fact, there was nothing to prevent the 'ineligible encroachers' from claiming that they indeed come under the category of 'the other forest dwellers' and it was for the District Level Committees to look into their claims.

It was around this time that a new Bill, namely, "Scheduled Tribes (Recognition of Forest Rights) Bill" was under the active consideration of the Government of India. The new Bill was steered by the Ministry of Tribal Affairs and not by the Ministry of Environment and Forests, which had been handling the matters relating to settlement of tribal rights since a long time. In this context, it may be mentioned that the Ministry of Environment and Forests during 2003 had constituted the National Forest Commission (NFC) under the Chairmanship of Justice B.N. Kirpal, ex-Chief Justice of India and six Members to review the working of the forest and wildlife sector with a number of terms of reference. One of the terms of reference of the NFC was "Establish meaningful partnership and interface between forestry management and local communities including the tribals." However, the opinion of the National Forest Commission was not taken before finalizing the Bill. However, the Bill was *suo moto* examined by the Commission and the recommendations of the Commission in respect of the Bill (with one dissent note) have been included in the Commission's Report submitted to the Government in 2006. The recommendations of the NFC with regard to the Bill as included in the Commission's Report are reproduced below:

"(340) The National Forest Commission is of the considered opinion that the proposed Scheduled Tribes (Recognition of Forest Rights) Act would be harmful to the interests of forests and to the ecological security of the country. It would be bad in law and would be in open conflict with the rulings of the Supreme Court. Another legislation, therefore, needs to be framed providing the forest dwelling communities a right to a share from the forest produce on an ecologically sustainable basis and Ministry of Environment and Forests could be asked to do the needful, after taking into account the inputs of the State Governments as recommended by the Sarkaria Commission as a subject under the concurrent list.

(341) Forest encroachments to the extent of 3.60 lakh hectares per annum have already been regularized. If any State feels that any encroachments done prior to 25-10-1980 still remains unsettled, the concerned State governments could appoint commissions, perhaps headed by judges, to finalize the claims within a time frame. Settlement of such claims and disputes arising there from should be done.

(342) The Bill implies that tribals would be permitted to exploit forests for commercial purposes and not only for bona fide livelihood purposes as was originally intended, with the concerned Gram Sabha empowered to decide as to what exploitation would be sustainable. The extent and nature of forest exploitation on an ecologically sustainable basis must be decided by forest managers in consultation with the local communities, who would have the first charge over any forest produce extracted, to meet their bona fide livelihood requirements, and an economic share of any surplus produce that may be disposed off thereafter.

(343) The proposed legislation should not apply to national parks and sanctuaries, which are the last havens of hope for the nation's forests, wildlife, wilderness and biodiversity. The villagers that remain within them have their pattas and rights and encroachments within them must not be condoned. Many communities themselves wish to resettle outside of such protected areas and this must be facilitated and alternative forestland

provided. The politically motivated and ecologically suicidal proposal of providing temporary rights in these protected areas for a period of five years and then if they are not relocated in that period the rights to become permanent, is a mere façade, and considering the past record and political motivations will never be achieved and grant of such rights will irrevocably impair the ecological viability of protected areas.

(344) The clause that no encroacher should be evicted from forestland under his occupation till the recognition and verification of his claims are completed, with no time limit for such a process, is again self-defeating and will give an impetus and license to more encroachments in forests and to corruption. Such a provision must not apply, at least to national parks and sanctuaries, if not to all forests.

(345) There is an ambiguity in the Bill about the applicability of laws. If the laws of the land pertaining to forests and wildlife are to apply to all tribals and non-tribals, this must be clearly stated and the current confusion about duality in the application of law to tribals and non-tribals, be done away with.

[Shri Chandi Prasad Bhatt, one of the seven Members of the Commission did not agree with the above recommendations from numbers 340 to 345 which pertained to the proposed Scheduled Tribes (Recognition of Forest Rights) Act.]"

As we all know, the above Bill was passed in December 2006 by the Parliament and became an Act, namely, 'The Scheduled Tribes and Other Traditional Forest Dwellers (Recognition of Forest Rights) Act, 2006 (Act No. 2 of 2007)'. The Act was followed up by the notification of "The Scheduled Tribes and Other Traditional Forest Dwellers (Recognition of Forest Rights) Rules, 2008". With the coming into force of the above Act and the Rules made there under, most of the encroachers, who were found to be ineligible for regularization by the Forest Department, made fresh claims as 'Other Traditional Forest Dwellers' and requested for their claims to be examined under the provisions of the new Act.

The eligibility to get rights under the new Act is confined to those who 'primarily reside in forests' and who depend on forests and forest land for a livelihood. Further, either the claimant must be a member of the

Scheduled Tribes scheduled in that area or must have been residing in the forest for 75 years. Evidently the Act provides true relief to a Scheduled Tribes person, as he does not have to provide any document as proof of residence. Quite expectedly, most of the persons who were earlier found ineligible have not been able to convince the concerned authorities under the new Act about their continued occupation in the forest for more than 75 years.

As of now, Karnataka has about 80,000 hectares of forest lands that are under encroachment. Eviction of old encroachments has been a difficult task for the Forest Department because of internal and external pressures. As already mentioned, the poor encroachers invariably garner sympathy from various sections of the society and support, at times very vocal, of powerful people and political leaders with vested interests. Encroachments carried out by the rich and the powerful are also difficult to remove. In a high profile case of encroachment in Tatkola State forest in Chikkamagaluru district, removal of the encroachment was possible because of the intervention of the Hon'ble Supreme Court of India. Removal of old encroachments continues to be a difficult task at the field level generally escalating into law-and-order situations. At times the forest officials, especially the field-level functionaries, are harassed or trumped-up charges are filed against them on atrocities cases. For the exercise of eviction of forest encroachments to be successful, it is absolutely necessary that the field-level functionaries get unstinted and wholehearted support from the top. It is also necessary that in all cases involving eviction of forest encroachment, which are always very sensitive in nature, the department, the government, the civil society and the political leadership are all on the same page. Conflicting signals emanating from these quarters lead to demoralization of the staff and, in the long run, the entire mission becomes counterproductive.

In the recent years, there has been growing awareness regarding protection of forest from the clutches of encroachment. This has enabled the Forest department to get favorable judgments from various courts. The Hon'ble High Court of Karnataka has also been monitoring the progress of eviction of forest encroachments by the Forest department. This has emboldened the younger generation of officers to take up eviction of forest encroachment cases head on and bring these to their logical ends. It must however be admitted that the Forest Rights Act (FRA), 2006 has come in the way of the Forest Department in evicting many of the encroachments, as the encroachers have staked their claim to land under the provisions of the new Act. This has seriously hampered the process of eviction and it has become a protracted exercise for the department to dispose of such claims. There was a glimmer of hope for the Forest Department when the Hon'ble Supreme Court of India on 13-02-2019 had ordered the eviction of the people whose claims have been finally rejected under the provisions of the Forests Rights Act. However, on 28-02-2019 the Hon'ble Court has stayed its earlier order responding to a plea that due procedure of law was not followed while rejecting the forest rights claims.

The implication of the above order is that all cases rejected under the FRA will need to be reviewed. While such a review is justifiable in genuine cases of Scheduled Tribes whose claims may have been rejected erroneously, the 'Other forest dwellers' most of whom belong to the category of encroachers found ineligible as per the Forest (Conservation) Act (FCA), 1980 and whose claims have been rejected under the FRA, appear to have been favored. The favor sought on their behalf appears to be intentional as it is well known that majority of the rejected cases pertain to non-tribal people who failed to prove their continuous residence for 75 years in the forest. It is definite that in the long run, the real truth about these ineligible encroachers will come out. But by that time irreversible and wanton damages would be done to the forests and it would be impossible to retrieve the situation. It is unfortunate that in the guise of helping the tribal people under the FRA, attempts are being made to espouse the cause of illegal forest encroachers who are required to be evicted under the Forest Conservation Act and the National Forest Policy. In retrospect, the whole idea of including the 'Other Forest Dwellers' in the FRA, after initially proposing it as only for tribal people, appears to be preplanned to favor the encroachers found to be ineligible as per FCA. Interestingly but not unexpectedly, the FRA has not stipulated any last date by which the people ought to claim their traditional rights on forest land. This has left a lot of scope for further encroachment of forest land and for schemers and manipulators to make use of the FRA as a tool for getting the encroachments regularized through dubious means.

The Act has virtually opened the floodgates for fresh encroachment of forest land. Considering the damages already caused to the forests by the implementation of the Forest Rights Act, and also considering its serious implications on the future of the limited forests that we are left with, it is necessary to review and repeal the Act.

A FEW PHOTOGRAPHS OF DRY DECIDUOUS AND THORN FORESTS OF KARNATAKA

Dry deciduous forest in the Western Ghats

Dry deciduous forest in the Eastern Plains (Ballari division)

***Hardwickia binata* forest (Chitradurga division)**

Shorea talura forest (Chikkaballapur division)

Scrub forest in the Eastern Plains (Daroji, Ballari division)

Thorn forest in interior Karnataka (Haveri division)

***Euphorbia* scrub in Chitradurga division**

[Photo credits: Mr. Vijay Mohan Raj, IFS, Mr. Arsalan, IFS, Mr. S. M. Malavalli (Retd. DCF), and Mr. S.M. Wali, ACF]

REFERENCES

1. Anon: India State of Forest Reports 1987, 1989, 1991, 1993, 1995, 1997, 1999, 2001, 2003, 2005, 2009, 2011, 2013, 2015, 2017 and 2019: Published by the Forest Survey of India (FSI), Dehradun

2. Anon: Annual Report of Karnataka Forest Department for 2018-19

3. Anon (2006): Land use-Land cover classification of various districts of Karnataka – Karnataka State Remote Sensing Application Center (KSRSAC), Bengaluru

4. Anon: Modern Mysore (1868)

5. Anon (1909): Provincial Series Hyderabad State (1909) – Gulbarga, Raichur and Bidar districts

6. Akbar Sha: Working Plan (Draft) Madikeri division (1986-1995)

7. Aralikatti K. S. (2003): Working Plan for Shimoga forest division

8. Buchanan Francis (1807): A Journey from Madras through the Countries of Mysore, Canara, and Malabar (Vol. I, II and III)

9. Campbell James M.: Gazetteer of Bombay Presidency: North Kanara district (Vol. XV, 1883), Belgaum district (Vol. XXI, 1884), Dharwar district (Vol. XXII, 1884), Bijapur district (Vol. XXIII, 1884) and Kolhapur district (Vol. XXIV, 1886)

10. Champion and F. C. Osmaston (Reprinted 1983): E. P. Stebbing's the Forests of India (Volume IV)

11. Das Dilip Kumar: Working Plan for Hunsur and Mandya forest divisions (2011-12 to 2020-21)

12. Devaraj N.: Working Plan for Chikkaballapur forest division (2013-14 to 2022-23)

13. Francis W: Madras District Gazetteers: Bellary district (1904)

14. Gaonkar D. S.: Working Plan for Mysore forest division (2013-14 to 2022-23)

15. Garg Seema (2013): Working Plan for Haveri forest division (2013-14 to 2022-23)

16. GOI (1988): National Forest Policy: Ministry of Environment and Forests, Resolution No. 3-1/86-FP, December, 1988

17. Goudar M. S. (2002-04): Working Plans for Bagalkote, Gadag and Bijapur forest divisions

18. Hameed Sajid: Working Plan for the forests of Shivamogga division (2011-12 to 2023-24)

19. Hanqin Tian, Kamaljit Banger, Tao Bo, and Vinay K. Dadhwal: [Global and Planetary Change 121 (2014) 78-88] – History of land use in India during 1880-2010: Large-scale land transformations reconstructed from satellite data and historical archives

20. John F. Richards and Elizabeth P. Flint (1994): Historic Land Use and Carbon Estimates for South and Southeast Asia for 1880-1980

21. Kelsall John: Manual of the Bellary district (1869)

22. Kumar H. R.: Working Plan for Bangalore Urban forest division (2013-14 to 2022-23)

23. Kshirsagar Yaspal: Working Plan for Gadag forest division (2012-13 to 2121-23)

24. Malkhede Subhash K. (2002-04): Working Plan for Belgaum forest division

25. Mallik Fiaz Uddin: Working Plan for Chikkamagaluru forest division (2013-2023)

26. Manjunatha B. K., Krishna V., Pullaiah T. (2004): "Flora of Davanagere District, Karnataka, India"

27. Manjunatha D.: Working Plans for the forests of the Ramanagara forest division (2012-13 to 2020-21) and Bhadravathi forest division (2014-15 to 2023-24)

28. Manjunath K. B.: Working Plan for the forests of Bangalore Rural division (2011-12 to 2020-21)

29. Manjunatha T. V.: Working Plan for Dharwar forest division (2012-13 to 2021-22)

30. Mishra Bishwajit (2002-04): Working Plan for Raichur forest division

31. Misra Ajai (2002-04) Working Plans for Haliyal and Hunsur forest divisions

32. Naik T. V.; Prashantha K. M.; Sayeswara H. A.; Patil H. S. R.: Study of flora and fauna distributed in selected areas of Hirekalgudda state forest: Environment Conservation Journal 2012 Vol. 13 No. 1/2 pp. 85-92 ref. 7

33. NarayanaSwamy K. M.: Approved Working Plans for Tumkur forest division (2015-16 to 2024-25) and Chikkamagaluru forest division (2012-13 to 2023-23)

34. Neginhal S.G. (2011): Forest Trees of the Western Ghats

35. Palanna R. M., Conservator of Forests, Kanara Circle, Karnataka, Eucalyptus in India

36. Purushotham D. S. (2002-04): Working Plans for Bellary, Chitradurga, Gulbarga and Bidar forest divisions

37. Ratan Anil Kumar: Working Plans for Bagalkote, Belgaum and Vijayapura forest divisions (2012-13 to 2021-22)

38. Rao C. Hayavadana: Mysore Gazetteer Vol. I, Vol. II, Vol. III, Vol.IV and Vol. V

39. Rao H. Shama: Modern Mysore (1936)

40. Ramachandra Chetty N. V.: Working Plan for composite Bangalore forest division (1976-1986)

41. Range Gowda (2002-04): Working Plans for Tumkur, Chikkamagaluru and Bangalore Rural forest divisions

42. Rangaswamy V. (2002-04): Working Plan for Bhadravathi forest divisions

43. Ribbentrop Berthold (1900): Forestry in British India

44. Rice Benjamin Lewis: Gazetteer of Mysore and Coorg- Vol. I, Vol. II and Vol. III

45. Sarmah Dipak (2018): Status of Forests of Karnataka

46. Sarmah Dipak (2019): Forestry in Karnataka – A Journey of 150 Years

47. Sarmah Dipak (2019): Forests of Karnataka – A Panoramic View

48. Sarmah Dipak (2019): Wildlife Management in Karnataka – A Forester's Perspective

49. Sarmah Dipak (2020): Forestry in British India – Karnataka Case-study

50. Sarmah Dipak (2020): Agroforestry in Karnataka – A Golden Opportunity for Green Growth

51. Singh Brij Kishore (2021): Forest Rights Act – Accelerated Deforestation

52. Singh Raj Kishore (2002-2004): Working Plan of Dharwar forest division (2002-03 to 2011-12)

53. Sir Harry G. Champion and S. K. Seth (1968): A Revised Survey of Forest Types of India

54. Sir Harry G. Champion and S. K. Seth (1968): General Silviculture for India

55. Srinivasamurthy K. M.-Working Plan for Kolar Forest Division (2012-13 to 2021-22)

56. Stebbing E. P. (1921): The Forests of India (Volume I)

57. Stebbing E. P. (1922): The Forests of India (Volume II)

58. Stebbing E. P. (1926): The Forests of India (Volume III)

59. Srinivasan C. (2002-04): Working Plan for Mysore and Kolar forest divisions

BOOK REVIEW

Title: Dry Deciduous Forests of Karnataka (Adding years to their life, and to ours)
Author: Dipak Sarmah, IFS (R)   **Language:** English
Pages: 220   **Year:** 2021   **Price:** Rs, 250/-
Publisher: Notion Press, Mylapore, Chennai – 600004.

[Reviewed by: Dr. B Raghotham Rao Desai, IFS(R)**]**

Dipak Sarmah lives up to his ability to create a compelling account and **a fantastic atmosphere of importance and utility of 'dry deciduous forests, adding years not only to their lives, but also to those of ours',** and how! He also enlists their dilemmas, and the pulls, and the tugs they face, due to the unprecedented anthropogenic interference, narrated like a thriller brilliantly, of the politics that engulf the vicious atmosphere that exists presently.

The impact will be vastly different, however, from the kind of impact that his earlier books had, because of the theme being so different.

A characteristic trait of almost all works of his is rooted in the reference to the milieu of Karnataka forests, strikingly in the native manner in which they are displayed with abiding love for the sanctified geography of Karnataka State -- consciously following the hoary tradition, painting vivid pictures of its vast, varied and lush forest types.

It looks like a Cindrella period, despite pandemic, as the New Year 2021 commenced and Dipak Sarmah is on a zoom-call with his seventh treatise on a trot, to adorn our bookshelves on which his earlier six beautiful works already occupy.

The book is also a comment on the times we live in, never overtly but as a hint here (as could be seen in the 5th chapter: "Present Status of……"), and a hint there (abundantly covered in the next chapter: "Restoration & Rejuvenation of ….") -- the book having no dearth of layers: "Classification of Dry Deciduous and Thorn Forests" (Chapter 2), and "Distribution of Tree Species Across…." (Chapter 4), etc., -- the book is thus branched out, and is open for interpretation. Perhaps that was exactly how the author intended it to be.

True to his name Dipak Sarmah sheds light in whichever direction he turns and nothing escapes his attention. He is indeed sharp-sighted -- **even a particle perhaps looks to him like the very universe,** to quote an idea of (Shaayere-Mashriq) Iqbal: the poet of the East! He deserves accolades to have written such an insightful book that describes and delineates -- the reader is all 'the better served' by the said 'anthology' (a derivative from the Greek word anthophilous).

In summation, this is a story told with a born raconteur's gift (i.e., a skilful story teller's gift) -- quaint (i.e., attractively unusual) but also thought-provoking. Isn't it true that **art is a creative expression that influences another being?**

After going through the text contained in the six chapters and the four annexures of the book through which the author tried to convey his view point of 'adding years to the life of the State's Deciduous Forests vis-à-vis to ours', we get to conclude that **our memories of the ocean will linger on, long after our footprints in the sand are gone!** While doing so, he was clear in his mind and had no-doubts, and no expectations -- just he went with the flow, his ability to embrace change being extraordinary, pleasantly surprising the people with his positive frame of mind. **One should not brood over what had happened in the distant past, and should not worry, but take it in one's stride & consider it as a transient phase which would be over sooner than one thinks. Changes do take place the way one perceives the situation around him, his professional life and himself --** this is what Dipak Sarmah firmly believed.

When something is precious to us it can mean the object itself, or our feelings about it! In the best traditions of speculative suggestions to improve the existing conditions of the dry deciduous forests (which have the potential to add years to our lives, while adding to theirs), Dipak Sarmah uses the lens of improbable events to show us the existing conditions in the interiors of such forests. **If it's about heartbreak, it's also about healing. The narration is conducive and sparse, yet effective style shines through,** making it one of the best books of recent times, being especially relevant in these days. The book has a unique narrative structure, taking the stance that systematic & scientific management of the forests (and woodlots) will eventually prevail over evil effects of promulgating Acts & Rules detrimental to the existence of grasslands and Reserve Forests.

The Forest Fraternity of the current generation would perhaps have felt a bit vulnerable in not finding a person of calibre which it had a century earlier ---- but in a few years of this decade it became evident, with the arrival of Dipak Sarmah on the scene, **all we really needed was someone capable of doing everything at an elite level of writing** a series of books on Forestry. If his earlier six treatises were a treat, the use of the medium to produce the very next book on **"Dry Deciduous Forests, to add years to their life (and to ours)"** has been equally delectable!